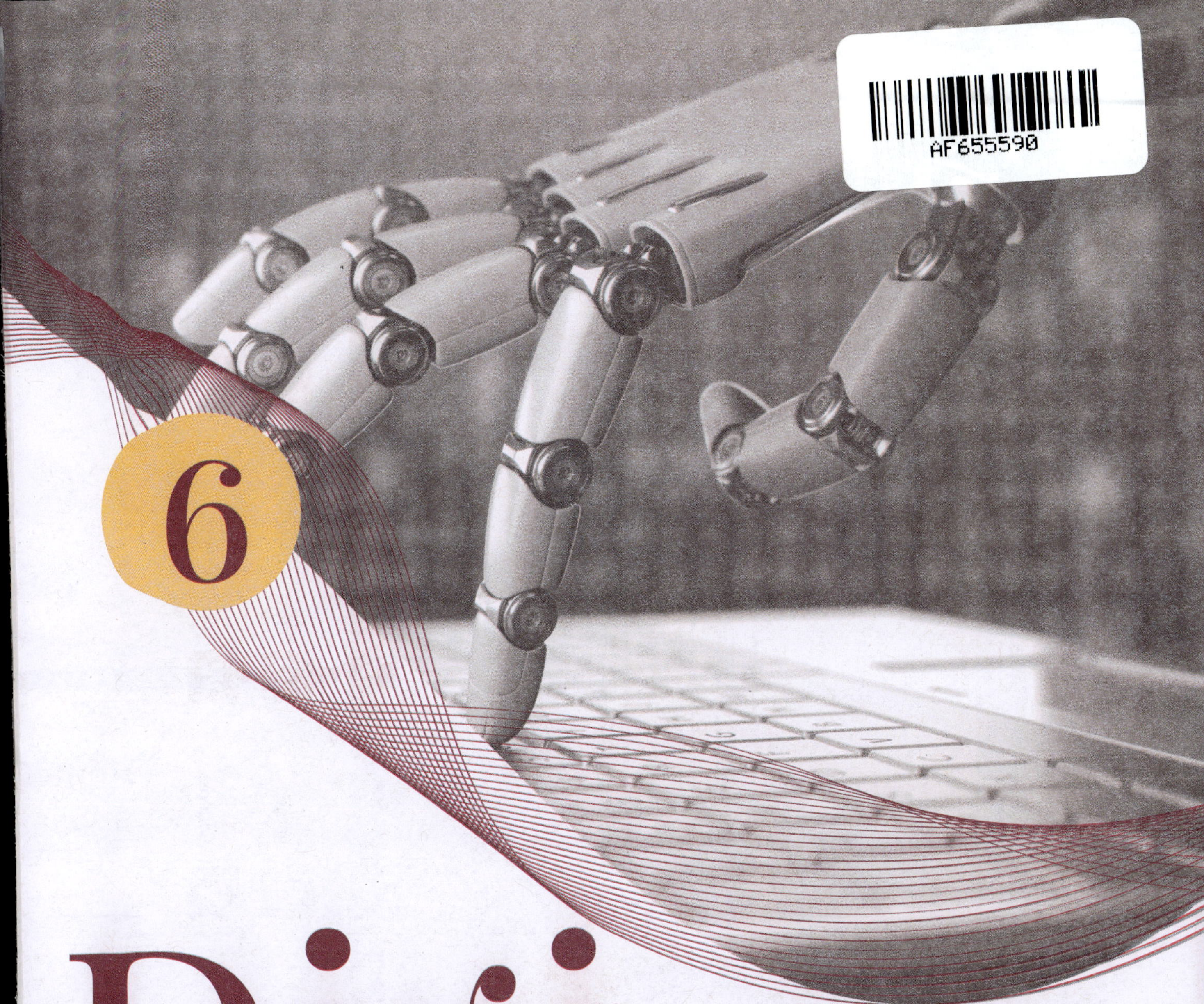

6

Digi Tech

Manasi Kashikar
Sneha Krishnan

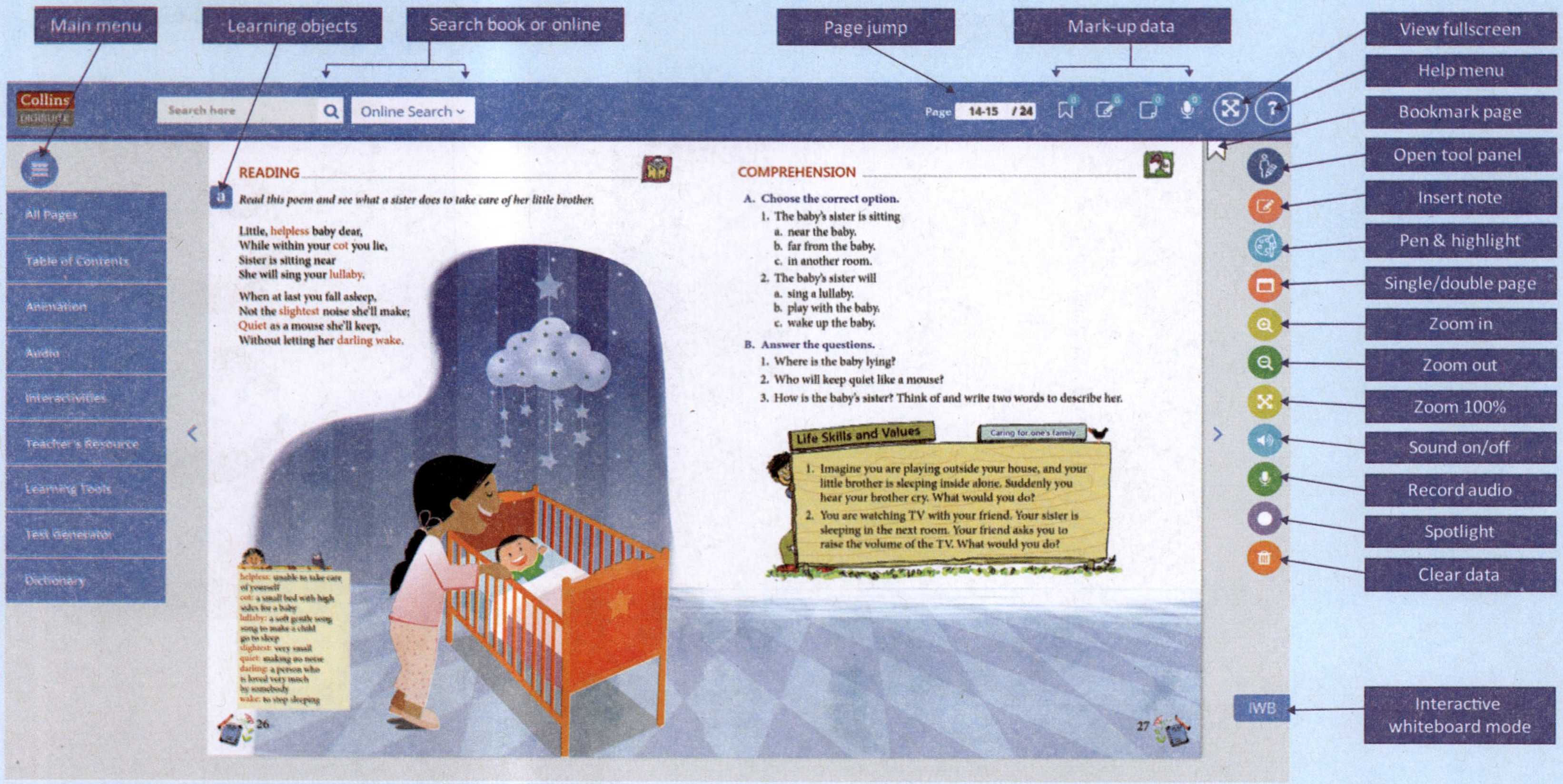

Student + Teacher			Teacher-only	
a animations	**ia** activities	**g** games	**lp** lesson plans	**tn** teacher's notes
ilt instructor-led tutorials	**w** worksheets	**v** videos	**w** worksheets	**ak** answer keys
	audio			

PREFACE

Over the last few decades, technology has touched almost all aspects of our lives. As technology continues to evolve more rapidly than ever, users are learning newer ways of harnessing the power of technology in their daily lives. In India, easy access to smartphones and affordable internet services have put the power of technology in the hands of millions.

In this backdrop, we believe, it is important for students to:

- ✓ Understand that technology is going to keep evolving. As citizens of the digital world that we all inhabit, keeping abreast of the latest advances is no longer optional, rather, it is an essential life skill.
- ✓ Appreciate that coding skills are as essential today as basic literacy and numeracy. This has been emphasized in the National Educational Policy of 2020 as well.
- ✓ Understand that technology is pervasive and they need to be able to comprehend its intersection with other disciplines. In other words, they need to learn to use technology as a tool to achieve a goal.
- ✓ Take control of regulating their usage and make constructive use of their access to computer devices.

While authoring this series, we have designed and presented the content with the intent of helping students in developing the skills described above. We have ensured that the topics are covered in a relatable manner and that the exercises are practical and applicable. The textbook along with its resources for teachers will enable them to deliver this subject effectively, while keeping the students engaged and interested.

In addition to the curriculum imperatives, we have included concepts as outlined in the National Education Policy 2020. Every grade has computational thinking–based practice problems that are aligned to Bloom's Taxonomy. Topics such as coding and app development have been given their due consideration as their relevance increases in the real world and while making career choices. Artificial intelligence has been woven into the chapters in an age-appropriate manner in the form of Fun with AI boxes, with the intent of enabling students to understand key concepts and applications of AI.

The series equips students with not only the skills required to excel in technology and make the most of it, but also exposes them to the practical applications of these in the world around them.

We would like to thank our intern Sejal Gupta in helping us shape the content.

KEY FEATURES

After reading this chapter, I will be able to:

- ✔ Define a table.
- ✔ Create a table and enter data in the table.
- ✔ Edit a table.
- ✔ Format the row/column/table.
- ✔ Apply borders and shading in tables.

Well-defined learning objectives that are mapped to the curriculum to help students identify the topics they will read about in the chapter

Activities and discussions based on real-life situations to set the context for what students are about to learn

Cross Curricular

Brainstorm and explore!

Sameer is organizing a seminar on cyber security in his apartment complex. He wants to invite friends and teachers to attend this seminar. He created a beautiful invitation using MS Word, mentioning the date, time and the venue details. He does not want to send a common letter to everyone. He wants to make sure that they receive personal invitation, with their names mentioned individually in the letter. What do you think Sameer should do? Discuss in your class.

Soak up!

By 1937, IBM was producing 10 million punched cards every day.

Additional information/facts about the topic being taught

Contextual meaning of difficult words

In Class 5, we learned that PowerPoint presentations can be enhanced with the use of pictures and charts. In this chapter, we will learn how to use animation and multimedia in a PowerPoint presentation.

animation: a film in which drawings or puppets appear to move

multimedia: a combination of movies, sound clips, SmartArt and animations

Technology Literacy

Crank up!

The default location of a saved list is My Documents/ My Data Sources.

Tips and shortcut tricks for the topics covered in the chapter to foster inquiry- and discovery-based learning

Clear up!

Create a Word doc and highlight the title and text with different styles available. Import the file in PowerPoint.

Hands-on tasks for revision, based on the application of the concept taught

Brush up!

In the computer lab, open both an image file and a text document. Which letters follow the full stop in the file names? Are they same or different? Note down your observations here.

Short questions to reinforce the concept learned and promote competency-based learning

Exemplifies the relevance and application of AI to the concept in the real world

Fun with AI

Machine learning is a field of study that focuses on imparting machines the ability to learn from data and improve with experience without coding them again and again. It is a means to achieve Artificial Intelligence.

Real-world examples and situations to help students establish linkages and connections to support the development of lateral thinking

Link up!

The major use of assembly languages today is in the writing of operating systems—the programs that control the hardware and make it more accessible to computer users.

Today I learned!

- Electronic mail is the system of sending and receiving messages across the internet.
- Email services are provided by various companies such as Google (Gmail), Microsoft (MS Outlook), Yahoo (Yahoomail), Rediff (Rediffmail), Apple (Apple Mail) and so on.
- Emails can be accessed on personal computers as well as smartphones and tablets.
- Cloud storage refers to a model of storage where data is stored in the cloud that is an external server and can be accessed via the internet.
- Google Drive is one of the most widely used storage services on the cloud. Other cloud storage services include Microsoft OneDrive and Dropbox.

Recapitulates all the important points covered in the chapter

Revision exercises comprising a blend of both objective and long-answer questions, including both fact- and application-based questions in a variety of formats

Revise and polish!

Learning Skills

1. Tick (✓) the correct answer.

a. Computers are broadly categorized on the basis of their use and ____________.

(i) data ☐ (ii) presentation ☐

(iii) USB ports ☐ (iv) processing power ☐

b. Which of the following computers are very affordable?

(i) Microcomputers ☐ (ii) Supercomputers ☐

(iii) Play stations ☐ (iv) Mainframes ☐

Lab Activities

Experiential Learning

Create the following tables using MS Word:

a. A table showing your top three favourite non-academic books and the names of the authors
b. A table with the names of any five historic monuments, the year they were built in and by whom
c. Time-table of your class
d. A table representing your favourite sports players and their top scores

Based on the practical application of the concepts taught to enhance comprehension and provide opportunities for peer tutoring

Practical applications of the concepts covered to help analyse and understand real-world situations, with some extra effort put into research and information gathering

Projects

We have learned that a large number of Indians have a smartphone and connectivity to the internet. Imagine you are the District Collector in an area where there are many small villages. How will you use the power of the internet to improve their lives?

(**Hint:** Think along the lines of water supply, electricity, basic education, roads, etc.)

Worksheet 1 (Chapters 4, 5, 6 and 7)

Competency-based question

Technology Literacy

1. The Principal of your school has given you the responsibility of inviting students, parents and alumni to the Independence Day celebrations in your school. The invitation will be sent via email. Create an invitation using the Mail Merge features and include required information. Add elements to make it appealing.

2. Did you know forests are home to 80% of Earth's terrestrial animals and cover 31% of the landmass? Create a presentation on any of the world's forests and explain what makes it unique. Include pictures, transitions and audio to make the presentation interesting and engaging.

Chapter-based revision worksheets focused on competency-based learning and one dedicated worksheet on developing computational thinking through playing games and problem-solving

NEP IN DIGI TECH

These are some of the key skills that you will see occurring throughout the books at various stages.

21st Century Skills

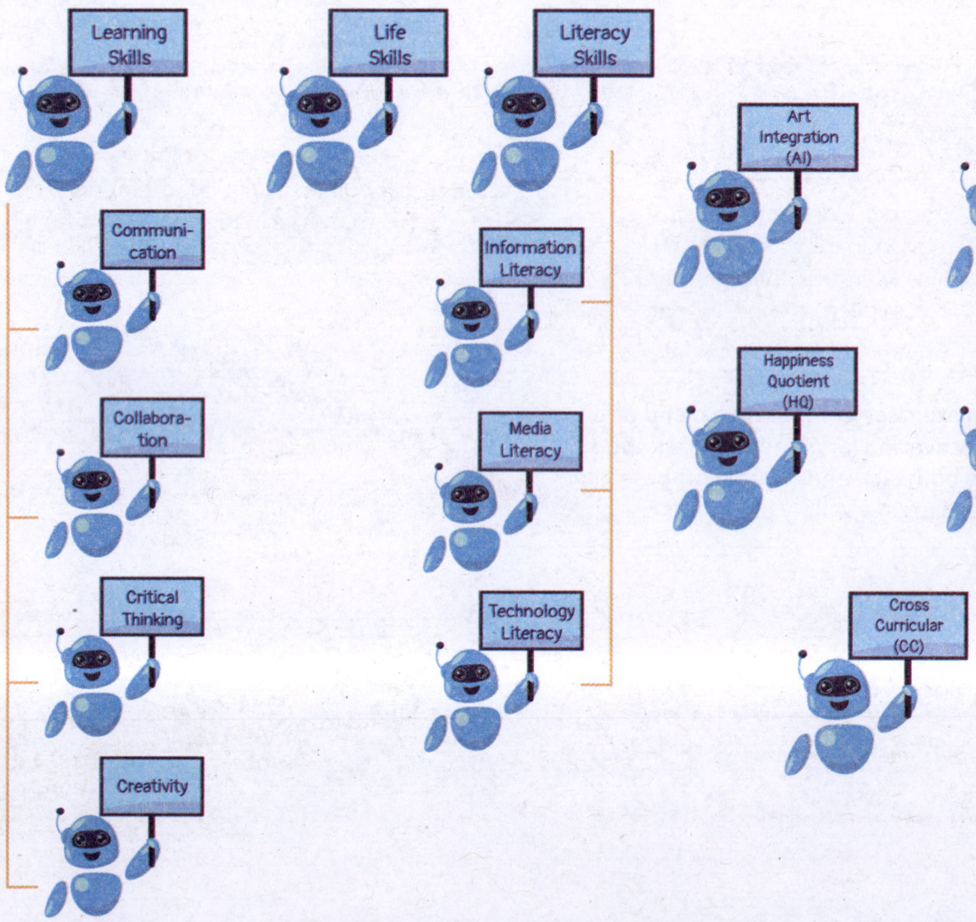

ABOUT THE AUTHORS

Sneha Krishnan and **Manasi Kashikar**, techies at heart, bond over their love of coding. They are co-founders of the company *MindChamp* where they teach coding to school students using fun, activity-based learning. They both love to teach students and that reflects in their work. Together with a team of educators, they have taught thousands of students to create computer games and websites. They want to make coding accessible to young students as well, so they are better equipped for the future.

CONTENTS

Chapter 1

Categories of Computers and Computer Languages

After reading this chapter, I will be able to:

- ✔ Describe the various ways in which computers are classified.
- ✔ Identify different categories of computers.
- ✔ Describe machine and high-level languages.
- ✔ Explain the importance of 4GLs.
- ✔ Explain the working of translators by differentiating between an interpreter and a compiler.

Brainstorm and explore!

Technology Literacy

Write down the name of the device that is best suited for each of the following tasks.

a. Making a video call to your grandparents while you are on vacation

____

b. Preparing a presentation at home for your Science project

____

c. Learning a new application in the computer lab

____

d. Printing a poster for an upcoming Fun Fair in the school

____

Notice how different devices are used for different purposes. Similarly, different kinds of computers are required for different tasks. Computers are broadly categorized on the basis of their size, use and processing power. For example, your home computer is sufficient for storing pictures and playing games. Is it powerful enough to track and predict the weather for the entire country? Definitely not! It may not even have the storage capacity required to store such huge amounts of data. A more powerful computer with huge storage capacity is required for this task. Such a computer would be more expensive, too. Thus, computers can be categorized based on various parameters such as processing power, storage capacity and cost. We will learn more about them in this chapter.

processing power: the ability of a computer to process data rapidly and efficiently

Types of Computers

Computers are used for a variety of tasks behind the scenes such as controlling aircraft or even packaging ice cream! On the basis of size and processing power, computers can be categorized as follows:

Microcomputers

A microcomputer is a small computer. It is designed for use by one person at a time for carrying out simple tasks such as writing an email, creating a presentation and listening to songs. Microcomputers are usually affordable. They are used in homes, schools, shops, hospitals, etc.

Soak up!

The word *micro* in *microcomputers* suggests that they have microchips that are responsible for processing information.

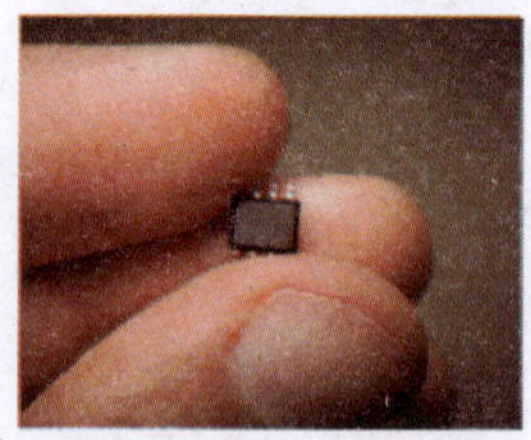

Microcomputers are the most commonly found type of computers today. Because they can be used by one person, they are also known as personal computers (PCs). Some of the commonly used microcomputers are as follows:

Desktop Computers

As the name suggests, desktop computers are placed on a desk (Fig. 1.1). They comprise of a CPU, monitor, keyboard and mouse.

Fig. 1.1 | *A desktop computer*

Laptops

Laptops are portable desktop computers. The CPU, mouse, speakers and monitor are bundled into a single device called laptop (Fig. 1.2). A key difference between a desktop computer and a laptop is that a laptop can be charged, whereas the former has to be connected to a power source while in use.

Fig. 1.2 | *A laptop*

Handheld Devices

A handheld device such as a smartphone or a tablet is small and light enough to be used while you are holding it. Let us learn more about these.

Fig. 1.3 | *A smartphone*

- **Smartphone:** Smartphones (Fig. 1.3) have become ubiquitous today. They have many of the functionalities of a laptop in less than a quarter of the size. They are lightweight and can be carried around easily.

Fig. 1.4 | *A tablet*

- **Tablets:** In terms of size and utility, tablets (Fig. 1.4) lie between a laptop and a smartphone. They are used for watching movies, reading, taking notes, showing presentations, etc.

Some of the other microcomputers are printers, scanners, digital camera and so on.

Gaming Console

A gaming console is a device that can be connected to a monitor and a game controller, which is used to play games (Fig. 1.5). The game controller can be a keyboard, mouse, joystick, steering wheel, touchscreen device and so on, depending on the game. The games are pre-installed in the console or can even be purchased online. Some of the popular gaming consoles are PlayStation by Sony, Xbox by Mixrosoft and Nintendo Switch.

Fig. 1.5 | *Gaming console with a joystick*

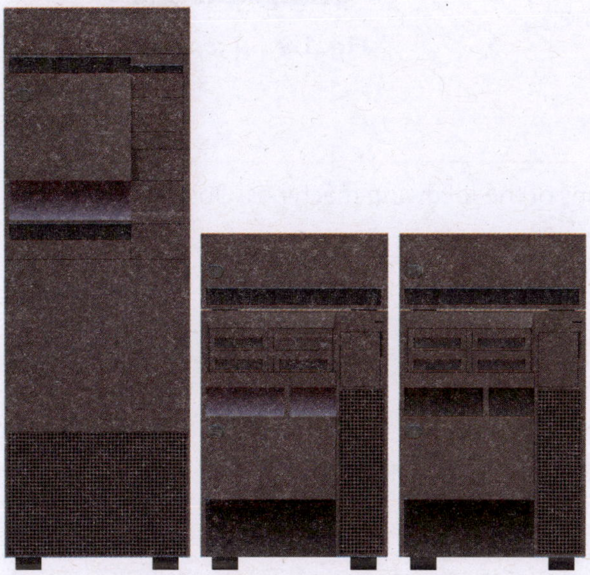

Fig. 1.6 | *Minicomputers*

Minicomputers

Minicomputers (Fig. 1.6) are the predecessors of microcomputers. They are larger than a microcomputer. They are used in large organizations for running scientific applications. Minicomputers were widely used in the 1970s and the 1980s but their use has fallen with the advent of microcomputers.

Mainframes

Mainframes (Fig. 1.7) have more processing power and storage capacity than mini-computers. A large amount of data is generated and needs to be processed by big organizations and governments. A mainframe can handle the processing of data. Unlike microcomputers, which have only a single processor, mainframes have multiple processors. Airline reservations, banking, and e-commerce are some of the areas where mainframes are used.

Fig. 1.7 | *Mainframes*

Soak up!

The picture given here shows how computers have evolved over the years.

Supercomputers

Supercomputers (Fig. 1.8), as the name suggests, have the greatest processing speed and storage capacity. They are usually of the size of a room or larger. They are used by meteorologists, nuclear scientists, space agencies, etc. They are very expensive. Param, Pratyush and Fukagu are some examples of supercomputers.

Fig. 1.8 | *A supercomputer*

Mini Scientist

Use Google to find out the type and applications of the following machines. Observe the answers and write down your analysis.

a. Param by Centre for Development of Advanced Computer, India

____

b. IBM AS/400e

____

c. Ninetendo Switch

____

d. iPhone 11

____

Embedded Computer Systems

Embedded systems are defined as the systems consisting of a software component that serves a specific function embedded on the hardware of the device. TV, refrigerators, microwaves, elevators, digital camera, printers and car dashboard are all examples of embedded systems.

Software with specific function + Hardware → Embedded system

Table 1.1 shows how we use embedded systems in our daily lives.

Table 1.1 *Commonly used embedded systems*

Device	Specific functions of the software	Hardware
 Washing machine	1. Selecting the quantity of water 2. Selecting what needs to be done—Rinse, Wash, Dry or All 3. The beep sound when the task is completed (timer) 4. Some advanced versions of washing machines also have temperature control	The body of the washing machine with the drum (tub), water inlet and outlet pipes, washing machine motor that helps it spin, etc.
 Elevator	1. Selecting the floor 2. As the lift moves up and down, the screen indicates the floor number	The cabin, electro-mechanical doors, motors to lift, brakes, etc.

In embedded systems, the user has to select from a menu of predefined inputs to achieve the desired output. Users cannot provide specialized inputs in such systems.

Another parameter to classify computers is the language used to communicate with computers.

Clear up!

Observe these devices in use. Write one difference between them.

a. Laptop and Smartphone: ______

b. Desktop and Tablet: ______

c. Smartphone camera and DSLR camera: ______

d. Tablet and Smartphone: ______

Fun with AI

Machine learning is a field of study that focuses on imparting machines the ability to learn from data and improve with experience without coding them again and again. It is a means to achieve Artificial Intelligence.

Computer Generations

To identify machines based on the progress of software and hardware qualities of computers over time, computers are classified into several generations.

As shown in Table 1.2, computers have improved significantly since the 1930s. From taking inputs in the machine language, computers today use the fourth generation of programming languages, abbreviated as 4GLs. 4GLs are characterized by user-friendliness and versatility, that is, they can be used in a wide range of applications. 4GLs are used for database management, web development, application development and so on. They are effective for working with large amounts of data.

Let us learn how 4GLs evolved from machine language, that is, the language of 0s and 1s understood by computers.

Table 1.2 | *Generations of computers*

Generation	Hardware used	Examples	Language/Software
First Generation (1946–1958)	Vacuum tubes **I/O:** Punched cards and paper tapes **Storage:** Magnetic drums **Speed:** 10,000 instructions per second **Size:** Up to the size of a room	Z1, ENIAC	Machine language
Second Generation (1958–1965)	Transistors **I/O:** Punched cards, paper tape (for input) and printers (for output) **Storage:** Magnetic drums, disk **Speed:** 30,000 instructions per second **Size:** Smaller than first-generation computers	IBM 1400 series	Assembly language

Third Generation (1965–1970)	Integrated circuits **Storage:** Magnetic drums **Speed:** 5 million instructions per second **Size:** Smaller than second-generation computers **Overall:** Multitasking possible	IBM 360, IBM 370	High-level languages such as BASIC, C, COBOL, FORTRAN and Pascal
Fourth Generation (1970–Present)	Microprocessors **I/O:** Keyboard, mouse, monitor, printer, etc. **Storage:** Semiconductor memory such as RAM and ROM **Speed:** Exceeding billions of instructions per second (supercomputers) **Size:** Small enough to carry **Overall:** Smaller, more efficient and cheaper	Macintosh, Lenovo computers	4GLs and object-oriented languages such as Java, C++, Python developed GUI-based operating system and computer networks developed
Fifth Generation (Present–Future)	▪ Will be able to understand patterns, such as face or human speech. ▪ Will be able to solve complex problems and take intelligent decisions. ▪ Will be able to learn from instructions and data, and thus, improve themselves.	Artificial Intelligence-driven computer systems such as voice recognition, self-driven cars and Internet of Things (IoT)	Mercury, Prolog

Machine Language to Programming Language

The language that machines understand is called machine language or binary language. Machine language is a series of 1s and 0s. For example in binary language, 5 = 0101, 9 = 1001 and so on. However, it is not simple or quick for humans to understand machine language. Today, we use high-level languages to give instructions to a computer.

Soak up!

At a physical level, transistors are used to store the 0s and 1s in a computer system. Transistors are tiny switches that control the flow of electricity. If current passes through the transistor, this represents 1. If current does not pass through, this represents 0.

Evolution of Programming Languages

Computer programming languages were developed to make it easier for humans to use computers to solve problems quickly and more efficiently. The earliest computers had to be programmed manually, bit-by-bit, using tools such as punched cards. Each punched card (*see* Fig. 1.9) was a rectangular card, which had the provision to punch numbers, symbols and letters. Computers at that time could punch the cards as well as retrieve messages from punched cards for both input and output.

> **Link up!**
>
> The first punched card, invented by Herman Hollerith, was used for the 1890 census in New York. Hollerith got the idea of punched cards after seeing them being used to control textile looms in France. Did you know that one of the last important uses of punched cards has been in voting?

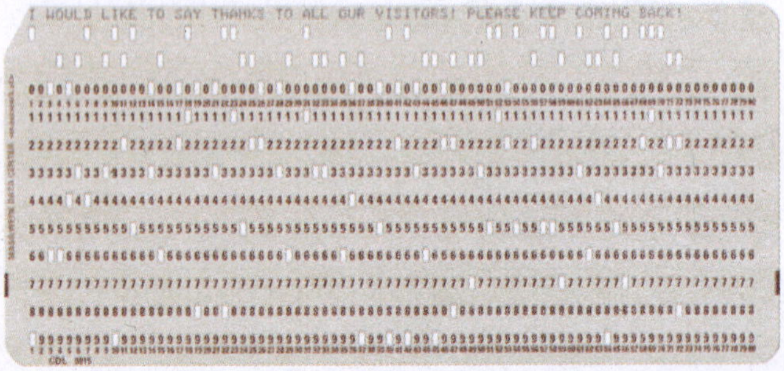

Fig. 1.9 | *Punched cards*

> **Soak up!**
>
> By 1937, IBM was producing 10 million punched cards every day.

Programming in machine language was very slow and led to errors. Hence, assembly languages were developed to express simple computer operations as **mnemonics** instead of numeric instructions. Although it is easier to use, assembly language is linked to the hardware used in the CPU. Programming in assembly language takes a lot of time. Both machine language and assembly language are called **low-level languages**.

> **Link up!**
>
> The major use of assembly languages today is in the writing of operating systems—the programs that control the hardware and make it more accessible to computer users.

High-level languages evolved to make programming simpler and less time-consuming. High-level languages are easily understandable by humans and close to human language in terms of structure. A single statement in a high-level language can produce hundreds of machine instructions. In contrast, a simple statement in assembly language will produce one or a few machine instructions.

With advancements of technology, computers became more programmable, that is, translators were developed to convert human instructions into machine language. Thus, high-level languages developed further. Figure 1.10 shows the evolution of computer languages. Some examples of high-level languages are Python, Java, C++, Javascript, JQuery and C#.

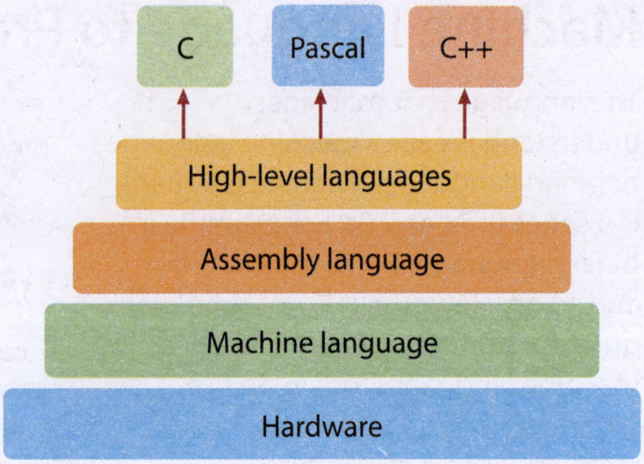

Fig. 1.10 | *Programming language to machine language*

Special programs called translators inside a computer convert instructions given in a high-level language to machine language. Figure 1.11 shows how high-level languages work.

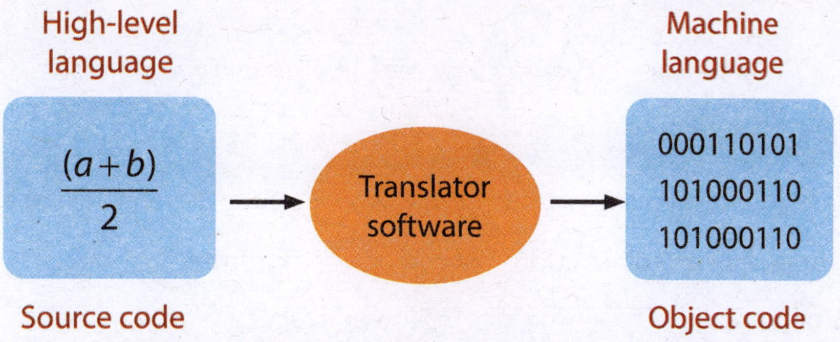

Fig. 1.11 | *How programming languages work*

> The formal way of giving instructions to the computer that produces a specific output is called a programming language or coding language.

Even though all high-level languages are written differently, they have the same underlying logical concepts. Table 1.3 shows codes of adding two numbers using Java and Python.

Table 1.3 | *Adding two numbers*

Java Code	Python Code
`int x = 5;`	`x = 5`
`int y = 6;`	`y = 6`
`int sum = x + y;`	`sum = x + y`
`System.out.println(sum);`	`print(sum)`

Translators

A translator/language processor is a type of system software. Before a program is executed, it is translated into binary language. A translator translates the programs into binary language and vice versa.

The code written in a high-level language is called the **source code** and the translated code in machine language is known as the **object code**. Some languages use compilers, while others use interpreters.

> Translators are programs inside the computer that convert high-level language into codes that machines can understand.

Compilers and interpreters can be understood with the help of the differences between them, as shown in Table 1.4.

Table 1.4 *Differences between compilers and interpreters*

Compilers	Interpreters
1. Scans the entire source code at once.	1. Scans the source code one line at a time.
2. Does not generate intermediate code.	2. Generates intermediate code.
3. Faster execution time.	3. Slower execution time.
4. C, C++, Java use compilers.	4. Python, JavaScript, RubyOnRails use interpreters.

Soak up!

Grace Murray Hopper (1906–1992) was one of the pioneers of computer programming. In addition to being a Mathematics professor, she also aided the war efforts of the United States of America during the Second World War, where she worked on the Mark I computer. She helped create one of the first compilers for computers, a historic contribution that led to advancement in Science and Technology. An annual set of conferences, named Grace Hopper Celebration of Women in Computing, takes place every year in her honour, which brings together women research and technology.

Today I learned!

- Computers are categorized on the basis of their processing power and storage capacity.
- The various categories of computers are microcomputers, minicomputers, mainframes and supercomputers.
- Embedded systems are defined as the systems consisting of a software component that serves a specific function embedded on the hardware of the device.
- Computers understand only machine language, which is a series of 0s and 1s.
- Assembly language uses mnemonics, but it is specific to the hardware of a computer.
- Machine language and assembly language, called low-level languages, are difficult and time-consuming to use.
- High-level languages can be easily understood by humans. Hence, programming using high-level languages is easier.
- 4GLs are characterized by user-friendliness and versatility, that is, they can be used in a wide range of applications.
- Translators are programs inside the computer that convert the high-level language into codes understandable by machines. Interpreters and compilers are different kinds of translators.

Revise and polish!

Learning Skills

1. Tick (✓) the correct answer.

a. Computers are broadly categorized on the basis of their use and ______________.

(i) data ☐ (ii) presentation ☐

(iii) USB ports ☐ (iv) processing power ☐

b. Which of the following computers are very affordable?

(i) Microcomputers ☐ (ii) Supercomputers ☐

(iii) Play stations ☐ (iv) Mainframes ☐

c. A ______________ is a portable computer.

(i) Mainframe ☐ (ii) Laptop ☐

(iii) Supercomputer ☐ (iv) Cloud ☐

d. Which of the following computers is a predecessor of microcomputers?

(i) Servers ☐ (ii) Supercomputers ☐

(iii) Minicomputers ☐ (iv) Mainframes ☐

e. Which of these computers use multiple processors?

(i) Laptops ☐ (ii) Tablets ☐

(iii) Desktop computers ☐ (iv) Mainframes ☐

f. Which of the following is not an example of a supercomputer?

(i) MacBook Pro ☐ (ii) Param ☐ (iii) Fukagu ☐ (iv) Pratyush ☐

g. TV, refrigerators, elevators and car dashboard are all examples of ______________.

(i) supercomputers ☐ (ii) embedded systems ☐

(iii) laptops ☐ (iv) mainframes ☐

h. Which generation of computers used vacuum tubes?

(i) First ☐ (ii) Second ☐ (iii) Third ☐ (iv) Fourth ☐

i. Which technology was used by the computers of third generation?

(i) Transistors ☐ (ii) Microprocessors ☐

(iii) Integrated circuits ☐ (iv) Artificial intelligence ☐

j. A translator is a type of ______________ software.

(i) system ☐ (ii) application ☐

(iii) utility ☐ (iv) processing ☐

2. Fill in the blanks.

a. ____________ are smaller than mainframes but larger than microcomputers.

b. The number of people who can use a microcomputer at a time is ____________.

c. The ____________ in an embedded system performs a very specific function.

d. There are ____________ generations of computers.

e. ____________ are translators that scan the entire code at once.

3. State whether the following statements are true (T) or false (F).

a. A tablet is smaller than a laptop but larger than a smartphone. ☐

b. A supercomputer sits comfortably on the desk. ☐

c. Machine language is a series of 0s and 1s. ☐

d. Instructions can be given to computers with the help of punched cards. ☐

e. The instructions written in a high-level language are known as code. ☐

4. Match the following

a.	4GL	(i)	Software on hardware
b.	Mainframes	(ii)	Used for airline reservations
c.	Embedded systems	(iii)	Assembly language
d.	5GL	(iv)	Python
e.	Mnemonics	(v)	Mercury

5. Arrange microcomputers, minicomputers, mainframes and supercomputers according to the given parameters.

	Highest			Lowest
Size				
Processing speed				
Price				

6. Categorize the following into low-level and high-level languages

Machine Language, Python, Java, C++, JQuery, C#, Assembly Language, Javascript, Mercury

a. High-level languages:

____

b. Low-level languages:

____

7. Fill in the diagrams with the correct steps.

a. How high-level languages are understood by the computer?

b. Categories of generation of languages

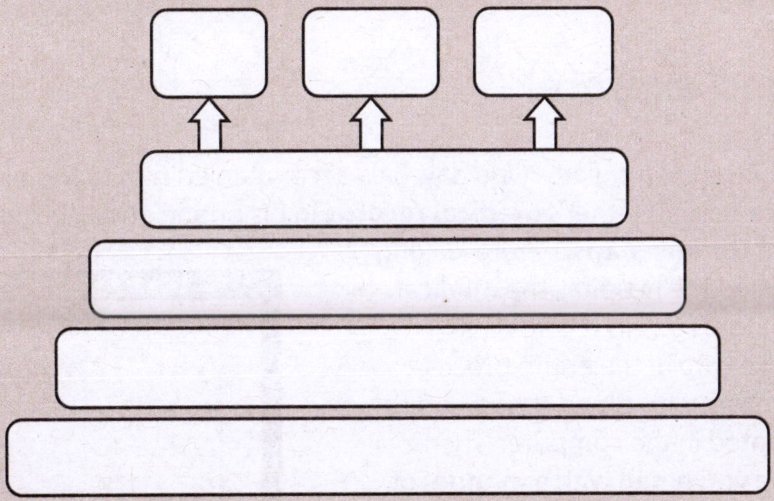

8. Answer the following questions

a. Explain how programming languages work.

b. What are some of the uses of supercomputers?

c. What is meant by generations of computers?

d. How did programming languages evolve?

e. What is the difference between interpreters and compilers?

Chapter

2

File Management and Data Organization

After reading this chapter, I will be able to:

- ✔ Define data, files, file formats and folders.
- ✔ Describe primary and secondary memory in a computer.
- ✔ Discuss moving/copying data from one drive to another drive.
- ✔ Explain how to move/copy data between storage devices.
- ✔ Use two or more applications at the same time.

Information Literacy

Brainstorm and explore!

Bala's father donates his blood regularly. One day, Bala accompanied him to the blood donation camp. Bala carried his father's **medical records** in his phone and checked the traffic status, using **Google Maps**, before leaving home. Once they reached the hospital, the medical staff checked **their systems** for his records and assigned a nurse to take care of the entire process. The nurse **carefully entered** his blood group and the quantity of blood donated in the computer. Then, the camp sent a **thank you email** with a **manual** of suggested food and beverages to avoid dizziness. Bala and his father came back home happy and satisfied!

Look at the words given in bold in the paragraph above. What do you notice? Do these words have anything in common? Write your observations in the space given below.

____

____

Data

Data is all around us—right from our personal records, such as name, age and date of birth, to the traffic information we use via Google Maps! A huge amount of data is generated as a result of the interaction between humans and machines in schools, offices, factories, airports and even on the road.

Storing, retrieving and processing data are, thus, an important part of computing. Data is constantly accessed and processed in the background for the smooth functioning of a computer.

Let us learn about how data is stored in a computer.

retrieve: pull out from saved information/objects

process: a software program manipulating or extracting data from a stored file

Soak up!

The scientific analysis and interpretation of a large amount of information held on computers is called data science.

Data is a collection of numbers, characters and symbols stored in a format that can be processed by a computer.

Files and Folders

We store documents, images, songs, videos and applications in computers. All these are made up of a sequence of numbers, characters and symbols. However, each of these is stored as a different kind of file in a computer. In a computer's memory, data is stored as the files and organized into folders.

A file is a container in a computer system that has information of a particular type.

Brush up!

Can you think of a few situations from everyday life where data is used? Write them here. Also, write where the data is stored. One is already done for you.

1. Timetable is written down in the school diary.
2. ______________________________
3. ______________________________
4. ______________________________
5. ______________________________

Since there are different types of files on a computer, it is important to organize them so that they can be located easily. This is done using a **folder** (Fig. 2.1).

A folder is the designated storage space used to store files and organize them in the computer. It can be created, modified and deleted.

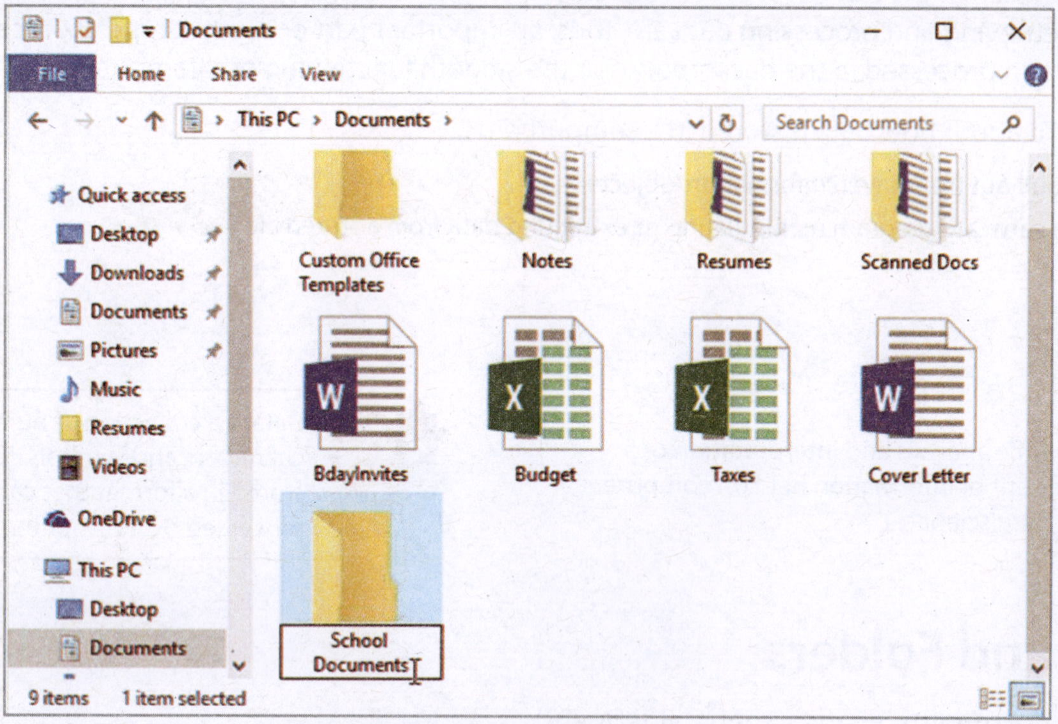

Fig. 2.1 | *Files and Folders in a computer*

File Formats

Files can be of different types—image files, audio files, video files, documents, application files and so forth. A video file is different from a document file because it has been encoded differently. Therefore, they have different file formats.

A file format is the way a file is encoded and saved into a computer. It tells the computer what to do when the file is opened.

encode: to change (information) into a set of letters, numbers or symbols that can be read by a computer

Brush up!

In the computer lab, open both an image file and a text document. Which letters follow the full stop in the file names? Are they same or different? Note down your observations here.

____

File formats describe the type of file with the help of extensions. Examples of some common extensions for different file types are discussed in Table 2.1.

Table 2.1 | *Different file formats*

Format	Extensions
Image	**.bmp:** stands for Bitmap image. **.jpeg:** stands for Joint Photographic Experts Group. **.png:** stands for Portable Network Graphics. **.gif:** stands for Graphics Interchange Format.
Audio	**.mp3:** was developed by Moving Pictures Experts Group. **.wav:** was developed by Microsoft and IBM. **.wma:** stands for Windows Media Audio. **.midi:** stands for Musical Instrument Digital Interface.
Video	**.avi:** stands for Audio Video Interleave. **.mpeg:** stands for Moving Picture Experts Group.
Document	**.docx:** used for Word documents. **.pdf:** stands for Portable Document Format. **.txt:** used for plain text.

extension: the character or group of characters after the full stop in the file name

Measuring File Sizes

Just like liquids and solids can be measured in liters and kilograms, respectively, files also have their unit of measurement. Can 10 litres of water be stored in a 1-litre bottle? No!

Similarly, a file larger than the storage capacity of the device cannot be accommodated there.

The smallest unit of measurement of a file is a **bit**. Bits come together to form **bytes**, which, in turn, come together to form larger file sizes. The different units used to measure file sizes are given in Table 2.2.

Table 2.2 | *Units of measurements of file sizes*

Units	Conversion	Example
Bit	Smallest unit of data	0 or 1
Byte	8 bits = 1 byte	'A' *A single character can be stored.*
Kilobyte (KB)	1024 bytes = 1 kilobyte	 *A text file can be stored.*
Megabyte (MB)	1024 kilobytes = 1 megabyte	 *An image file can be of 1 MB to several MBs, depending on the quality.*
Gigabyte (GB)	1024 megabytes = 1 gigabyte	 *A video file can be of several GBs.*
Terabyte (TB)	1024 gigabytes = 1 terabyte	 NASA's Hubble Telescope generates 10 TB data per year.

Brush up!

1. Radha loves learning new things and always participates in quiz competitions. One day at school, a friend told her about a new quizzing app that has more than 50 quiz topics. She went home from school and excitedly told her parents about it. However, when she tried to download the app on her mother's phone, it displayed the message—"Storage space not available". Why do you think this happened?
2. Luna has pictures from her birthday party last week. She wants to email them to all her friends. However, the email service restricts the size of the attachment to 25 MB. How can she make sure she can send pictures 50 MB large over email?

____

____

Searching for Files and Folders in a Computer

A computer is capable of storing hundreds of images, songs, documents and videos. Manually searching for these is time-consuming. Operating systems allow users to search for files with file names.

To search for a file in Windows 10, type the name of the file in the search bar on the bottom left corner of the Desktop (Fig. 2.2). Click on the desired result to open the file.

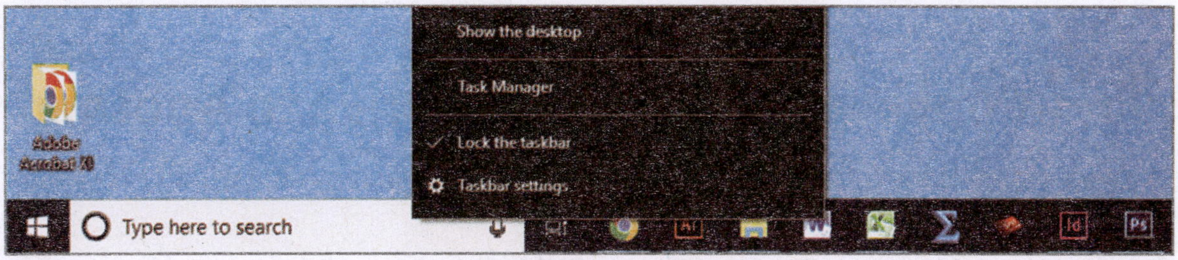

Fig. 2.2 | *Search bar in Windows 10*

Wildcard Characters

The brain has the ability to connect the dots. Similarly, the computer can search for incomplete file names with the help of a wildcard character.

A special character used to replace one or more missing letters in a file name is called a wildcard character.

Some of the commonly used wildcards in Windows operating system are discussed in Table 2.3.

Table 2.3 | *Commonly used wildcard characters*

Wildcard	Search term	Results
?	Shows all files bearing the missing character	**Search term:** Test?.png **Sample results** TestToday.png Test1.png
*	Shows all files bearing the missing term	**Search term:** Flower.* **Sample results** Flower.mp4 Flower.jpeg **Search term:** *.png **Sample results** Displays all .png image files on the computer

Clear up!

Fill in the missing letters to complete the names of these flowers.

L__L__   J______I__E   SU__FLO__ER   R__S__

Moving/Copying Data from One Drive to Another

Data is always stored in the form of a file/folder. The steps to move/copy data within a computer are as follows:

1. Locate the file/folder you want to move/copy. Right-click on it and click on the **Copy** option (Fig. 2.3).

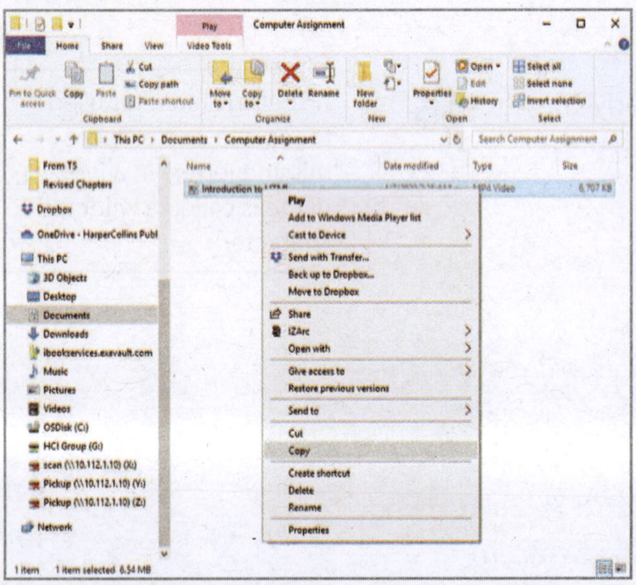

Fig. 2.3 | *Copying a file from a drive*

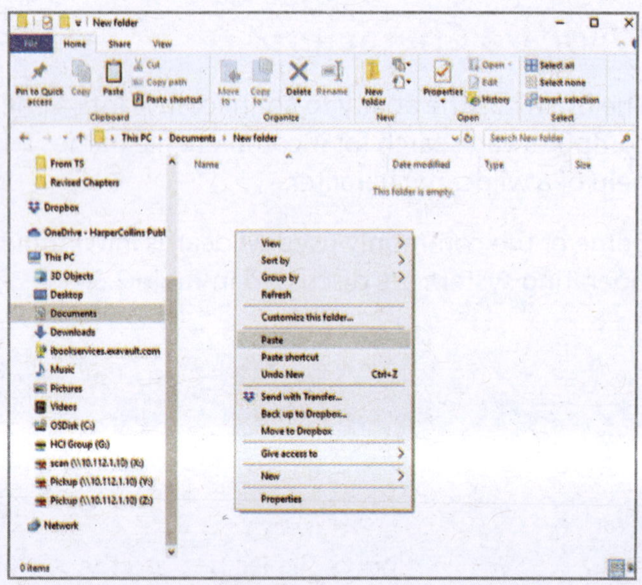

Fig. 2.4 | *Pasting the file on another location on a drive*

2. Now, open the folder where you want to paste the file.

3. Right-click anywhere in this folder and click on the **Paste** option (Fig. 2.4).

Remember that the Copy and Paste options are used to duplicate or copy a file/folder and paste it in another location on your computer. If you want to move your file from one location to another, select the **Cut** option and then **Paste** it on the desired location.

Soak up!

The cut/copied part of the picture is stored in a temporary folder called the Clipboard.

Moving/Copying Data from a Storage Device to Computer

Storage devices such as a USB drive or an external hard disk can be connected to the computer. The steps for moving/copying files are similar to the steps for moving files within a computer.

1. Connect the storage device to the computer.
2. Locate the folder/file in your computer that you want to copy. Right-click and select the **Copy** option.
3. Once the folder opens, right-click and select the **Copy** option. Alternatively, you can select the file by clicking on it and use the keyboard shortcut Ctrl+C to copy the file.
4. Now, open the folder on the storage device where you want to paste the file.
5. Right-click anywhere in this folder and select the **Paste** option. Alternatively, you can use the keyboard shortcut Ctrl+V.
6. Once all the files are moved, click on the **Eject Media** icon on the bottom right (Fig. 2.5). Once it indicates it is safe to remove the storage device, unplug it from the device.

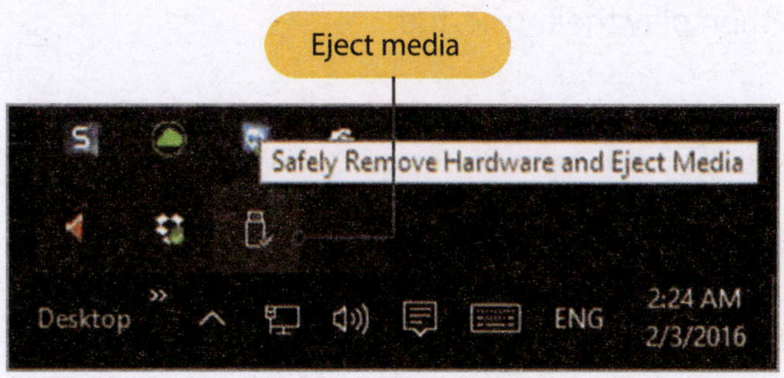

Fig. 2.5 | *Eject media*

Crank up!

Important keyboard shortcuts are given below:

Action	Keyboard Shortcut
Copy a file/folder	Ctrl+C
Cut a file/folder	Ctrl+X
Paste a file/folder	Ctrl+V

Clear up!

Open a folder containing many files. Press the keyboard shortcut Ctrl+A. Note down what happens and the functionality of the shortcut.

___

___

___

Working with Multiple Applications

The computer allows us to open and work with files of different file formats at once. For example, while preparing a presentation for the Science project in MS Power Point, we can play videos to check if they need to be included. We can also draw pictures using MS Paint and insert them into our presentation. This way, our computer enables us to do multitasking.

The steps to play music while browsing the web are given below.

1. Open the folder in which the music file is stored.
2. Double-click on the song you want to play. The song is now playing on the Windows Media Player or the music application of your choice.
3. Click on the **Minimize** button on the top right corner of the music player window. This will hide the music player from the Desktop.
4. Once the music player is minimized, the song folder would be open. Minimize the song folder as well, using the same Minimize button from the top right corner.
5. Open the browser window by double-clicking on the browser icon on the desktop. If you are unable to find the icon, type its name in Cortana bar and click on the browser's icon to open it.
6. Enter the URL of the website you want to visit.

Note: The order in which we open applications does not matter. We can first open the browser and then play the music, too.

Technology Literacy

Crank up!

A provision called Task Manager in Windows 10 allows us to view all the applications open at any given time. The shortcut to open the windows manager is Ctrl+Alt+Del → Click on Task Manager.

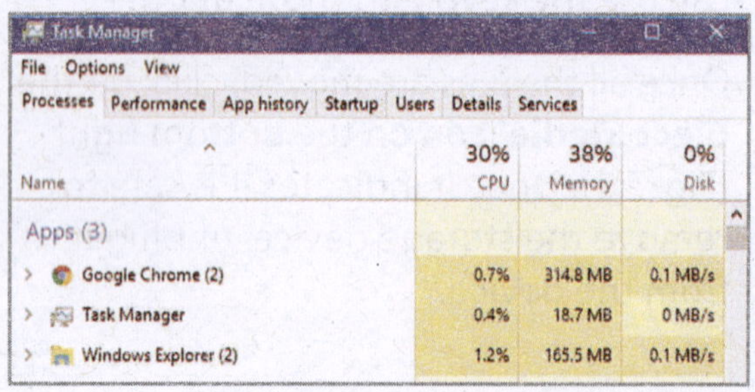

Today I learned!

- Data is a collection of numbers, characters and symbols coded into a format that can be stored in and processed by a computer.
- A file is a container in a computer system for storing information of a particular type.
- The different file formats are images, documents, audio, videos and applications. They can be recognized by their file extensions.
- A folder is a division of space in a computer used to store files. Folders are named by users.
- A wildcard is a symbol used to represent one or more missing characters in a file name.
- A file extension shows the format of the file.
- Files can be moved/copies between drives of a computer and storage devices.
- Copy and Paste options are used to duplicate or copy a file/folder and paste it in another location on the drive or a storage device.
- Cut and Paste commands are used to remove or delete a file/folder and paste it in another location on the drive or a storage device.

Revise and polish!

Learning Skills

1. Tick (✓) the correct answer.

a. While of the following is a typical size of a song?

(i) A few MBs ☐ (ii) More than a GB ☐

(iii) One KB ☐ (iv) A few TBs ☐

b. In the computer memory, data is organized as ____________.

(i) files ☐ (ii) images ☐

(iii) songs ☐ (iv) videos ☐

c. The operating system allows users to search for ____________ files.

(i) videos ☐ (ii) music ☐

(iii) documents ☐ (iv) videos, music and documents ☐

d. To which of the following locations, files can be copied or moved?

(i) Folder ☐ (ii) Drive ☐

(iii) Storage device ☐ (iv) All of the above places ☐

e. Which of the following terms is used to represent a missing character or symbol?

(i) Wildcard character ☐ (ii) Blank card ☐

(iii) Alphanumeric key ☐ (iv) Numeric key ☐

f. NASA's Hubble Telescope collects data in the order of magnitude of ____________.

(i) KBs ☐ (ii) MBs ☐ (iii) GBs ☐ (iv) TBs ☐

g. File format can be identified by its ____________.

(i) extension ☐ (ii) links ☐ (iii) location ☐ (iv) size ☐

h. Which of the following is a music file format?

(i) .mov ☐ (ii) .mp3 ☐ (iii) .xls ☐ (iv) .pdf ☐

i. Which of the following is an image file format?

(i) .mp3 ☐ (ii) .avi ☐ (iii) .xls ☐ (iv) .png ☐

j. Files can be organized into ____________.

(i) folders ☐ (ii) boxes ☐

(iii) bags ☐ (iv) compartments ☐

2. Fill in the blanks.

a. Data is a collection of ____________, ____________ and symbols coded into a format that can be stored and processed by a computer.

b. A ____________ is a container in a computer system for storing information of a particular type.

c. The different file formats are audio, ____________, images, documents, etc.

d. A ____________ is a division of space in a computer used to store files.

e. ____________ refers to the use of an external server for storage and processing of data and accessed via the internet.

3. Match the following.

a.	Bit	(i)	1024 gigabytes
b.	Byte	(ii)	1024 kilobytes
c.	Kilobyte (KB)	(iii)	1024 bytes
d.	Megabyte (MB)	(iv)	8 bits
e.	Terabyte (TB)	(v)	Smallest unit of data

4. Define the following terms.

a. Data
b. File
c. Folder
d. GB
e. File format

5. Answer the following questions.

a. Define file, folder and file format.

b. You have one song in a folder full of class projects. What are the steps to move the song file to another folder?

c. Your friend has given you a USB drive with pictures of your birthday. What are the steps to copy it to your desktop computer?

d. What is a wildcard and what is it used for?

e. Write a note on units of measurement of file sizes.

6. Neha has saved the following files in a folder called "My Collection". List the different folders that can be created to organize these files.

Cat.jpg	swan.jpeg	lion.jpeg
duck.png	Birthday.mp3	New Year.mp3
Project.pdf	Assignment.doc	Jungle Safari.mov

____

____

____

7. **Varsha's family computer has the following files stored in it. Give the file types for these extensions.**

	File	File type
a.	 sunflower.png	
b.	 ScienceProject.docx	
c.	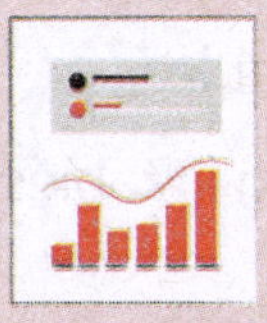 ReportCard2022.pdf	
d.	 VandeMataram.mp3	
e.	 FamilyTaxInfo.xls	
f.	 OotyVacationPicsVideos.rar	

Experiential Learning

Lab Activity

Using the internet, find the full forms of the following file extensions.

a. .jpeg
b. .png
c. .mov
d. .pdf
e. .xls
f. .avi
g. .mp3
h. .mp4
i. .ppt
j. .doc

Chapter 3

Word Processor—Tabular Presentation

After reading this chapter, I will be able to:

- ✔ Define a table.
- ✔ Create a table and enter data in the table.
- ✔ Edit a table.
- ✔ Format the row/column/table.
- ✔ Apply borders and shading in tables.

Brainstorm and explore!

The teacher had asked two students of class 6 to prepare timetable for Monday. Rachit made the timetable shown in the first box and Priya made the timetable shown in second box.

Rachit's Timetable

The first period on Monday is Science, the second period is Geography and the third period is EVS. Then, there is a short break of 20 minutes. The fourth period is Mathematics, the fifth period is History and the sixth period is Computer Science. The first period on Tuesday is ....

Priya's Timetable

Period	Subject
1	Science
2	Geography
3	EVS
Lunch break (20 minutes)	
4	Mathematics
5	History
6	Computer Science

Which of the two timetables is easy-to-read and recall? Give reasons for your choice.

____

____

There are situations where we want to organize data in such a way that it occupies less space and can be compared easily. In such situations, we can choose tables to present the data. A table is a good and simple way of representing text and numerical data in rows and columns (Fig. 3.1).

A table is a good and simple way of representing text and numerical data in the row and column format.

- **Row:** It is the arrangement of cells in the horizontal direction.
- **Column:** It is the arrangement of cells in the vertical direction.
- **Cell:** It is the intersection of a row and a column.

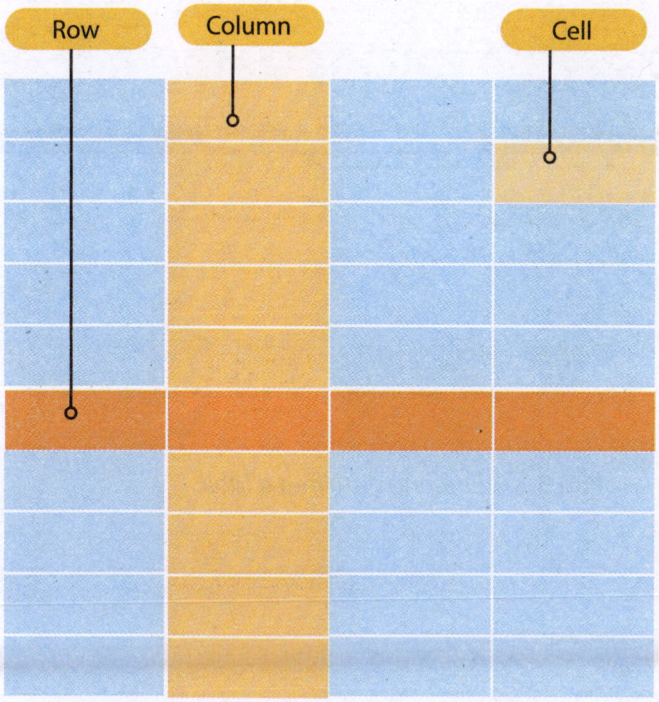

Fig. 3.1 | *Rows, columns and cells in a table*

Link up!

We see different types of data organized into tables around us. For example, board games, timetable, etc.

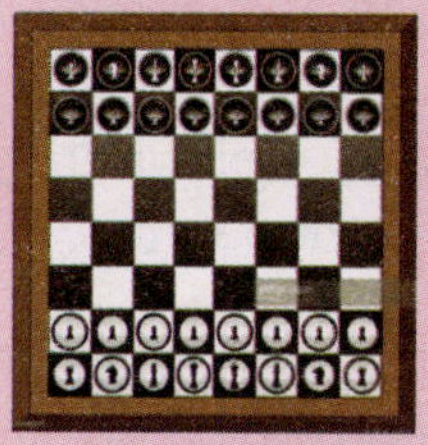

Creating a Table

The steps to create a table are as follows:

1. Place the cursor at the location where a table needs to be inserted.
2. Select the **Table** option on the **Insert** tab (Fig. 3.2).

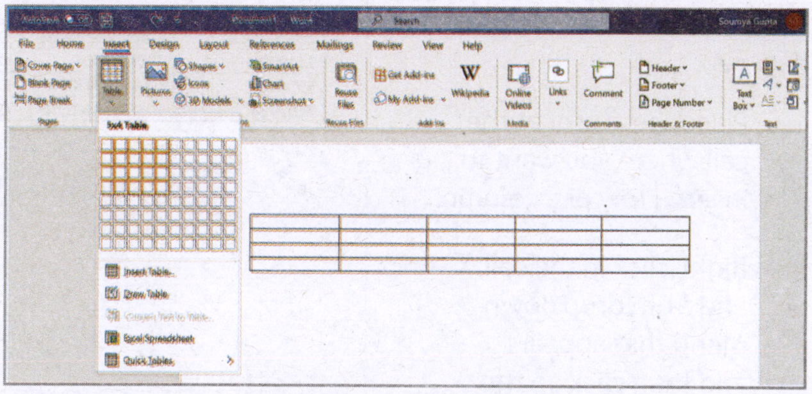

Fig. 3.2 | *Creating a table*

3. Fix the number of rows and columns in the table by moving the pointer over the grid.

4. Click the left mouse button when finished. The table will be inserted.

Technology Literacy

Crank up!

We can also use the **Insert Table...** option to create a table. When we click on this option, the **Insert Table** dialog box appears. We can create a table by specifying the number of columns and rows in this box.

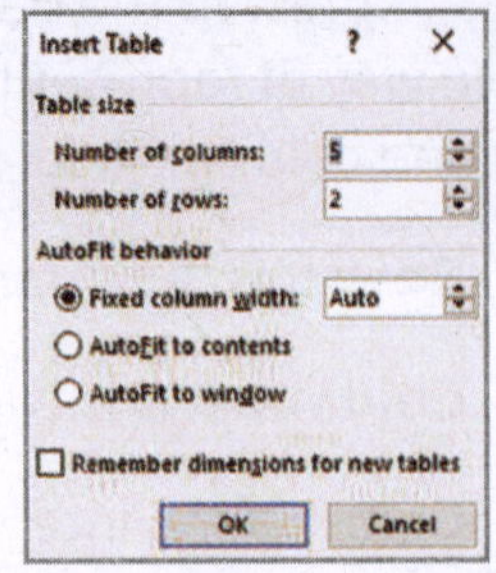

Entering Data in a Table

After creating a table, we can insert data into it (Fig. 3.3). The steps to enter data into a table are given below:

1. Click in the cell where you want to enter data.

2. Type in the information that needs to be displayed in the rows and columns.

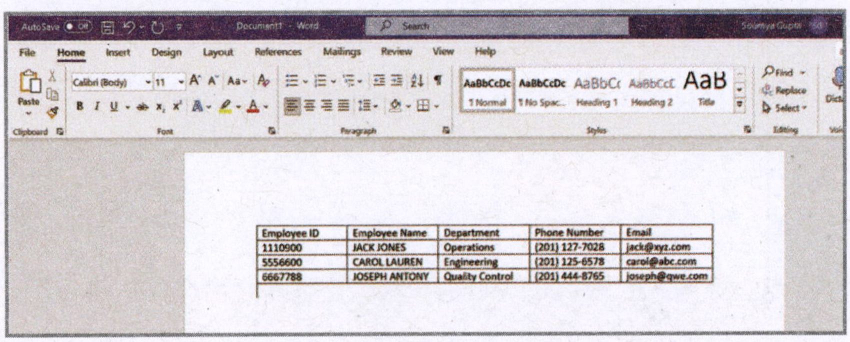

Fig. 3.3 | *Entering data into a table*

Editing a Table

A table can be edited in four ways as discussed below:

Inserting Rows and Columns in a Table

Here are the steps to add rows or columns to the table (Fig. 3.4).

1. Place the cursor at the cell where you want to insert a row or a column.

2. Right-click in the cell, and from drop down menu that appears and then click on the arrow next to the **Insert** option.

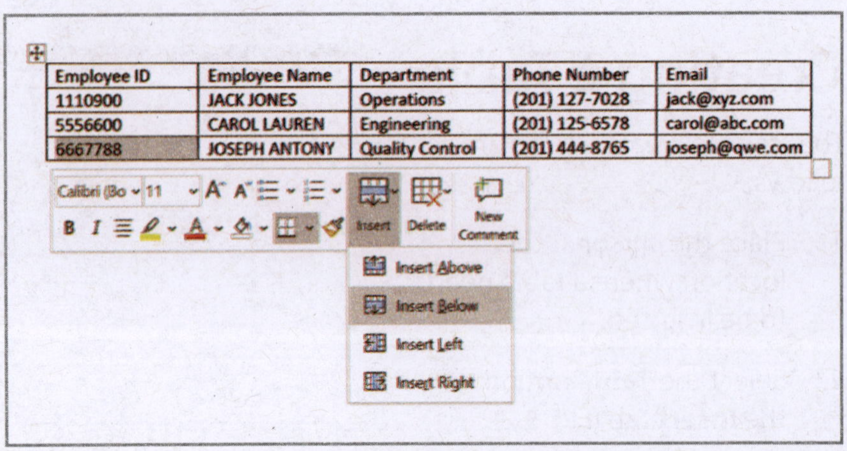

Fig. 3.4 | *Insert and Delete options*

3. Another submenu will appear for adding rows and columns. Click on the desired option.
   - **Insert Above:** Adds a row above the current cell.
   - **Insert Below:** Adds a row below the current cell.
   - **Insert Left:** Adds a column to the left of the current cell.
   - **Insert Right:** Adds a column to the right of the current cell.

Deleting Rows and Columns in a Table

Follow these steps to delete a row or column from the table:

1. Select the row or column that needs to be deleted.
2. Right-click, and in the drop down menu that appears, click on the **Delete Rows** or **Delete Columns** option. To delete the entire table, click on the **Delete Table** option (Fig. 3.5).

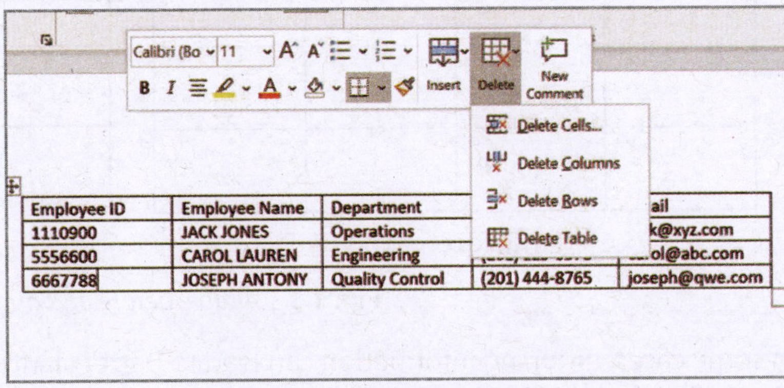

Fig. 3.5 | *Deletion options in a table*

Brush up!

Which of the following tables represents the data of students and teachers in a better way? Give reasons for your choice.

Table 1

Teacher		Student	
Name	Age	Name	Age
Shakti	30	Vikas	12
Rajesh	40	Sameera	12
Kiran	43	Aditya	11

Table 2

Teacher		Student	
Name	**Age**	**Name**	**Age**
Shakti	30	Vikas	12
Rajesh	40	Sameera	12
Kiran	43	Aditya	11

____

Soak up!

To select the entire table at once, click on any cell within the table and use the keyboard shortcut Ctrl+A.

Merging and Splitting Cells in a Table

A table with 4 columns and 5 rows is given in Fig. 3.6(a). If we merge the first and second columns of the first row and the third and fourth columns of the same row, we will get a merged table, as shown in Fig. 3.6(b).

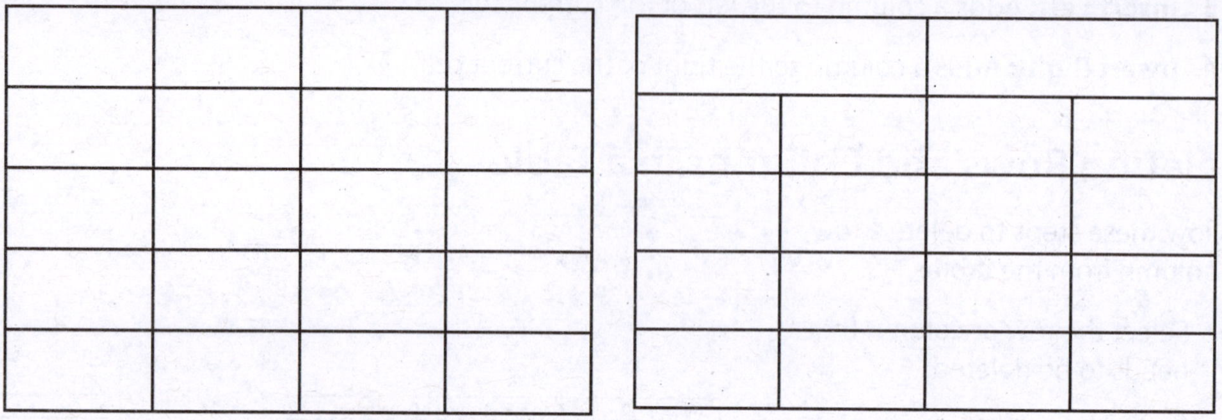

(a) Before mering (b) After merging

Fig. 3.6 | *A table before and after merge*

In some cases, grouping information can lead to better clarity and neater presentation. Tables in MS Word allow us to organize information by merging cells. The steps to merge cells are as follows:

1. Select two or more cells that need to be merged.
2. Right-click in the selected area.
3. Click on the **Merge Cells** option from the submenu that appears (Fig. 3.7). The desired cells will be merged into one cell.

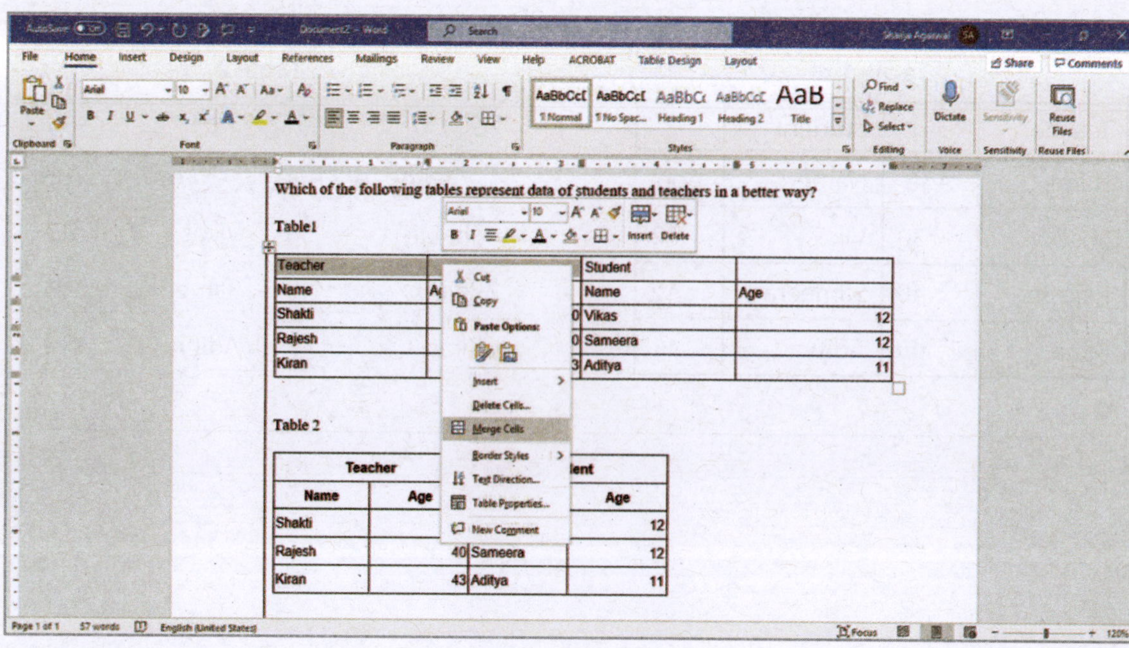

Fig. 3.7 | *Merging cells*

To split merged cells, right-click on the cell and then select the **Split Cells** option (Fig. 3.8).

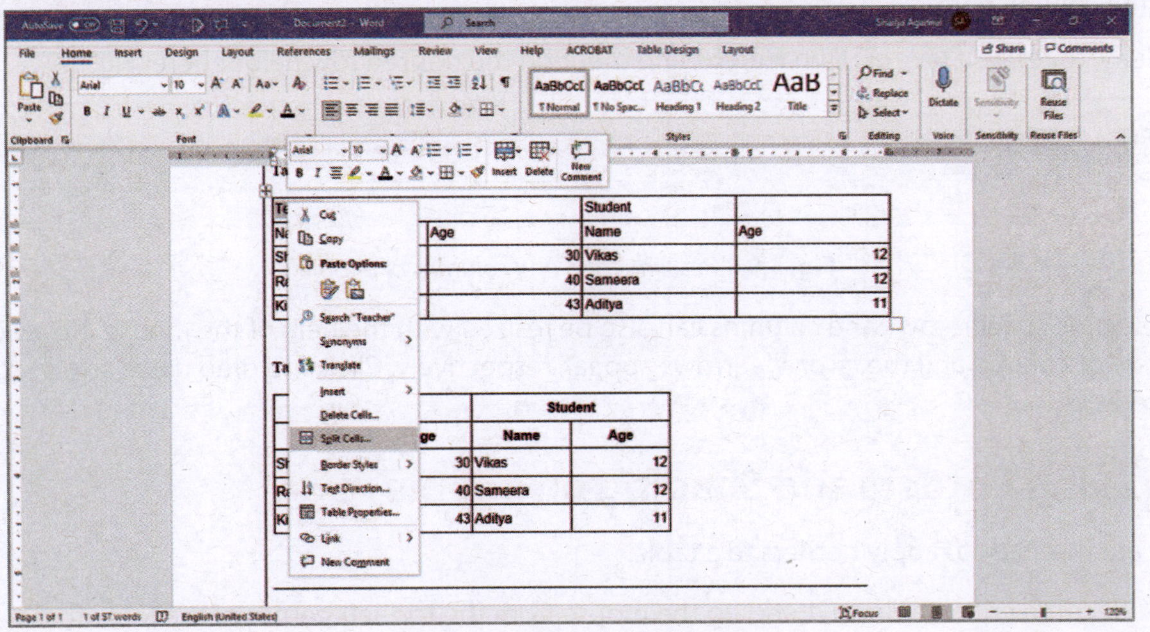

Fig. 3.8 | *Splitting merged cells*

Soak up!

When we create a table in MS Word, notice the additional two tabs that appear on the top.

These tabs are **Table Design** and **Layout**.

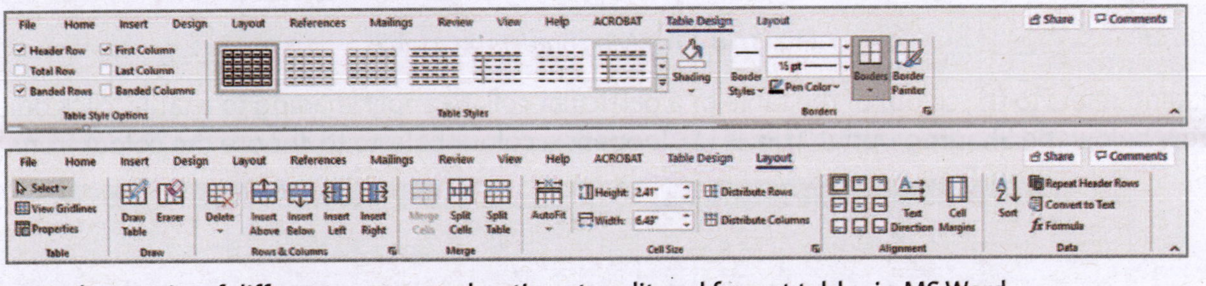

These tabs consist of different groups and options to edit and format tables in MS Word.

Formatting a Table

Formatting a table highlights the important information and helps us better organize it. Let us learn about the different ways in which we can format a table.

Resizing Rows and Columns

MS Word allows us to adjust the width and height of columns and rows, respectively. Here are the steps to change the width of a column:

1. Click on the cell to be resized.

2. On the **Layout** tab, in the **Cell Size** group, click on **Width**. Mention the desired size of the column here.

Similarly, to resize a row, click on **Height** and mention the desired row height here (Fig. 3.9).

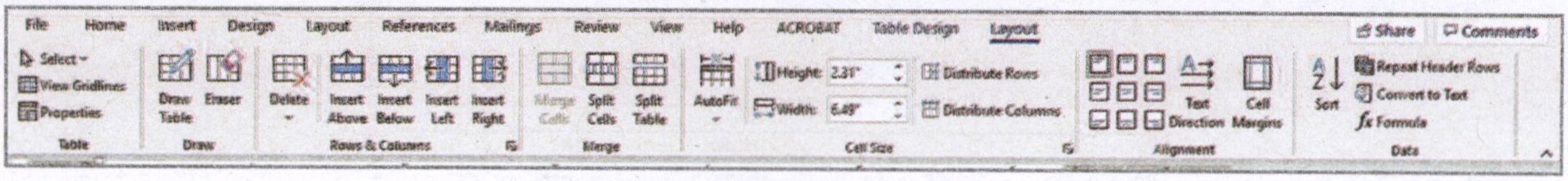

Fig. 3.9 | *Resizing rows and columns of a table*

Note: Some specific rows and columns can also be resized with the help of the mouse. Hover over the row or column and the ⇳ or ◂||▸ arrows appear, respectively. Click and drag these arrows to the desired size.

Applying Borders and Shading on a Table

Here are the steps to apply borders to a table:

1. Select the entire table by dragging the mouse from the top-left corner of the table to the bottom-right.

2. Click on the **Table Design** tab and navigate to **Borders** group (Fig. 3.10). The border style, colour and thickness can be created using this group.

Fig. 3.10 | *Applying borders on a table*

Shading refers to the colour of the table or a particular cell. To apply shading to a table, click on the arrow below the **Shading** option (Fig. 3.11). It opens a colour palette to choose the colour from.

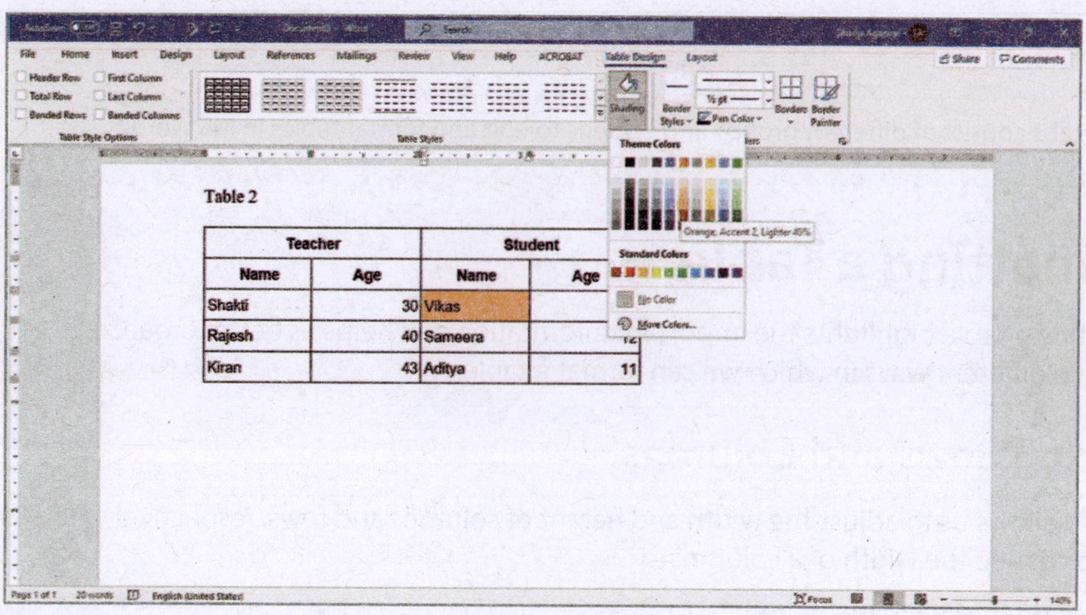

Fig. 3.11 | *Applying shading on a table*

The similar steps can be followed to change the colour in a table cell. In Step 1, select the cell instead of the entire table and follow the steps (Fig. 3.12).

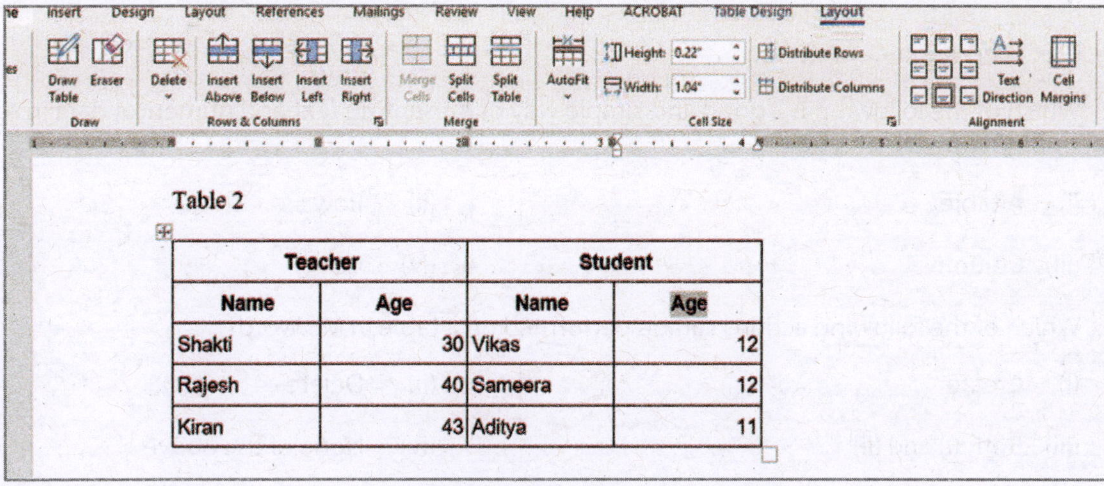

Fig. 3.12 | *Aligning text in a table*

Aligning the Text

The steps to align text within a cell or table are as follows:

1. Select the entire table or a cell in which you want to align text.
2. From the **Layout** tab, select the desired alignment option from the available nine options.

Clear up!

Create the following table. List the tabs you have used to create it.

Top Left	Top Center	Top Right
Middle Left	Center	Middle Right
Bottom Left	Bottom Center	Bottom Right

Today I learned!

- A table helps to present the text and numerical data in a row and column format.
- The arrangement of cells in the horizontal direction is called a row.
- The arrangement of cells in the vertical direction is called a column.
- The intersection of a row and a column is called a cell.
- We can create a table using the Insert tab.
- We can add, delete and resize rows and columns in a table.
- Two or more cells in a table can be merged to organize data. We can also split a cell into a number of cells.
- We can apply different borders to a table.
- Shading changes the colour of the table or a particular cell.
- We can align text within a cell in nine different ways.

Revise and polish!

Learning Skills

1. Tick (✓) the correct answer.

a. Which of the following is a good and simple way of presenting text and numerical data in row and column format?

(i) A table ☐ (ii) Row ☐

(iii) Column ☐ (iv) Cell ☐

b. Which of the following actions can be performed on a table in MS Word?

(i) Create ☐ (ii) Delete ☐

(iii) Both (i) and (ii) ☐ (iv) None of the above ☐

c. Which of the following formatting options can be used on a table in MS Word?

(i) Borders and Shading ☐ (ii) Alignment ☐

(iii) Both (i) and (ii) ☐ (iv) Shading ☐

d. Two cells in a table are joined together with the help of the ____________ option.

(i) Mix cells ☐ (ii) Join cells ☐

(iii) Merge cells ☐ (iv) Connect cells ☐

e. Merging cells is a way of ____________.

(i) Organizing data neatly ☐ (ii) Making the table smaller ☐

(iii) Making the table larger ☐ (iv) All of the above ☐

f. Which of the following are the components of a table?

(i) Row and columns ☐ (ii) Columns and cells ☐

(iii) Rows, columns and cells ☐ (iv) Rows and cells ☐

g. The intersection of a row and a column is a ____________.

(i) cell ☐ (ii) box ☐ (iii) rectangle ☐ (iv) square ☐

h. Moving the position of text within the cell is known as changing its ____________.

(i) position ☐ (ii) alignment ☐ (iii) spot ☐ (iv) place ☐

i. Under which tab is the Merge Cells option is present?

(i) File ☐ (ii) Design ☐ (iii) Table ☐ (iv) Layout ☐

j. Which of the following tabs consists of the Shading option?

(i) Layout ☐ (ii) Design ☐ (iii) Table ☐ (iv) Outline ☐

2. Fill in the blanks.

a. Once a table is created, ____________ can be entered in the table.

b. The intersection of rows and columns is called a ____________.

c. ____________ information can lead to better clarity and neater presentation.

d. ____________ refers to the colour of the table or a particular cell.

e. Just as cells can be merged, they can also be ____________.

3. Match the following.

a.	Rows	(i)	Grouping cells together
b.	Columns	(ii)	Vertical
c.	Merging cells	(iii)	Layout tab
d.	Formatting	(iv)	Horizontal
e.	Alignment	(v)	Shading and Borders

4. Read the following table carefully. Then, answer the questions given below.

	C1	C2	C3	C4	C5
R1	apple	fox	lion	sheep	giraffe
R2	rose	banana	jasmine	sunflower	hibiscus
R3	yellow	pink	orange	blue	green
R4	circle	triangle	rectangle	litchi	square
R5	cheetah	dragon	bear	tiger	pineapple

a. Give the values in the following cells.

(i) R1C4 ____________

(ii) R5C2 ____________

(iii) R3C3 ____________

(iv) R2C3 ____________

(v) R5C2 ____________

b. What are the cell references for the following values?

(i) lion ____________

(ii) square ____________

(iii) cheetah ____________

(iv) orange ____________

(v) rose ____________

Lab Activities

Experiential Learning

Create the following tables using MS Word:

a. A table showing your top three favourite non-academic books and the names of the authors

b. A table with the names of any five historic monuments, the year they were built in and by whom

c. Time-table of your class

d. A table representing your favourite sports players and their top scores

Group Activity

Collaboration

Brainstorm with your lab partner and list five uses of tables in everyday life.

Chapter

4

Word Processor—Mail Merge

After reading this chapter, I will be able to:

- ✔ Explain what Mail Merge does in MS Word.
- ✔ Demonstrate the various steps to effectively use Mail Merge for a document.
- ✔ Show how to print documents.

Technology Literacy

Brainstorm and explore!

Sameer is organizing a seminar on cyber security in his apartment complex. He wants to invite his friends and teachers to attend this seminar. He created a beautiful invitation using MS Word, mentioning the date, time and the venue details. He does not want to send a common letter to everyone. He wants to make sure that they receive a personal invitation, with their names mentioned individually in the letter. What do you think Sameer should do? Discuss in your class.

Mail Merge helps us create and send personalized documents containing similar information to many people. The main document is to be typed only once. The unique information in each document comes from a list containing the names of the recipients and other required details, called the **data source**. Mail Merge combines the main document and the data source to create a personalized copy for each recipient.

> The feature of MS Word with which a document can be emailed to multiple people with customized information about them is called Mail Merge.

Clear up!

Can you think of three situations where you can use Mail Merge? Write them here.

1. ________________________________

2. ________________________________

3. ________________________________

Mail Merge can be broken down into four phases, comprising six steps, as shown in Fig. 4.1.

		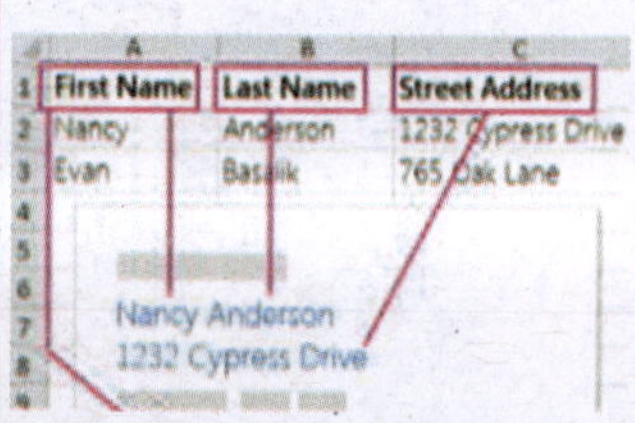	
1. Set up the main document a. Select the document type b. Select the starting document	**2. Create the data source** a. Select recipients	**3. Add merge fields** a. Write your letter	**4. Preview and complete the merge** a. Preview your letters b. Complete the merge

Fig. 4.1 | *The Mail Merge process*

Set Up the Main Document

The Mail Merge process starts with setting up of the main document, the steps for which are as follows:

1. Select the **Mailings** tab. Then, click on **Start Mail Merge → Step by Step Mail Merge Wizard** (Fig. 4.2).

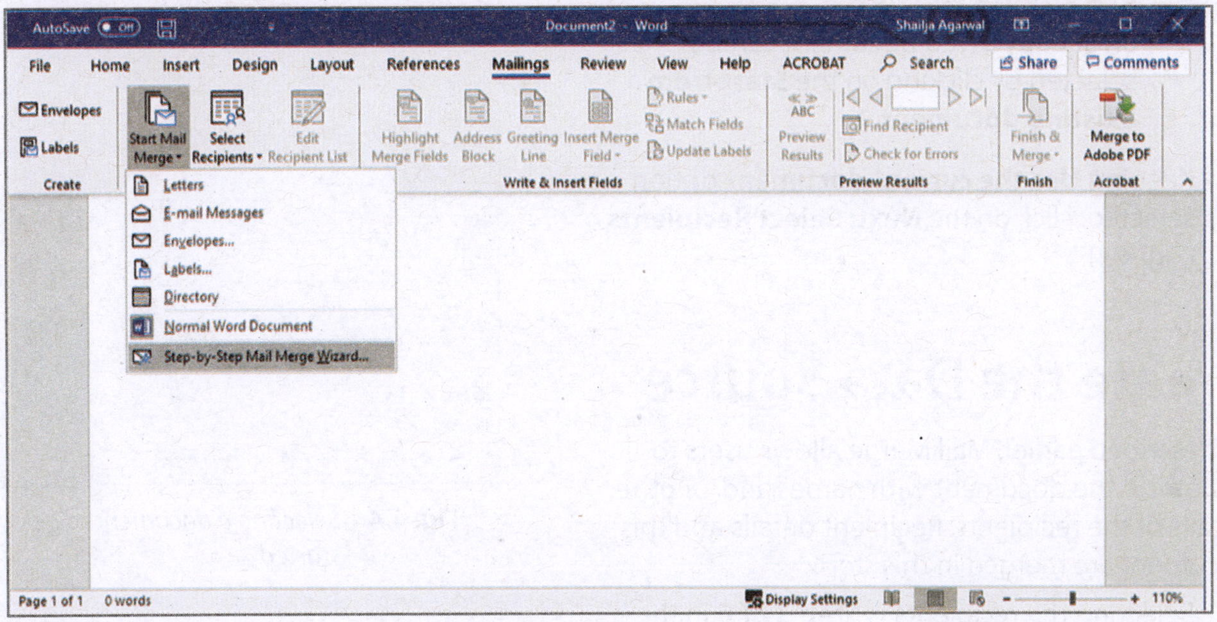

Fig. 4.2 | *Start Mail Merge*

2. The Mail Merge task pane opens on the right side of the MS Word window. Selecting the document type is **Step 1 of 6**. Here, the **Letters** option is selected by default. Notice how the small description below the options is displayed when each of the options is selected. With **Letters** selected, click on **Next: Starting document** (Fig. 4.3).

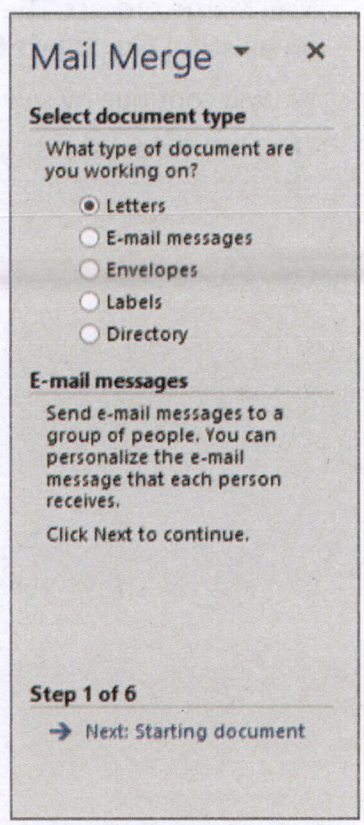

Fig. 4.3 | *Selecting the document type*

Soak up!

In the **Start Mail Merge** option, **Letters** is the default option. We can choose other type of documents, as well. Each document type displays a description.

3. Selecting the starting document is **Step 2 of 6**. Here,
   a. the currently opened document can be selected by checking the option next to **Use the current document**.
   b. a template can be selected by clicking on **Start from a template**.
   c. an already saved document can be selected by clicking on the **Start from existing document**.

   Keeping **Use the current document** option selected, click on the **Next: Select Recipients** (Fig. 4.4).

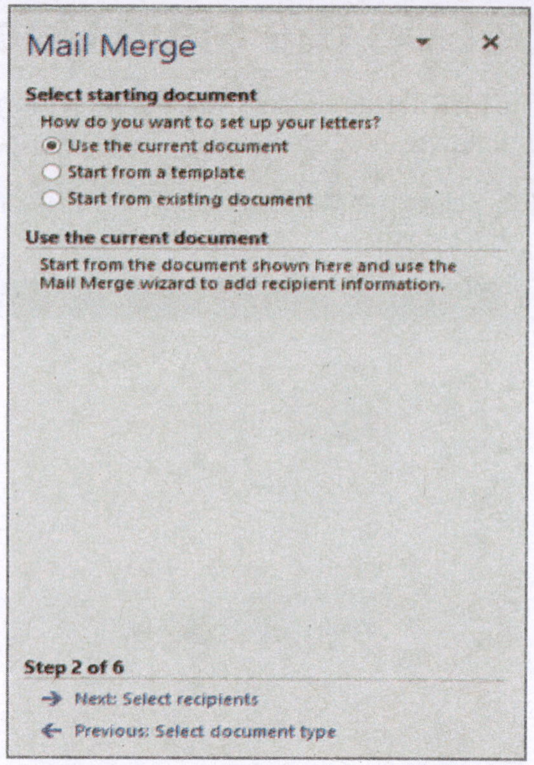

Fig. 4.4 | *Selecting a document to get started*

Create the Data Source

As described earlier, Mail Merge allows users to customize the document with names and/or other details of the recipients. Recipient details and this document are merged in this step.

4. Selecting the recipients is **Step 3 of 6** in the Mail Merge process. These details can be imported by selecting one of the three options: **Use an existing list, Select from Outlook contacts, Type a new list**.

   We will continue by selecting the last option, **Type a new list → Create** (Fig. 4.5).

   The **New Address List** dialog box will appear (Fig. 4.6).

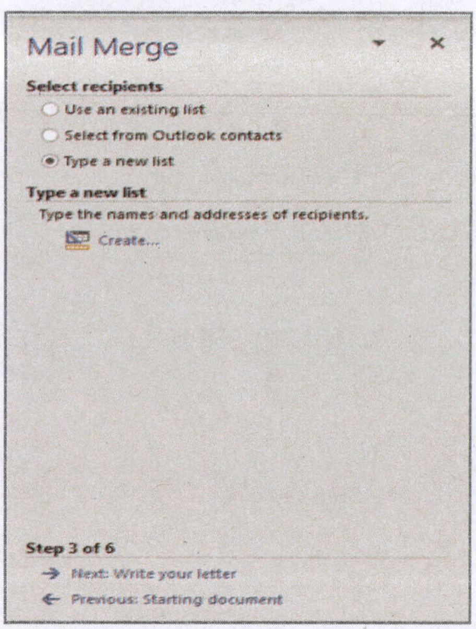

Fig. 4.5 | *Selecting recipients*

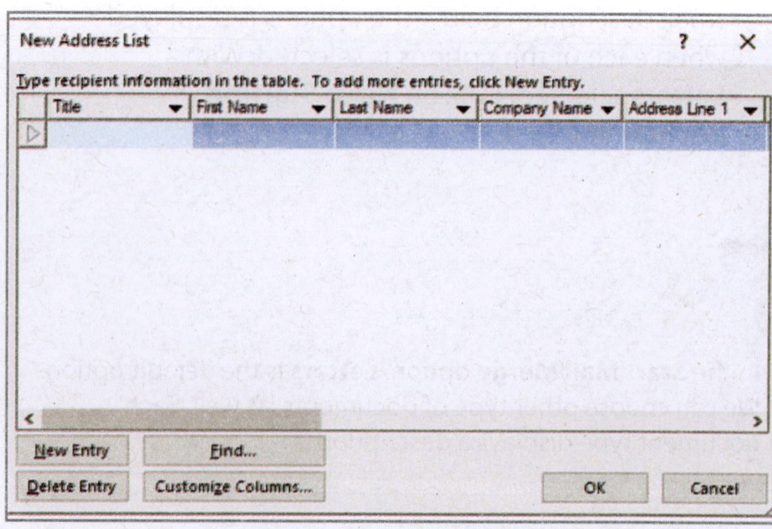

Fig. 4.6 | *New Address List dialog box*

5. In the **New Address List** dialog box, select the **Customize Columns** option. A **Customize Address List** dialog will appear (Fig. 4.7). Note that any field can be added, renamed or deleted. At this point, select the fields you want in your list. Click on **OK**.

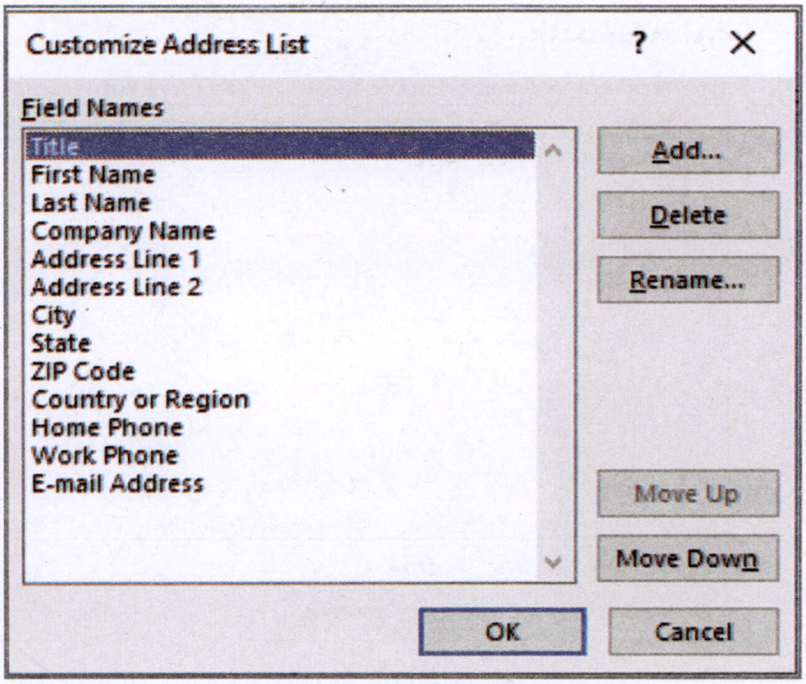

Fig. 4.7 | *Customize Address List*

6. The **New Address List** dialog box is displayed again (Fig. 4.8). To enter new recipients, click on the **New Entry** button. Click on **OK** after all the recipients are added (Fig. 4.9).

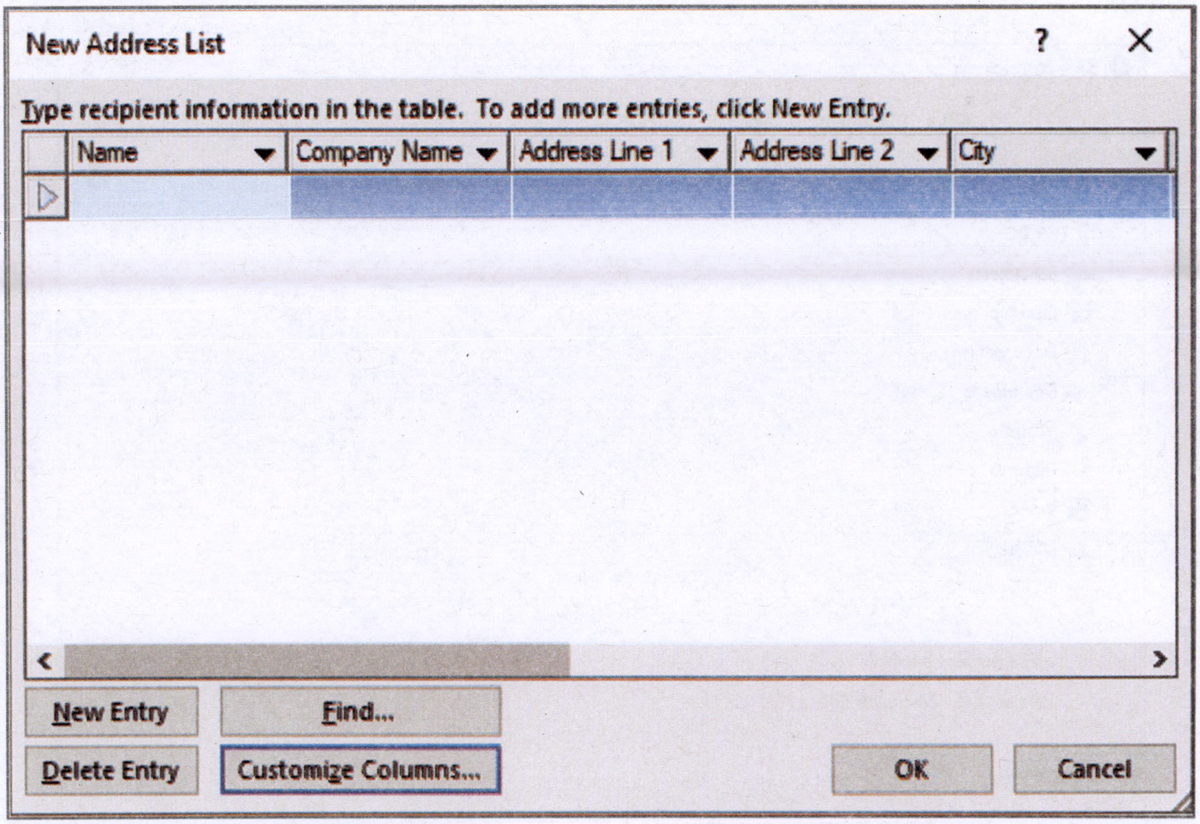

Fig. 4.8 | *New Address List dialog box after customizations*

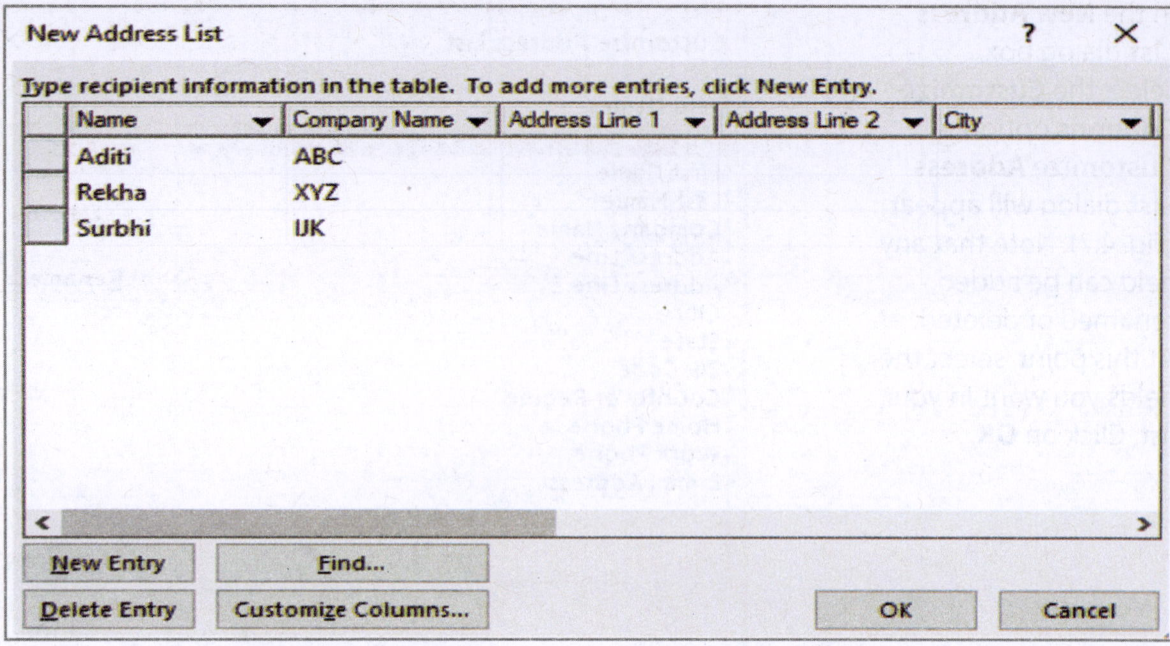

Fig. 4.9 | *New Address List dialog box with the list of recipients*

7. This opens the **Save Address List** dialog box (Fig. 4.10), which can be used to save the list created in a location on your computer. Choose a filename and click on the **Save** button. This opens the **Mail Merge Recipients** window (Fig. 4.11). This allows us to view and edit the data entered and to select individual recipients. After the suitable recipients have been selected, click on **OK.**

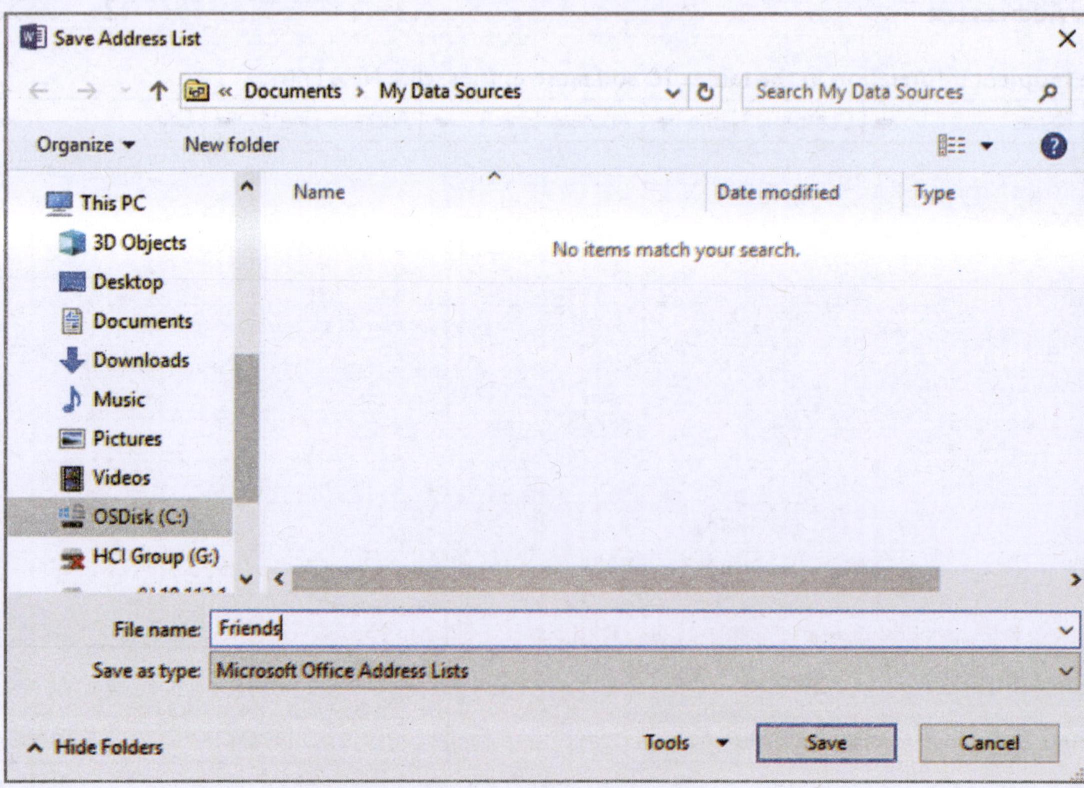

Fig. 4.10 | *Save Address List dialog box*

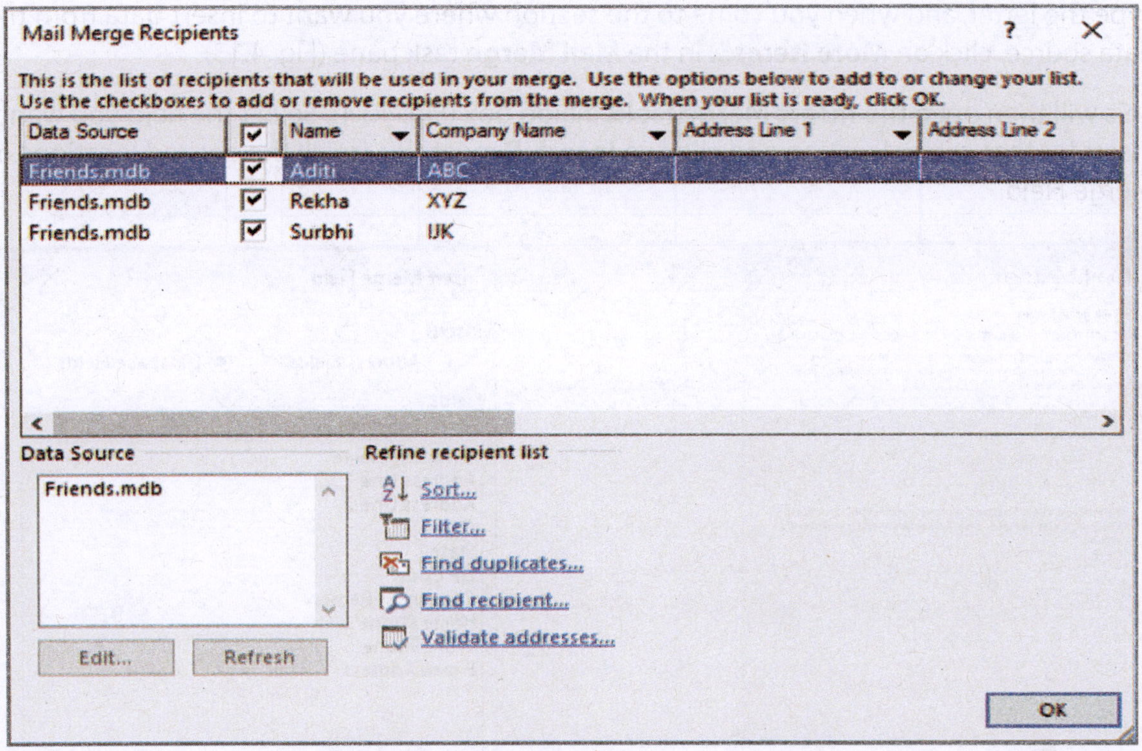

Fig. 4.11 | *Mail Merge Recipients window*

8. The list of recipients is now saved. Click on **Use an existing list** from the **Mail Merge** task pane (Fig. 4.12). Now, select **Next: Write your letter** to begin **Step 4 of 6**.

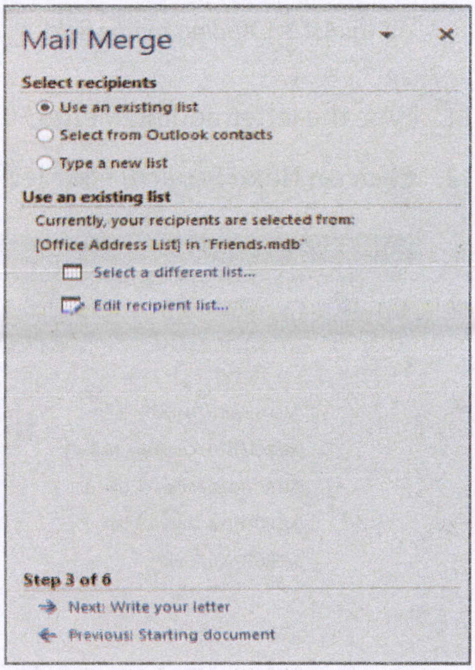

Fig. 4.12 | *Selecting recipients using an existing list*

Technology Literacy

Crank up!

The default location of a saved list is My Documents/My Data Sources.

Add Merge Fields

In this step, the letter is merged with the recipient details added in the previous steps. After composing the letter and making sure all the details are correct, come to the part of the letter where you want to insert data from the data source.

For example, this could be at the start of the letter, where you mention the address and the name, or at the bottom, where you would want to take their signature.

9. Type the letter, and when you come to the section where you want to insert data from the data source, click on **More Items...** in the **Mail Merge** task pane (Fig. 4.13).

10. This will then open the **Insert Merge Field** dialog box (Fig. 4.14). Select the field you want to insert for that cursor location and click on **Insert**. Repeat this for all the desired locations of Merge Field.

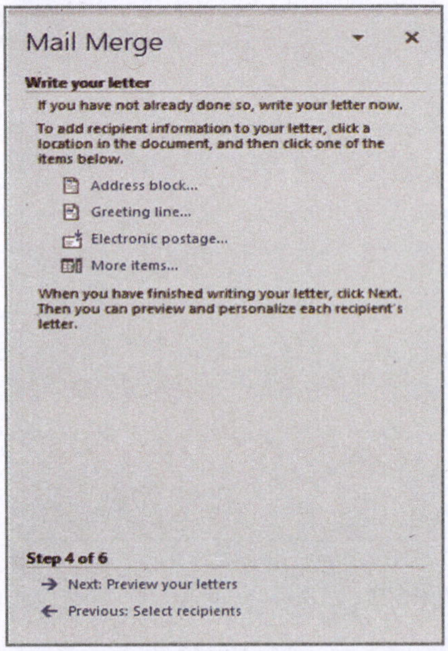

Fig. 4.13 | *Adding merge fields*

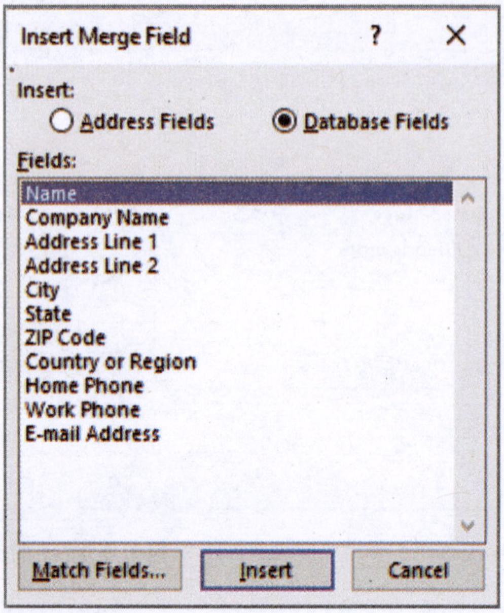

Fig. 4.14 | *Insert the Merge Field dialog box*

11. Type the letter, adding Merge Field at suitable places until the letter is finished (Fig. 4.15).

12. **Click on Next:** Preview your letters when you finish typing to proceed to **Step 5 of 6**.

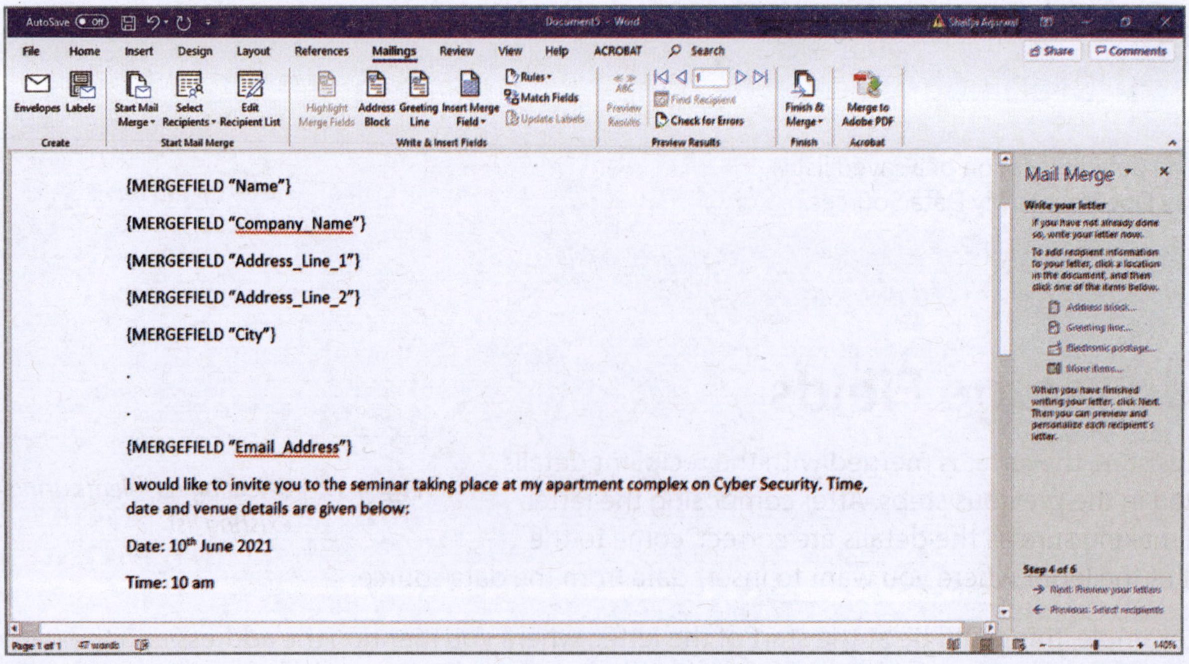

Fig. 4.15 | *Example of a letter with merged fields*

Preview and Complete the Merge

This step allows us to preview the letters for each recipient to make sure all information is correct.

13. Clicking on **Previous: Write your letter** allows us to go back to Step 4. We can also edit the recipient list.
14. After we verify that the letters are correct, click on **Next: Complete the merge.** This is the last step of Mail Merge (Fig. 4.16).

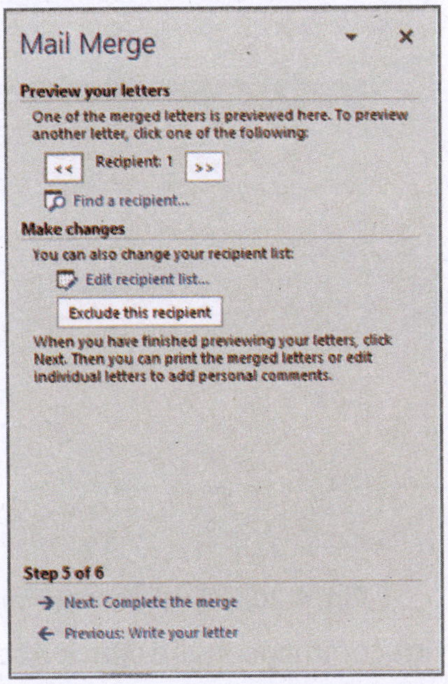

Fig. 4.16 | *Previewing the letter*

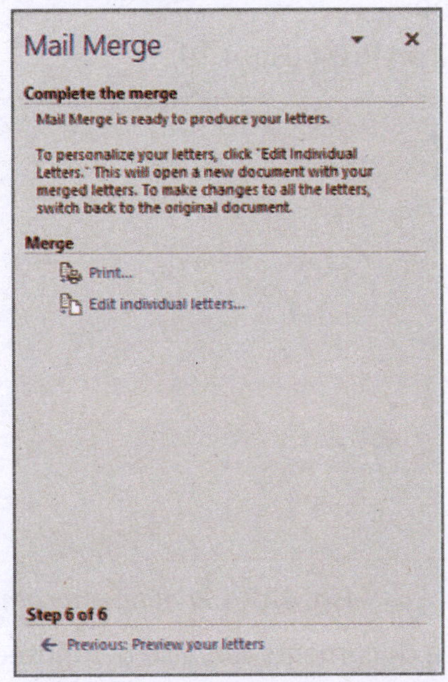

Fig. 4.17 | *Customize address list*

15. The merge fields are replaced by the recipient information in this step. You can print, edit and read the recipient details (Fig. 4.17).

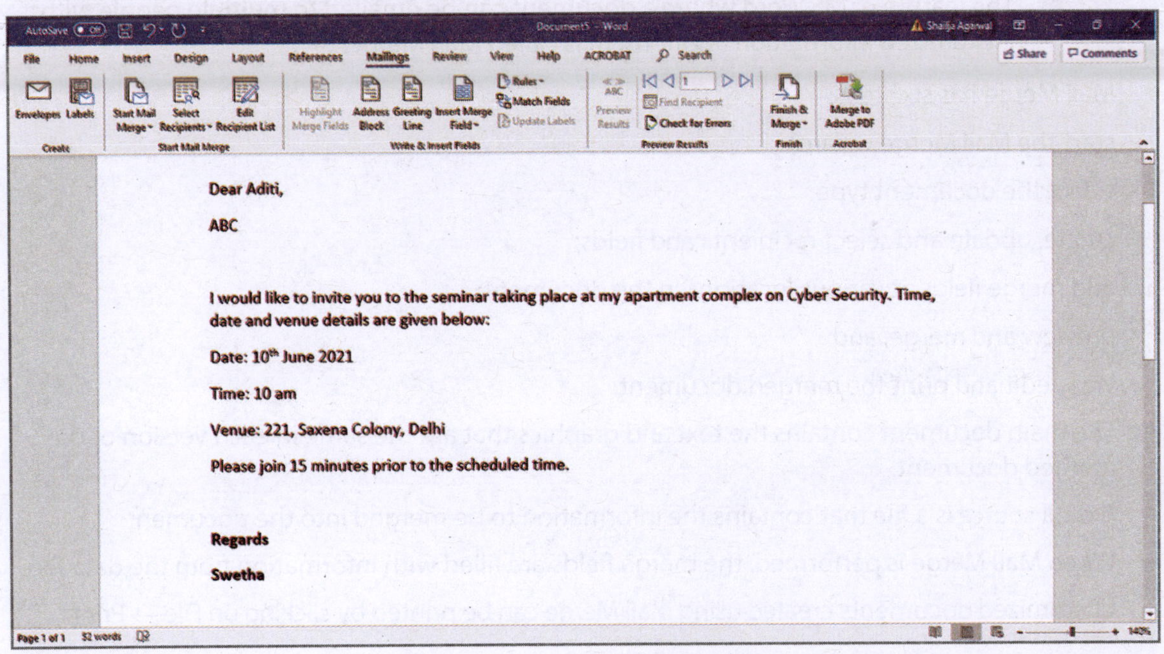

Fig. 4.18 | *Successful Mail Merge*

Printing a Document

Customized documents created using Mail Merge can be printed by following these steps:

1. After opening the document, click on **File → Print**.
2. Select your preference of the number of copies, pages you want to print, whether you want to print on one side or both, collated copies, paper size, orientation and margins.
3. After selecting your preference, select the printer connected to your computer in the printer list box.
4. Click on **Print** (Fig. 4.19).

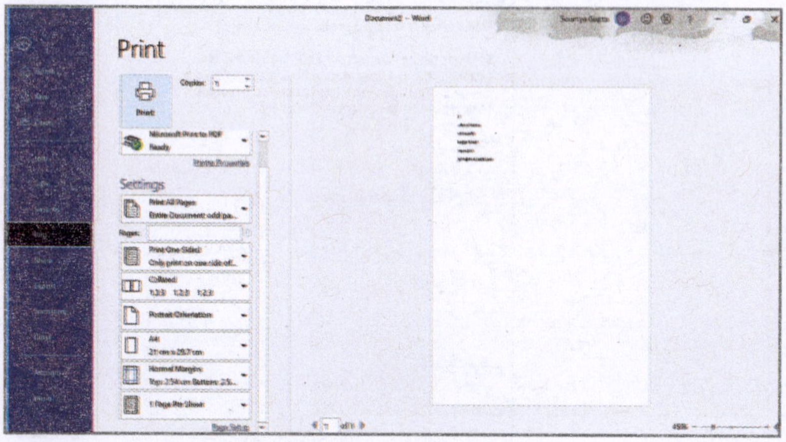

Fig. 4.19 | *Printing a document*

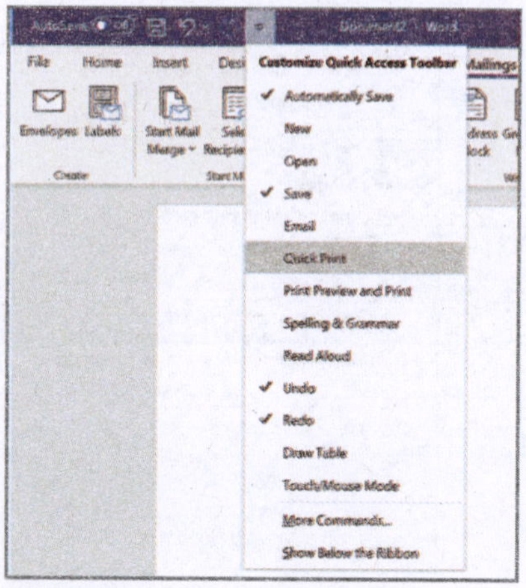

Fig. 4.20 | *Quick Print command*

Note: The documents can also be printed from the **Quick Print** command in the **Quick Access Toolbar** (Fig. 4.20).

Today I learned!

- The feature of MS Word where a document can be emailed to multiple people with customized information about them is called Mail Merge.
- Mail Merge has six steps:
  start the Mail Merge wizard;
  select the document type;
  create, update and select recipients and fields;
  add merge fields at various locations in the document;
  preview and merge; and
  view, edit and print the merged document.
- The main document contains the text and graphics that are the same in each version of the merged document.
- A data source is a file that contains the information to be merged into the document.
- When Mail Merge is performed, the merge fields are filled with information from the data file.
- Customized documents created using Mail Merge can be printed by clicking on File → Print.

Revise and polish!

1. Tick (✓) the correct answer.

a. Which of the following is the first step in setting up Mail Merge?

(i) Setting up document ☐	(ii) Create Data Source ☐
(iii) Add Mail Merge ☐	(iv) Print the mail ☐

b. Start Mail Merge is available on which of the following tabs?

(i) Design ☐	(ii) Layout ☐
(iii) Mailings ☐	(iv) Review ☐

c. Mail Merge allows users to customize the document as per people's ____________.

(i) Name ☐	(ii) Address ☐
(iii) Name and address ☐	(iv) Date of birth ☐

d. Which of the following commands is used to print documents?

(i) Quick Print Command ☐	(ii) Printer ☐
(iii) Print ☐	(iv) Print Access ☐

e. Which of the following is used to protect documents in MS Word?

(i) Lock ☐	(ii) Gate ☐
(iii) Encryption ☐	(iv) Secret key ☐

f. Mail Merge is also helpful in ____________.

(i) Sending emails ☐	(ii) Writing a note ☐
(iii) Editing notes ☐	(iv) Printing customized documents ☐

g. Which of the following is the last step in setting up Mail Merge?

(i) Setting up document ☐	(ii) Create Data Source ☐
(iii) Add Mail Merge ☐	(iv) Preview and Complete ☐

h. Recipient details in Mail Merge can be imported from ____________.

(i) An existing list ☐	(ii) From the MS Outlook contacts ☐
(iii) Create a new list ☐	(iv) From smartphone contacts ☐

i. Which of the following options are allowed by Mail Merge?

(i) Number of copies ☐	(ii) Pages you want to print ☐
(iii) Both (i) and (ii) ☐	(iv) None of the above ☐

2. Fill in the blanks.

a. ____________ is the first step in the Mail Merge process.

b. The process of protecting a document is called ____________.

c. Clicking on ____________ on the Mail Merge pane allows you to go back to Step 4.

d. ____________ is the last step in the Mail Merge process.

e. The list that contains the data of people you want to send the document is known as the ____________ list.

3. Match the following.

a.	Without Mail Merge	(i)	Password
b.	Encryption	(ii)	Custom prints
c.	Edit Recipient information	(iii)	No customization
d.	After Mail Merge	(iv)	Preview your letters

4. Answer the following questions.

a. What are the uses of Mail Merge?

b. What are the types of documents that can be created using Mail Merge?

c. What are the three ways to select a document for Mail Merge?

d. Define data source and main document.

Experiential Learning

Lab Activities

1. Draft an invitation to all members of the alumni, inviting them to the 100-year celebration of your school.

2. Compose a notice to the citizens of an area from the Municipality, outlining the importance of segregating waste.

Chapter

5

Presentation—Visual Effects

After reading this chapter, I will be able to:

- ✔ Use the different views of a presentation.
- ✔ Run a slide show.
- ✔ Apply animation effects through custom animation.
- ✔ Apply transitions to slides.
- ✔ Insert media clips (movie and sound).
- ✔ Add action buttons in the presentation.
- ✔ Import data from other applications.

Brainstorm and explore!

Learning Skills

Look at the two boxes given below. Which one is more visually appealing to you and why?

Box 1

Popular Breeds of Dogs

1. saint bernard
2. newfoundland
3. old english sheepdog
4. mastiff
5. great dane
6. greyhound

Box 2

Breeds of Dogs

____

____

In Class 5, we learned that PowerPoint presentations can be enhanced with the use of pictures and charts. In this chapter, we will learn how to use animation and multimedia in a PowerPoint presentation.

animation: a film in which drawings or puppets appear to move

multimedia: a combination of movies, sound clips, SmartArt and animations

Let us first learn the different views that can be used to create a presentation.

Viewing a Presentation

A presentation can be viewed through various view options in Microsoft PowerPoint—normal view, slide sorter view and slide show view. Each view has its own use. These view buttons are available at the bottom right corner of the PowerPoint window.

Let us learn about them in detail.

Normal View

The Normal view is the default view. It is the main editing view used to write and design a presentation.

To navigate to the Normal view, either click on the Normal button shown in Fig. 5.1 or follow the steps given here:

1. Click **View** in the **Menu** bar
2. Click the **Normal** button.

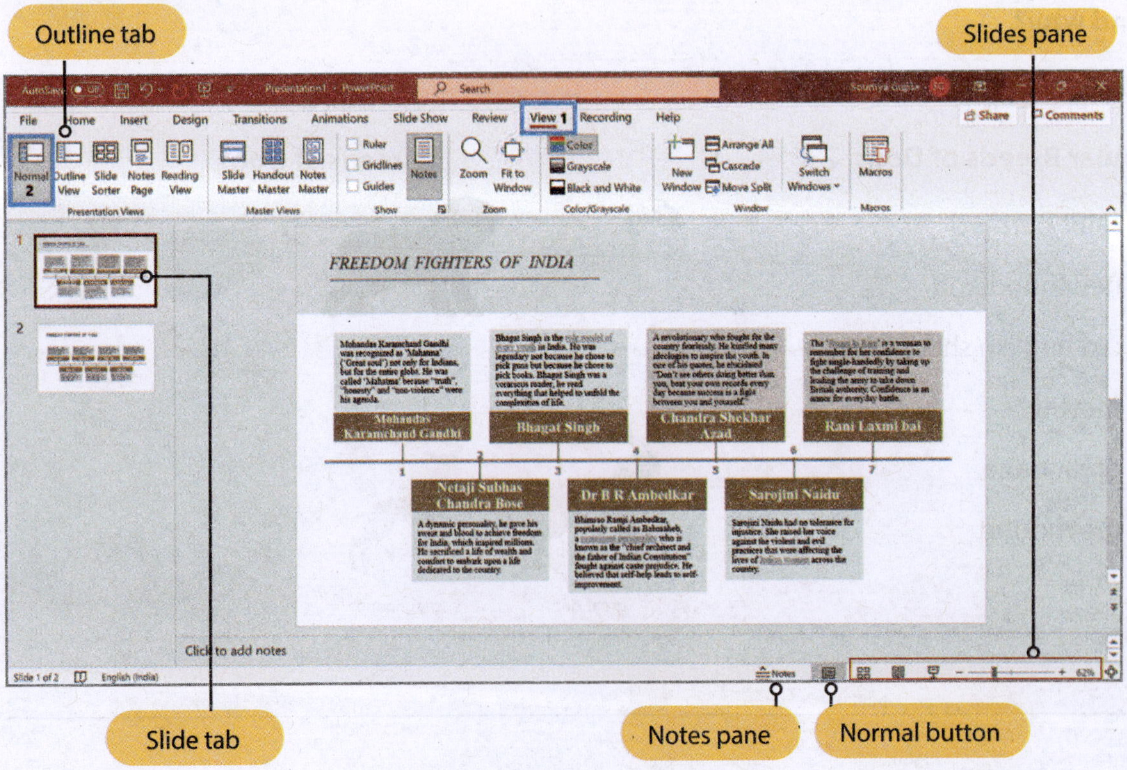

Fig. 5.1 | *Normal view*

The Normal view has three working areas (Fig. 5.1):

- On the left, there are tabs that alternate between an outline of slide text (**Outline** tab) and the slides displayed as thumbnails (**Slides** tab).
- On the right, there is the **Slides** pane, which displays a large view of the current slide.
- At the bottom, there is the **Notes** pane, which is used to type notes that are required to accompany a slide.

Slide Sorter View

The **Slide Sorter View** (Fig. 5.2) shows a thumbnail image of each slide in the presentation. This view is best when rearranging the order of slides, or just wanting to see each slide in the presentation with the formats and colours chosen. In the Slide Sorter View, it is not possible to edit the contents of a slide, but one can quickly switch to the Slide View for editing the contents.

To navigate to the Slide Sorter View:

1. Click **View** in the Menu bar.
2. Click the **Slide Sorter View** button.

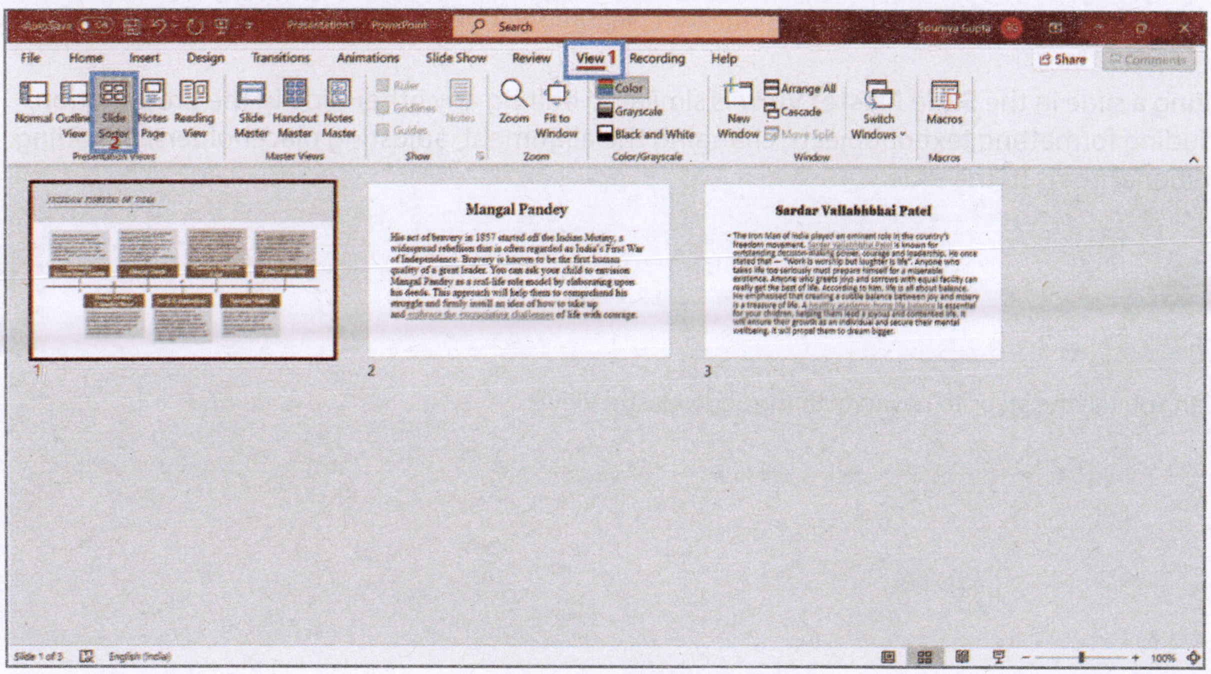

Fig. 5.2 | *Slide Sorter View*

When creating and editing a presentation, the Slide Sorter View gives an overall picture of it, making it easy to reorder, add or delete slides, and preview transitions and animation effects.

Slide Master View

The Slide Master View (Fig. 5.3) controls all aspects of a slide's appearance, including its background colour, font style, and any recurring text or pictures.

To exit the Slide Master View, click the **Close Master View** button.

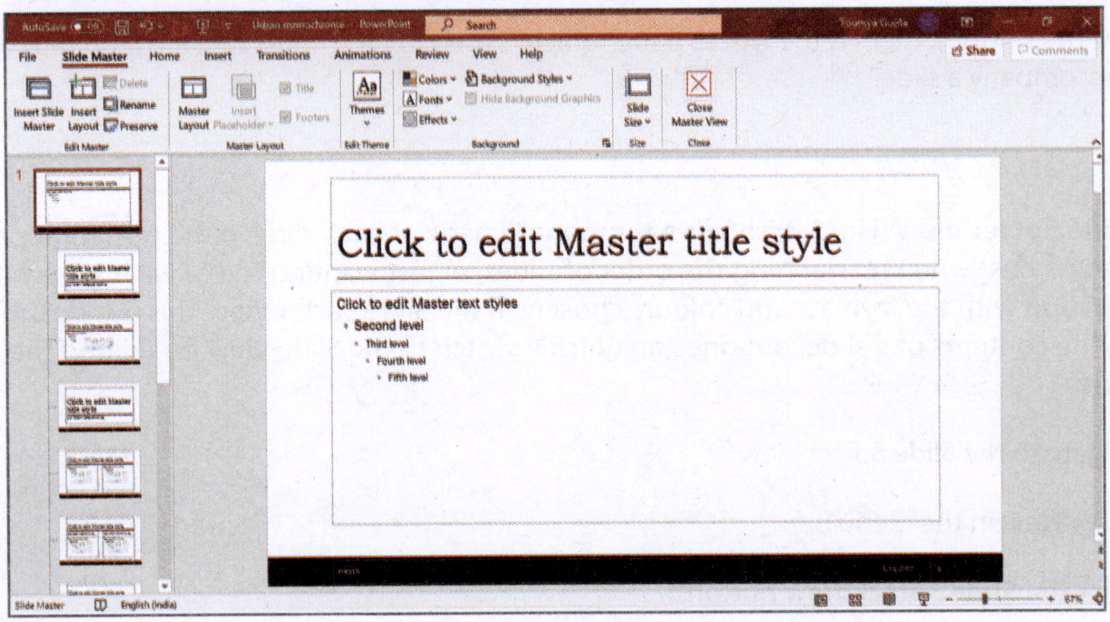

Fig. 5.3 | *Slide Master View*

Editing a slide in the **Slide Master View** is similar to editing any other slide in the presentation, including formatting text or objects, changing the alignment, adjusting placeholders, or adding additional items to the slide.

Brush up!

Can you tell the steps to navigate to the Slide Master View?

____

____

____

Slide Show View

The **Slide Show View** (Fig. 5.4) shows the presentation as it will look to the audience when it runs. This view displays one slide at a time in full-screen mode. Graphics, timings, movies, animated elements and transition effects are provided here to showcase how they will be looking when the show actually runs.

To navigate to the Slide Show View, follow these steps:

1. Click **View** in the **Menu** bar.
2. Click the **Slide Show View** button.

To exit the **Slide Show View**, press the **Esc** key on the keyboard.

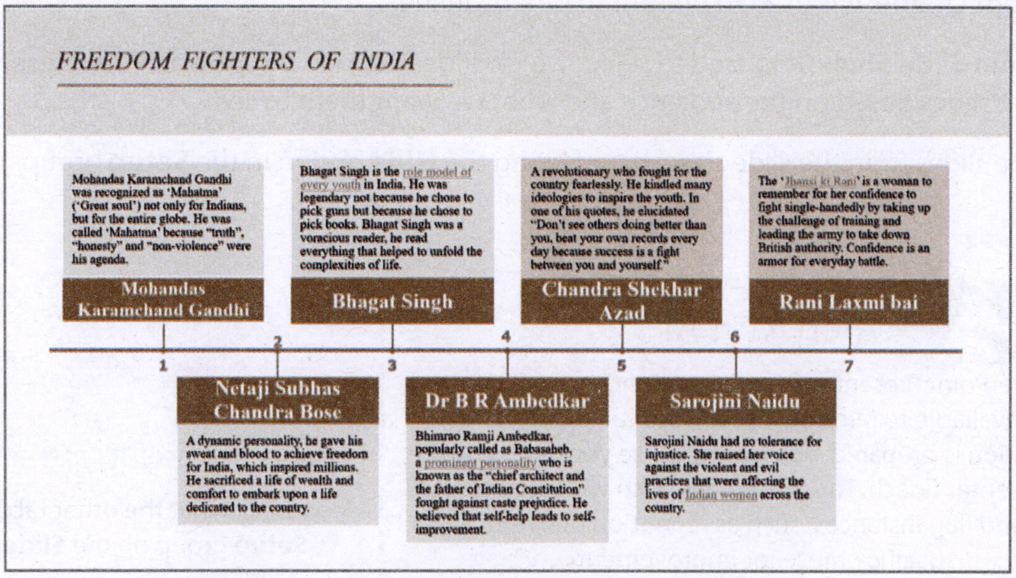

Fig. 5.4 | *Slide Show View*

Run a Slide Show

Once the presentation is prepared, it is time to run it in full screen.

To run a slide show, select the **Slide Show** tab on the ribbon (Fig. 5.5).

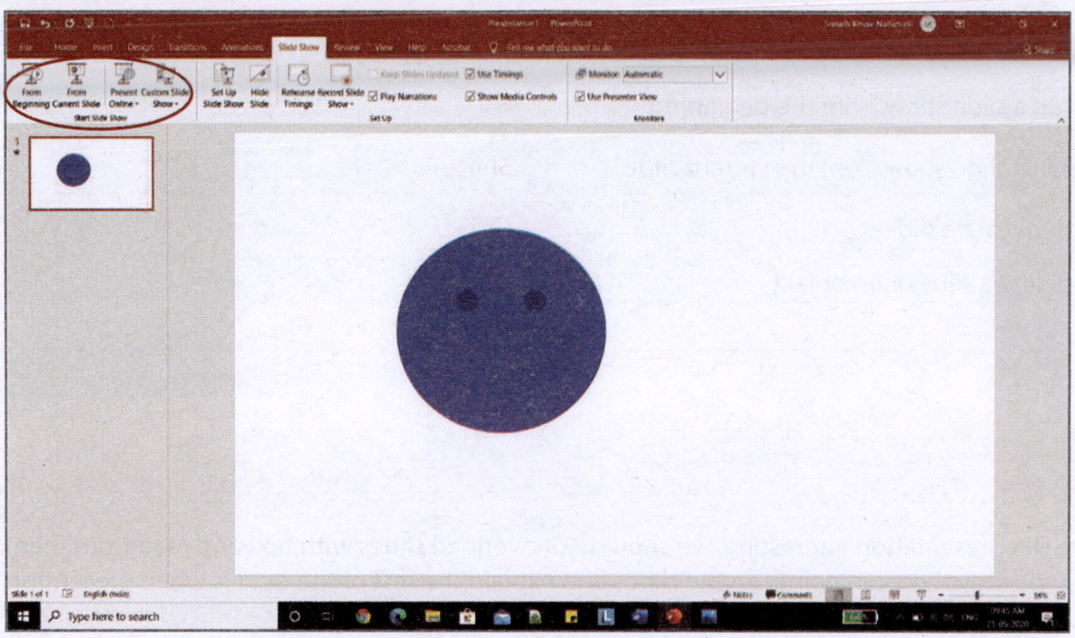

Fig. 5.5 | *Running a slide show*

In the **Slide Show** toolbar, we have **Start Slide Show** group with the following options:

- **From Beginning**: It is used to start the slide show from the beginning.
- **From Current Slide**: It is used to start the Slide show from the current slide, that is, selected on the presentation.
- **Present Online**: It is used to present to others online.
- **Custom Slide Show**: It is used to select which slides need to be shown in the presentation. Select slides based on the audience and what we want them to see.

We can hide slides from the slide show by selecting the **Hide** option in the **Setup** group.

Fun with AI

PowerPoint Presenter Coach was launched in 2019. It is available to Microsoft 365 subscribers. After the presentation is prepared, you can rehearse your speech with the Presenter Coach. The Presenter Coach will listen to the speech and flag instances, such as repetition or overuse of a specific phrase for improvement.

Clear up!

Check what the other tabs on the **Setup** group on the **Slide Show** toolbar do.

Technology Literacy

Crank up!

Important keyboard shortcuts for MS PowerPoint 2016 are given below:

Action	Keyboard Shortcut
To run a slide show from the beginning	F3
To run a slide show from the current slide	Shift+F3
To duplicate a slide	Ctrl+D
To delete a slide or an object	Delete

Soak up!

To make the presentation interesting, we should not overload slides with text and read from them. We should type only the main points on the slides and explain the rest of the details when presenting them.

Creating Animations

Animations add a lot of visual interest to PowerPoint slides. We can animate objects that we have added to our presentation, using the tools provided in MS PowerPoint. The **Animation** tab is present on the ribbon and has various functions (Fig. 5.6).

Fig. 5.6 | *Inside the Animations tab*

We can add animation to any part of the presentation that is displayed. So, a shape, picture, textbox and so forth can be animated using the tools provided. To insert an animation into our presentation, follow these steps:

1. Select the object that you want to animate.
2. Click the **Animations** tab on the Ribbon and select the animation displayed or click the **Add Animations** option under it.
3. A dropdown list will be displayed, from which we can select the animation to be inserted.
4. Select any animation to display, and the animation preview will be displayed in the presentation.

Animation Pane

Under the **Advanced Animation** group is the **Animation Pane** button. Click on it to display the Animation Pane (Fig. 5.6). It helps in the following functions:

1. We can record multiple animations on the same object by using the ▲ ▼ arrow buttons.
2. The green-, yellow-, and red-coloured stars for the animation indicate the type of animation.
3. There are four types of effects:
   - **Entrance**: Used to make the text or object enter the screen
   - **Emphasis:** Used to add an effect to your text or objects already visible on the screen
   - **Exit**: Used to make the text or object leave the screen
   - **Motion Paths**: Used to make the text or object move in a specified pattern
4. We can run the animation by clicking on the **Play** button.
5. To remove an animation effect, select the effect to be removed and click on the **Remove** option.

Timing

The **Timing** group has the **Start** options—**On Click**, **With Previous** and **After Previous**. These options show the time on which the animation will be played. We can set the duration of the animation using the **Duration** tab.

After adding all the settings to the animation, take a brief preview of the animation by selecting the **Preview** option on the top left corner (Fig. 5.7).

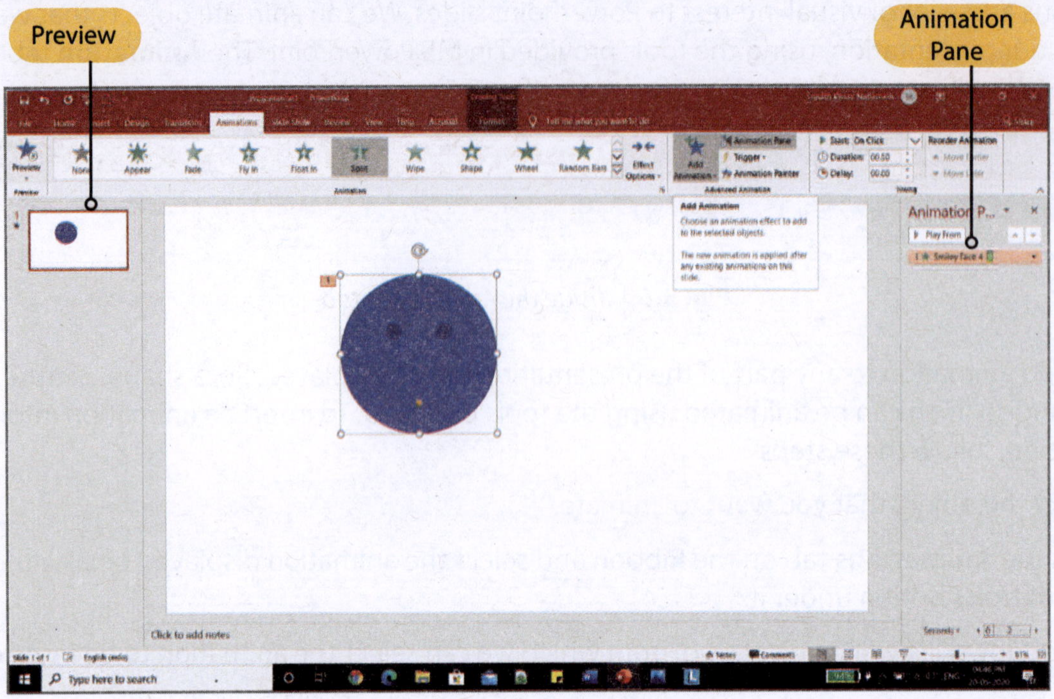

Fig. 5.7 | *Animations Pane and Preview*

Applying Transitions

We can add special effects between each slide of the presentation. These are called slide transitions. A transition can be as simple as fading to the next slide or as complex as a flashy, eye-catching effect. We can choose transitions to fit the style of any presentation.

There are three categories of transitions to choose from, all of which can be found under the **Transitions** tab—**Subtle**, **Exciting** and **Dynamic Content** (Fig. 5.8).

- Subtle

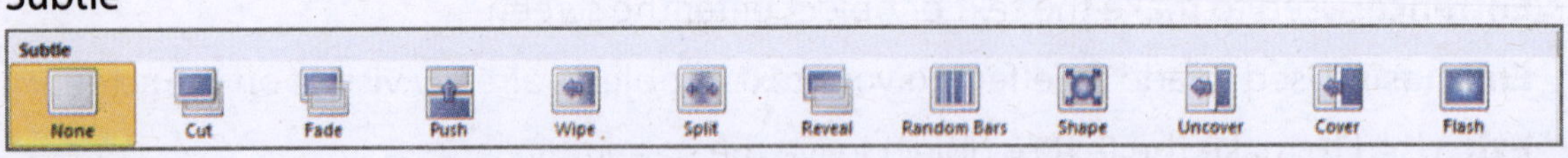

- Exciting

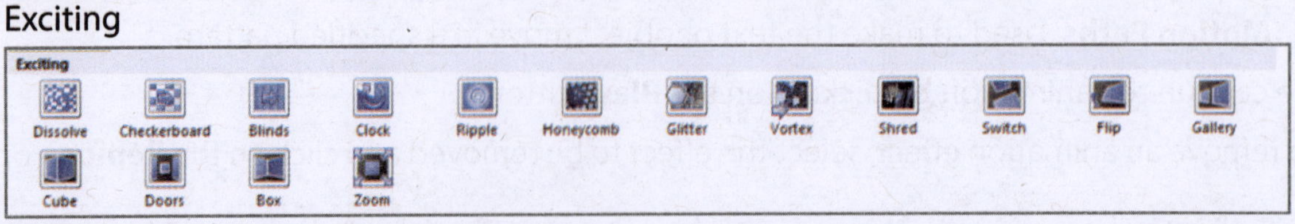

- Dynamic Content

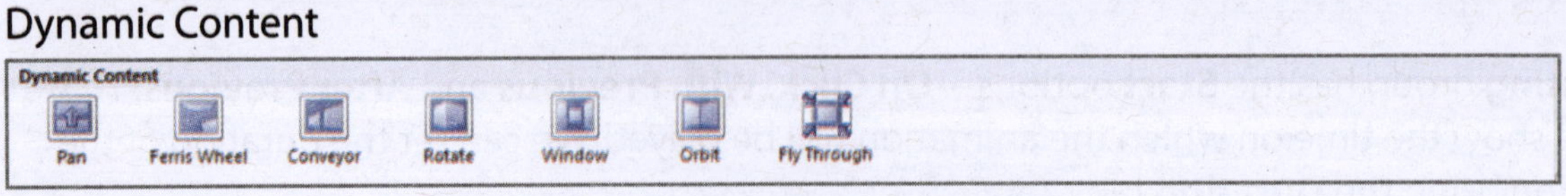

Fig. 5.8 | *Categories of transition*

Steps for Applying Transitions to a Presentation

To apply a transition to a presentation, follow these steps (Fig. 5.9):

1. Select the slide to which a transition needs to be applied.
2. Click on the **Transitions** tab.
3. Select the transition of your choice. The applied transition effect can automatically be reviewed.

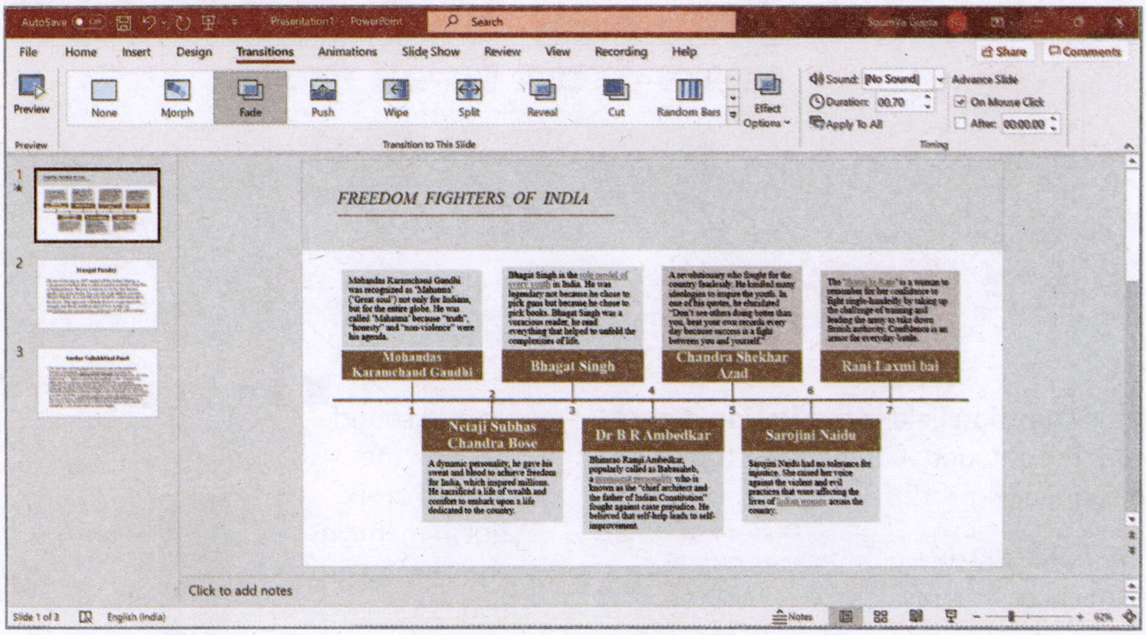

Fig. 5.9 | *Applying transitions*

4. Click on the **Effect Options** to choose features of the transition, including the direction and nature (Fig. 5.10).

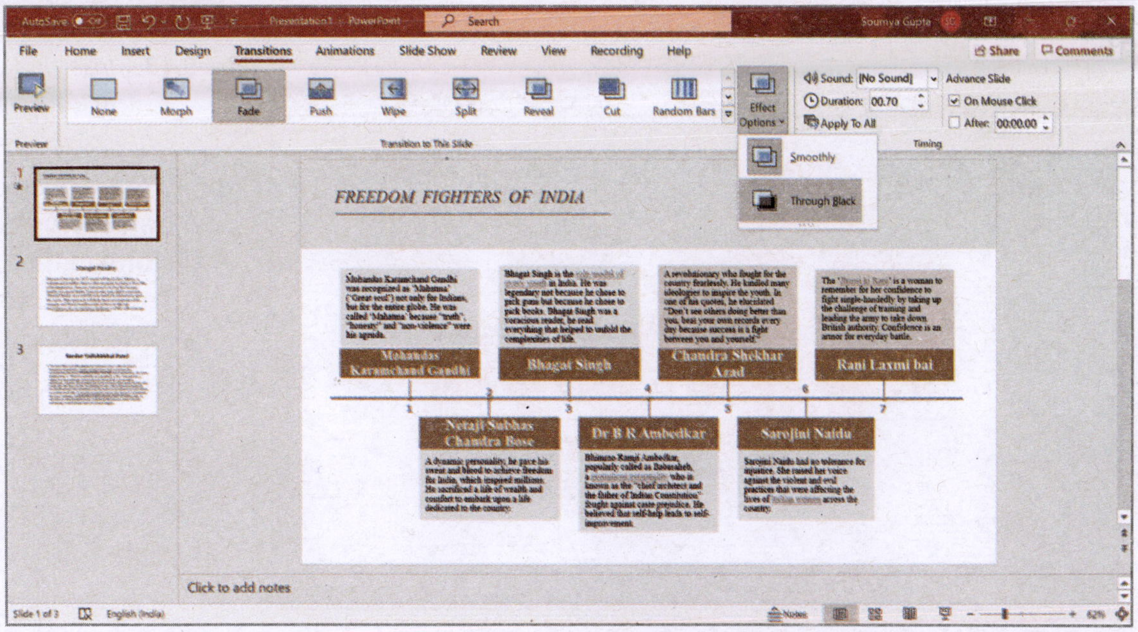

Fig. 5.10 | *Applying different effects to the slide*

5. Select **Preview** to see what the transition looks like (Fig. 5.11).

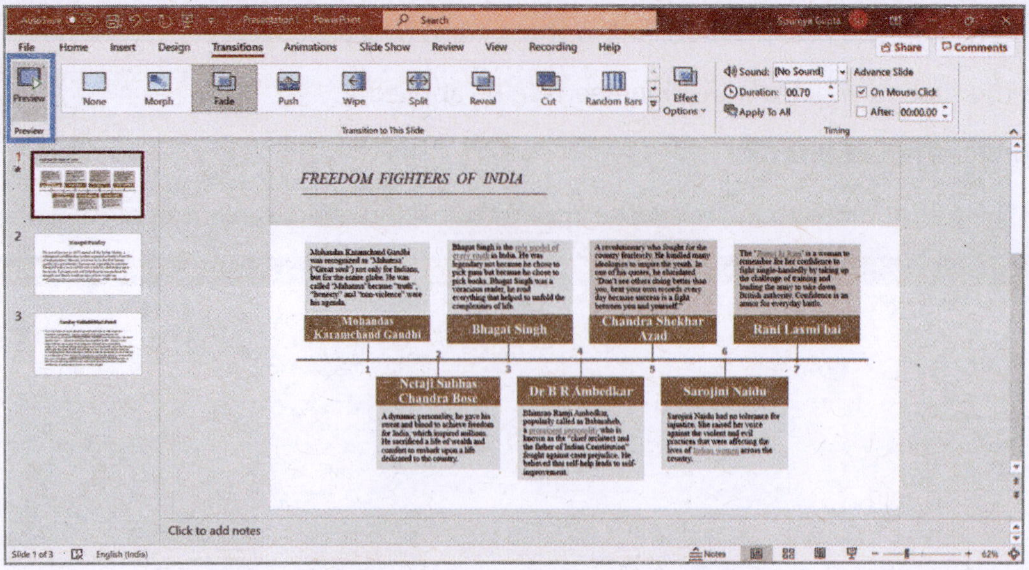

Fig. 5.11 | *Selecting Preview*

6. In the **Duration** field in the **Timing** group, enter the amount of time for the transition to happen (Fig. 5.12).

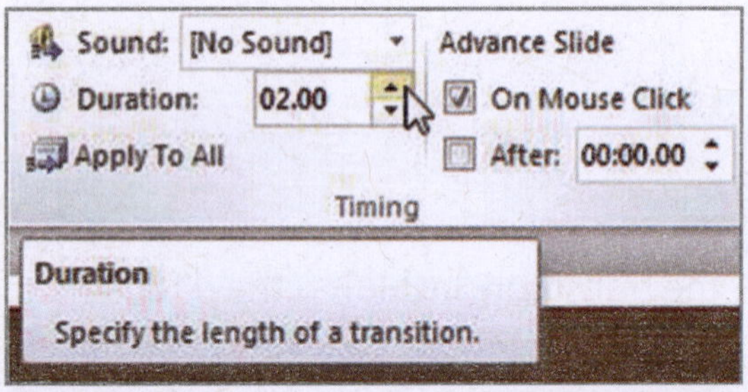

Fig. 5.12 | *Changing the duration of transition*

7. To add sound, click on the **Sound** drop-down menu in the **Timing** group (Fig. 5.13). Click on a sound to apply it to the selected slide.

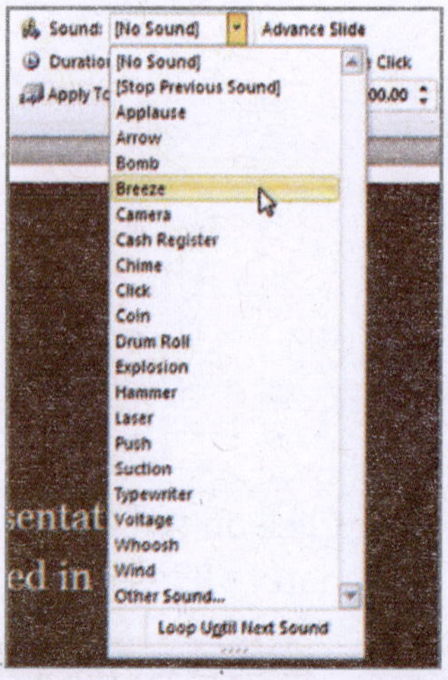

Fig. 5.13 | *Inserting sound in transition*

8. To remove any transition, choose **None** in the **Transition to This Slide** group (Fig. 5.14).

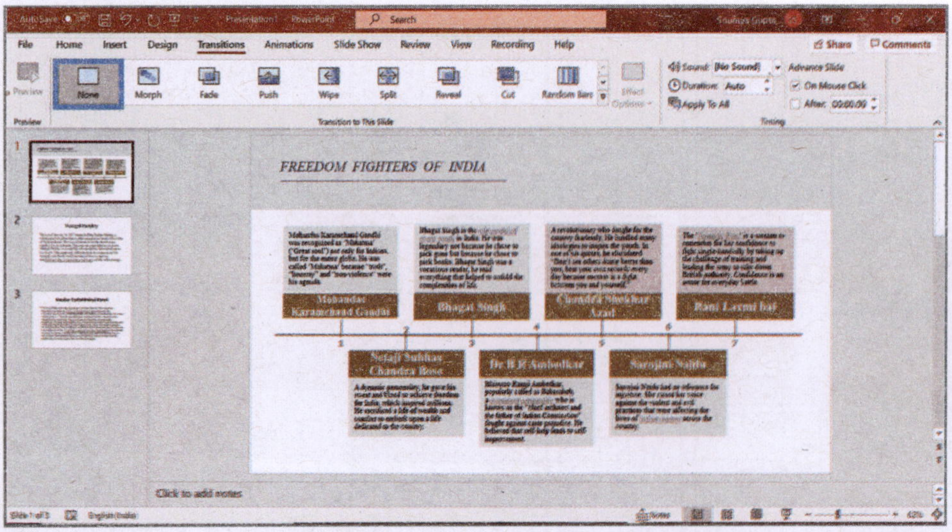

Fig. 5.14 | *Removing transition*

Inserting Sound Clips

MS PowerPoint allows us to insert sound or movie clips into presentations.

When inserting an audio file in the slide, the clip will be embedded in the presentation by default and will appear as a speaker icon on the slide. Once inserted, we can edit the audio clip in much the same way as for editing video clips. Audio clips can be inserted using the **Audio** command on the **Insert** tab and then edited using the commands on the **Playback** tab.

Adding Sound from the Computer

To add a sound clip from the computer, follow these steps:

1. Select the **Insert** tab and click on the **Audio** drop-down arrow in the **Media** group; then, select **Audio on My PC** (Fig. 5.15).

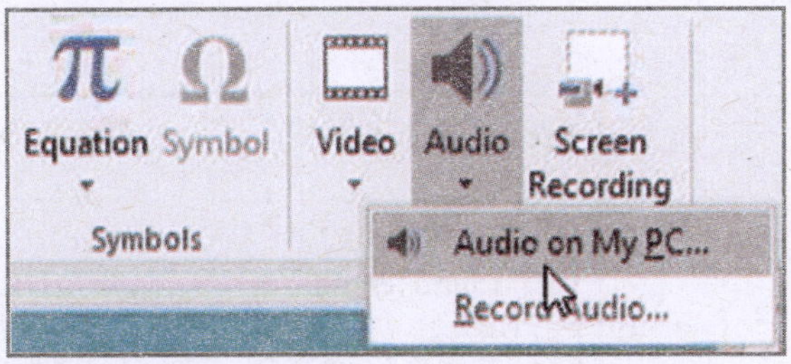

Fig. 5.15 | *Adding sound from the computer*

2. Locate and select the desired audio file and then click on the **Insert** option (Fig. 5.16).

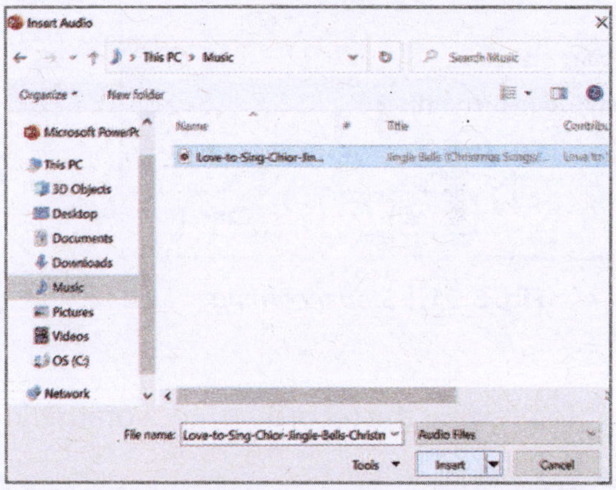

Fig. 5.16 | *Selecting sound and clicking on the **Insert** option*

3. The audio file will be added to the slide (Fig. 5.17).

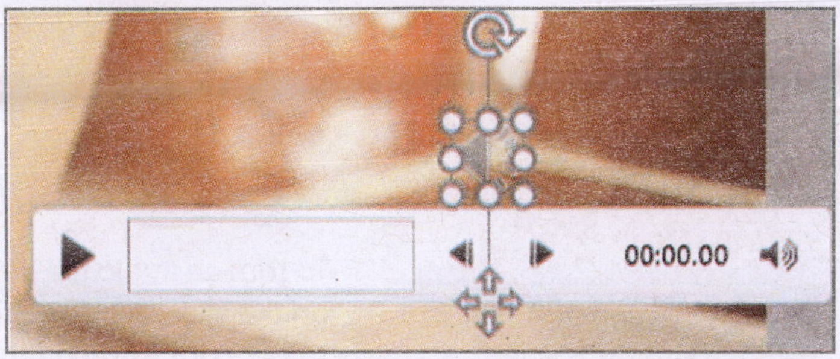

Fig. 5.17 | *Audio added to the slide*

Adding Sound through Recording

To record an audio and add the sound, follow these steps:

1. From the **Insert** tab, click on the **Audio** drop-down arrow and then select the **Record Audio...** option (Fig. 5.18).

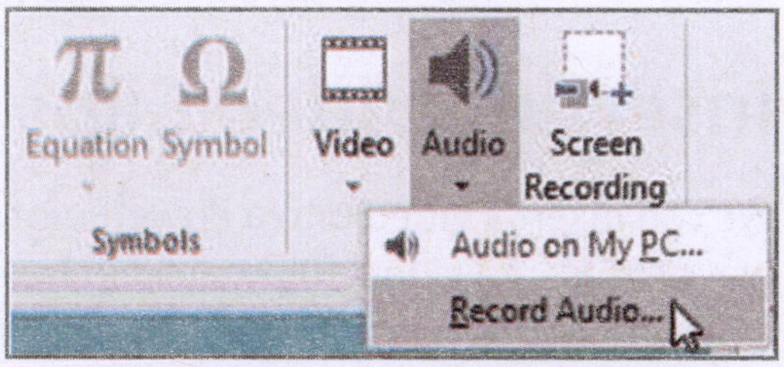

Fig. 5.18 | *Record Audio... option*

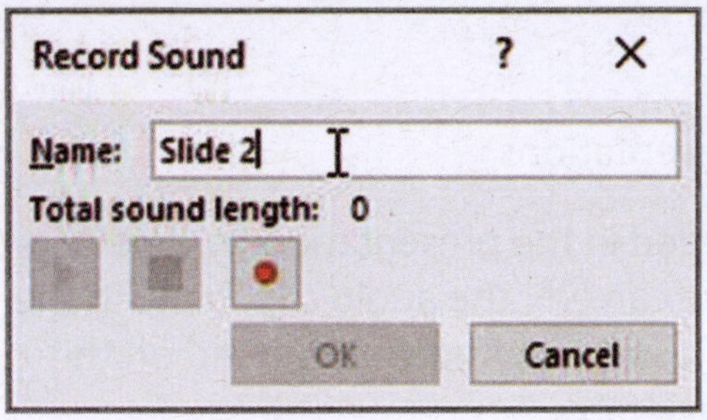

Fig. 5.19 | *Add name to the sound file*

2. Type a name for the audio recording (Fig. 5.19).

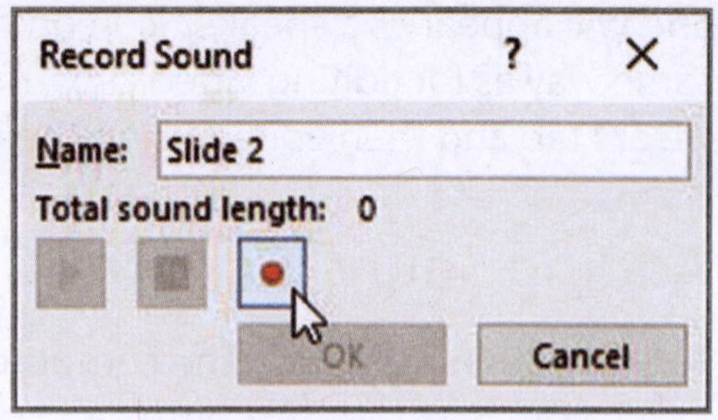

Fig. 5.20 | *Start recording*

3. Click on the **Record** button to start recording (Fig. 5.20).

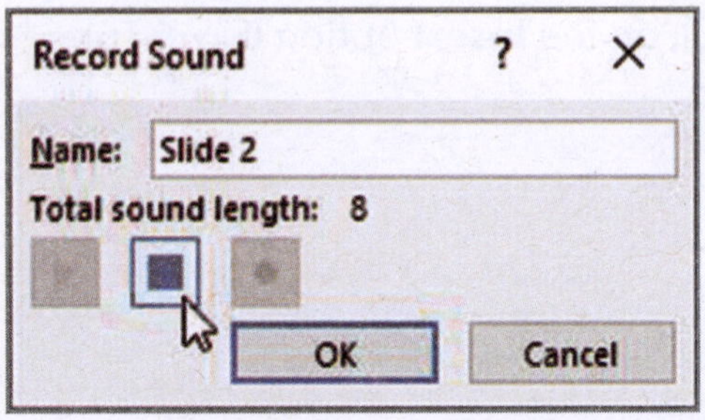

Fig. 5.21 | *Stop recording*

4. When recording is done, click on the **Stop** button (Fig. 5.21).

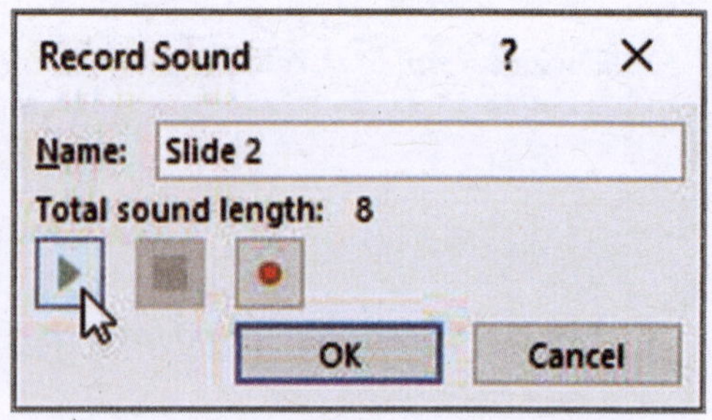

Fig. 5.22 | *Select **Play** to preview recording*

5. To preview the recording, click on the **Play** button (Fig. 5.22).

6. When done, click **OK**. The audio file will be inserted in the slide (Fig. 5.23).

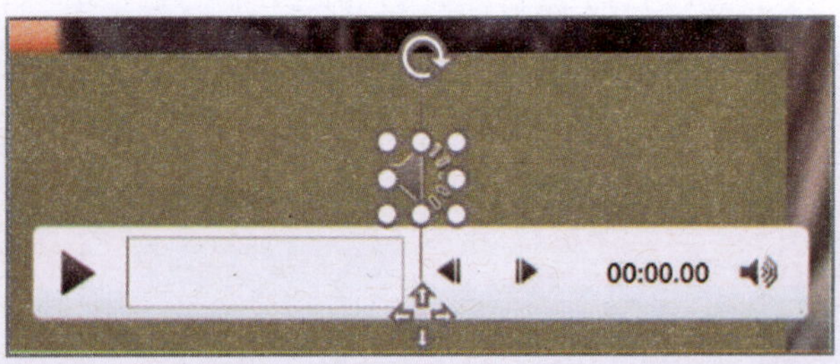

Fig. 5.23 | *File inserted in the slide*

Crank up!

To trim an audio file, select the audio object on the slide, click on the **Playback** tab and select **Trim Audio** in the **Editing** group. Media clips are objects. They can be moved, resized and positioned.

Inserting Video Clips

We can insert a video into a PowerPoint slide and play it during our presentation. There are two ways to insert a video: (i) by clicking **Insert Media Clip** in a content placeholder, or (ii) where a placeholder is not available using the relevant commands on the **Insert** tab.

To insert a video in a slide, follow these steps:

1. From the **Insert** tab, click **Media**, click the **Video** drop-down arrow and then select **This Device** (Fig. 5.24).

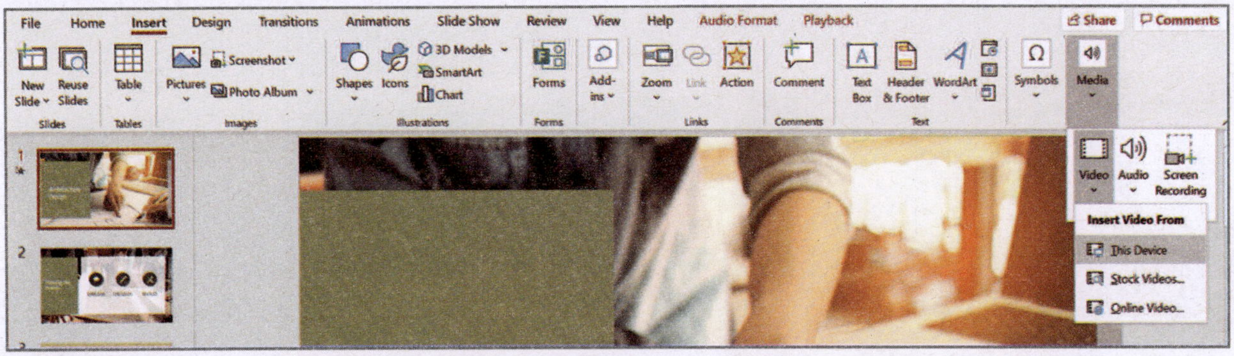

Fig. 5.24 | *Inserting video clips*

2. Locate the clip and click **Insert** (Fig. 5.25).

   The video will be added to the slide (Fig. 5.26).

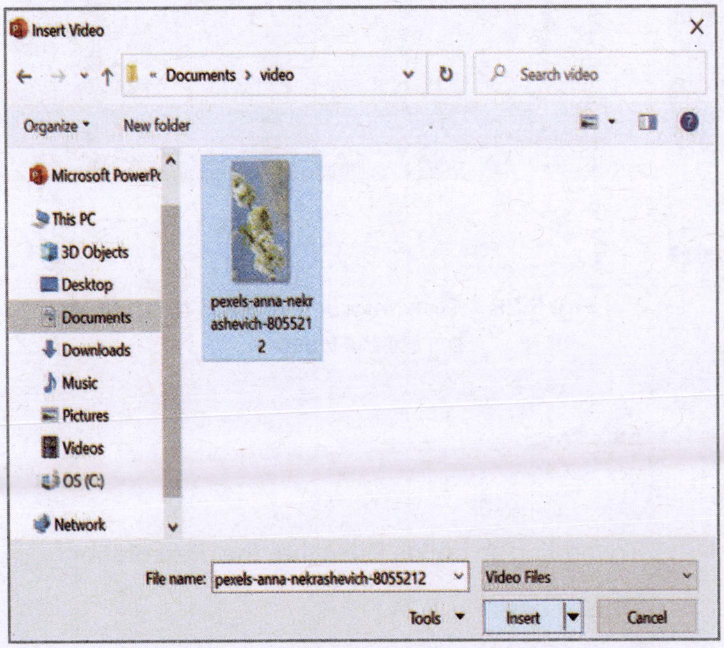

Fig. 5.25 | *Select clip from browser*

Fig. 5.26 | *Video added successfully*

To preview a video, follow these steps:

1. Click a video to select it.

2. Click the **Play/Pause** button (Fig. 5.27) below the video. The video will begin playing and the timeline next to the **Play/Pause** button will advance.

3. To jump to a different part of the video, click anywhere on the timeline (Fig. 5.28).

Fig. 5.27 | ***Play/Pause*** *button*

Fig. 5.28 | *Click anywhere to jump to a different part of the video*

4. For editing and formatting videos, the **Format** and **Playback** tabs have several options. To trim a video, add **Fade in** and **Fade out** and also add **Bookmark** to the video.

Clear up!

Try Adding an online video into the presentation.

(**Hint:** Check Fig. 5.24.)

Using Action Buttons

Action buttons are built-in shapes that can be added to a presentation and set to link to another slide, play a sound or perform a similar action. Action buttons let users navigate quickly and efficiently within a slideshow. They can also be used to activate hyperlinks, letting users jump outside of the show to visit useful websites. If we want one or more buttons on all slides, they can be added to the Slide Master and will show up automatically on all slides. Or, specific buttons can be created just for specific slides.

Steps for Inserting Action Buttons

To insert an action button on a slide, follow these steps:

1. Display the slide to which the button is to be added. To keep the button to be on all slides, do this with the Slide Master slide.

2. Select the **Insert** tab and click on the **Shapes** button. At the bottom of the **Shapes** menu is the **Action Buttons** section (Fig. 5.29). Each button comes with a different default action. For example,

   - The **Back** or **Previous** button will navigate to the previous slide.
   - The **Next** or **Forward** button will navigate to the next slide.
   - The **Beginning** button will navigate to the first slide.
   - The **End** button will navigate to the last slide.
   - The **Home** button will navigate to the first slide. This button has the same action as the **Beginning** button.

3. Select an action button.

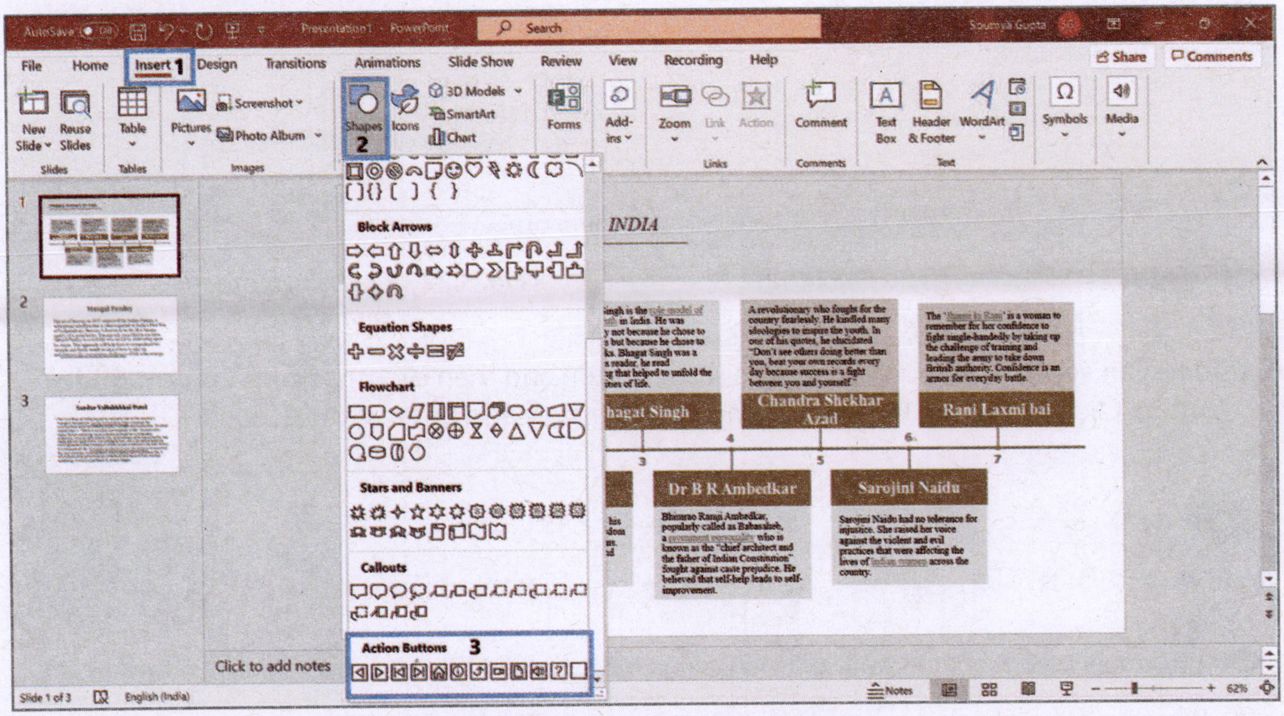

Fig. 5.29 | *Selecting* ***Action Buttons***

4. Click and drag to draw the button on the slide. The **Action Settings** dialog box will appear (Fig. 5.30).

5. Select the **Mouse Click** or **Mouse Over** tab. Selecting the **Mouse Click** tab means the action button will perform its action only when clicked. Selecting the **Mouse Over** tab will make the action button perform its action when the mouse is moved over it.

6. In the **Action on click** section, select **Hyperlink to:** then, click the drop-down arrow and choose an option from the menu (Fig. 5.31).

7. Check the **Play sound** box if you want a sound to play when the action button is clicked. Select a sound from the drop-down menu or select **Other sound** to use a sound file on your computer. When you are done, click **OK** (Fig. 5.32).

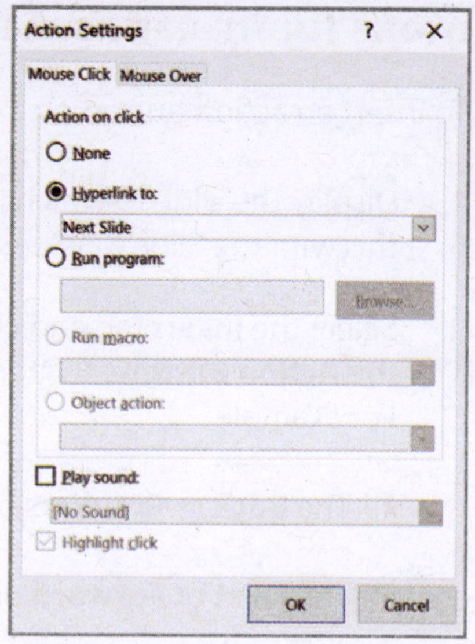

Fig. 5.30 | *Selecting **Mouse Click***

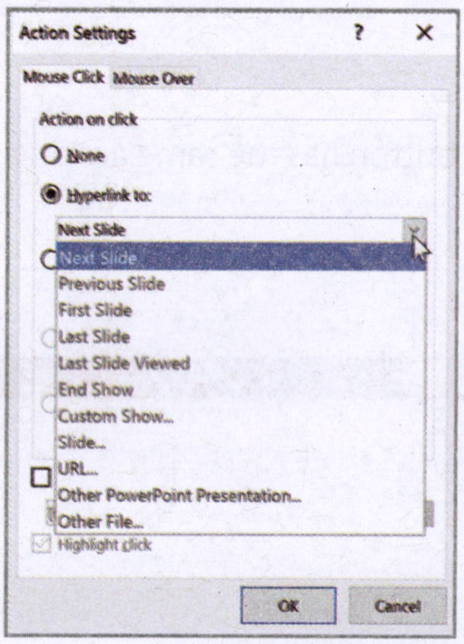

Fig. 5.31 | *Selecting **Hyperlink to:** and then selecting an option*

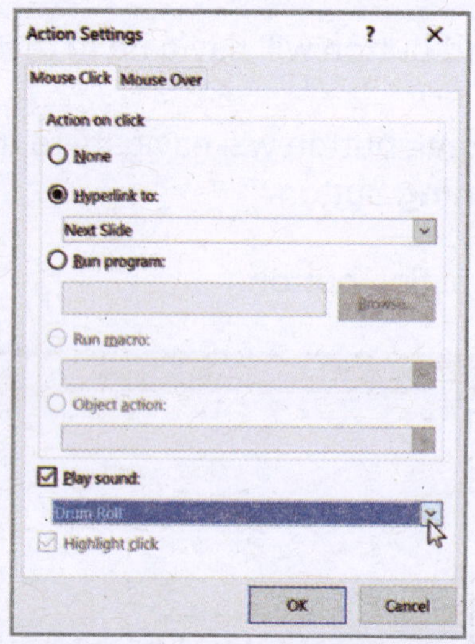

Fig. 5.32 | *Checking the **Play sound** box*

8. To test an action button, click the slide show button and then click the **From Current Slide** button. Click the **Action Buttons** during the slideshow and observe the action.

Crank up!

Technology Literacy

- For a more precise control while drawing action buttons, hold down the **Alt** key while drawing.
- When we copy and paste selected action buttons to other slides in the presentation, they will appear on the other slides in the same location as their original position.

Importing Data from MS Word

MS PowerPoint provides the option to import data from other applications such as MS Excel, Word and so forth, and use it in presentations. To use a Word document as an outline to build your presentation, follow these steps:

1. Open Microsoft Word 2016. In the Word document, click **Home**.
2. Create a new Word document. Under the **View** tab, click on the **Outlining** button. Type the text you want.
   - Highlight the content for your slide title and then select Level 1 in Styles.
   - Highlight the content for your slide text and then select Level 2 in Styles (Fig. 5.33).

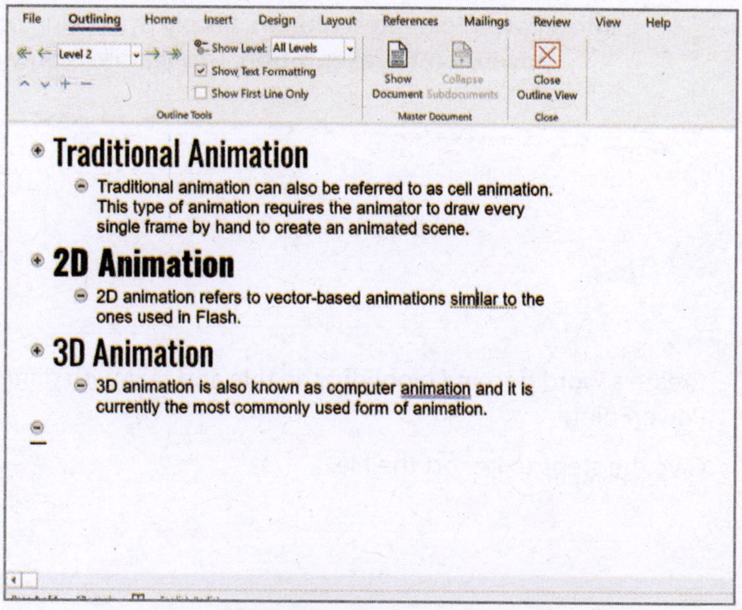

Fig. 5.33 | *Outlining the text*

3. In the Word document, Go to **File**, click **Save** and then click **File** > **Close**.
4. Open PowerPoint and click **Home** > **New Slide** (Fig. 5.34).

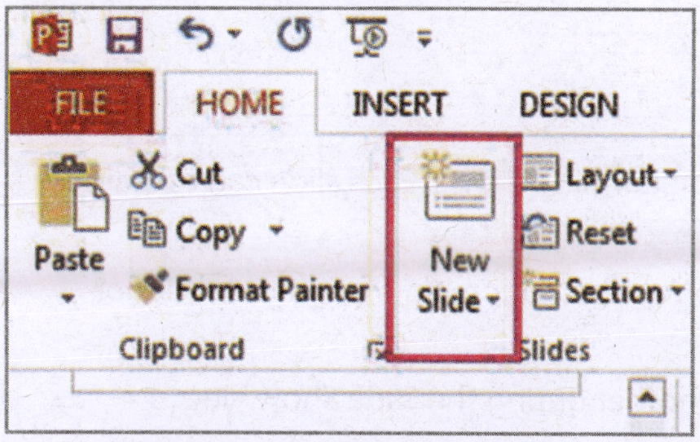

Fig. 5.34 | *Selecting New Slide*

5. Choose the **Slides from Outline** option (Fig. 5.35).
6. Locate and select the Word document in the **Insert Outline** dialog box and click **Insert**. A new slide will be created for each Heading 1 in your document.
7. The word document will be inserted in your slide.

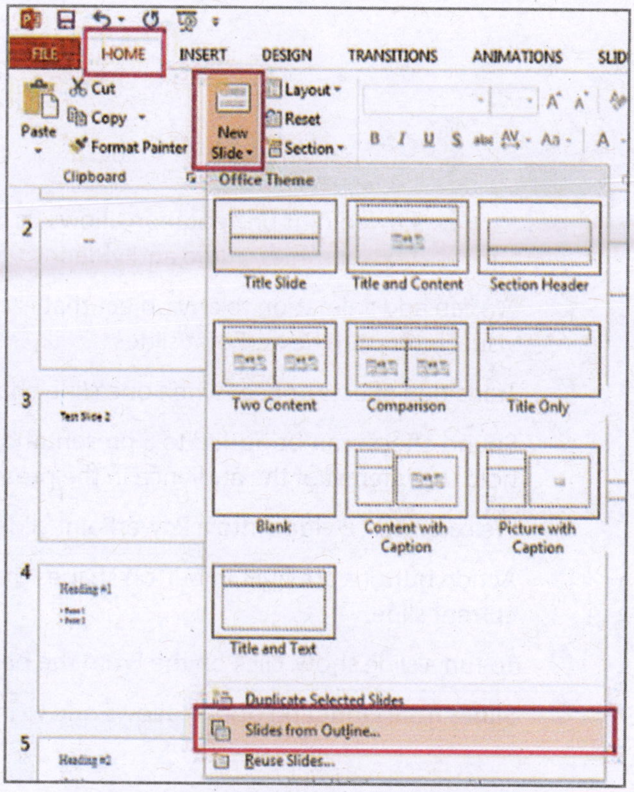

Fig. 5.35 | *Go to* ***Slides from Outline***

Fun with AI

Microsoft has recently come out with a new feature called Transform command. This **artificial intelligence feature** is designed to automatically convert your Word documents into a PowerPoint presentation, simply by clicking on **File menu → Export → Export to PowerPoint presentation**. This feature is only available for Word for the web.

Clear up!

Create a Word doc and highlight the title and text with different styles available. Import the file in PowerPoint.

Give the steps to import the file.

____

____

____

____

Today I learned!

- PowerPoint presentation allows us to create digital slide shows. Each slide can contain text, graphics, audio and video.
- We can add animation to any object that is added in our presentation. Animations add a lot of visual interest to PowerPoint slides.
- Transition effects appear when one slide changes to another during the Slide Show view.
- Sound effects can be added to a presentation to give importance to a specific content and to hold the interest of the audience in the presentation.
- We can insert a video into a PowerPoint slide and play it during our presentation.
- Action buttons are built in button shapes that can be used to link any other application to the current slide.
- To run a slide show, click on the From the beginning button of the Slide Show tab.
- Slides from Outlining option allows one to import data from MS Word to PowerPoint.

Revise and polish!

Learning Skills

1. Tick (✓) the correct answer.

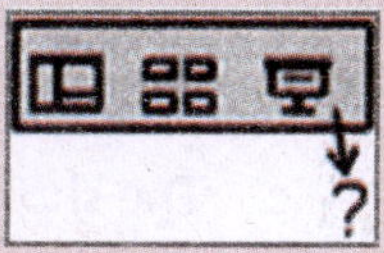

a. What does the arrow-marked icon of the view toolbar represent?

(i) Slide view ☐ (ii) Normal view ☐

(iii) Slide show ☐ (iv) Slide sorter view ☐

b. In MS PowerPoint, F5 is the shortcut key for ____________.

(i) normal show ☐ (ii) slide sorter view ☐

(iii) outline view ☐ (iv) slide show ☐

c. Select the correct sequence of steps used to add a picture from a file on the computer into a PowerPoint presentation.

(i) Choose the Menu option, click Insert → Picture → Clip Art ☐

(ii) Choose the Menu option, click Insert → Picture → From file ☐

(iii) Choose the Menu option, click Insert → Add Picture → From file ☐

(iv) Choose the Menu option, click View → Add Picture → From file ☐

d. What are the special effects used for introducing slides in a presentation called?

(i) Effects ☐ (ii) Custom animations ☐ (iii) Transitions ☐ (iv) Slide show ☐

e. __________ are communicative buttons that can be added on the slides to perform various actions during the slide show.

(i) Insert buttons ☐ (ii) Action buttons ☐

(iii) Delete buttons ☐ (iv) Review buttons ☐

f. How many types of slide transitions are there in a PowerPoint presentation?

(i) 3 ☐ (ii) 2 ☐ (iii) 4 ☐ (iv) 5 ☐

g. Aakash wants to give sound effects to his presentation. Where will he find sound options?

(i) Insert → Comment ☐

(ii) Insert → Media → Video → Video from file ☐

(iii) Insert → Media → Audio → Audio on my PC ☐ (iv) View → Comment ☐

h. Where can we find Custom Animation under the menu bar in MS PowerPoint?

(i) Edit menu ☐ (ii) Slide Show menu ☐

(iii) File menu ☐ (iv) Review tab ☐

i. What does the Apply Design Template option do?

(i) Adds functionality to the slide ☐ (ii) Changes the content of the slide ☐

(iii) Changes the look of the slide without changing the content ☐

(iv) All of the above ☐

2. Fill in the blanks.

a. In an MS PowerPoint presentation, the default view of the slide layout is ____________.

b. Animation can be removed from a slide by selecting the ____________ button from the Animation Pane.

c. The shortcut keys to create a new slide are ____________.

d. ____________ effects are applied when one slide changes to another.

e. ____________ is the shortcut key to run a slide show.

3. State whether the following statements are true (T) or false (F).

a. Slide transition merges the next slide during the slide show. ☐

b. The function key to start slide transition is F5. ☐

c. You can insert online audio but not online videos in a slide. ☐

d. You can record your own voice in a slide. ☐

e. The very first slide of the presentation opens in the Slide Master view. ☐

4. Match the following.

a.	Audio and video	(i)	Illustrations group in the Insert ribbon
b.	SmartArt and shapes	(ii)	Media group in the Insert ribbon
c.	Sound	(iii)	Advanced Animation group of the Animations ribbon
d.	Add animation	(iv)	Timing group in Transition ribbon
e.	Action button	(v)	Shapes in Insert tab

5. Answer the following questions in brief.

a. What is custom animation?

b. What is an action button?

c. What is meant by transition?

d. What is a Slide Master?

e. Write the steps to run a slide show.

6. Answer the following questions in detail.

a. What are Action Buttons? What functions do they serve?

b. Name the different views in MS PowerPoint. Explain the purpose of each of them.

c. Define animation. What are the different animation effects in MS PowerPoint?

d. What is Slide transition? What are the steps to add transitions to all the slides of a PowerPoint presentation?

e. What are the steps to add one's own voice in a presentation?

Lab Activities

Experiential Learning

1. Create a small presentation on *'How to Keep your Classroom/ School Clean'*.

   Add 2–3 slides to your presentation.

   Add images and use audio as well.

2. Sejal needs to give a presentation to introduce the new AI model she has built. She has created a video for the model as well. Can you write down the steps she should use to add the video in her presentation? Try replicating the same in the lab.

3. Vikram's father runs a pet shelter. Can you help Vikram create a presentation introducing all the animal breeds that are available there to help his father find a home for them?

   Remember, this presentation is going to be shared with all interested prospective adopters; so, add attractive images and videos wherever needed.

   Also, make it attractive by using animations to catch the attention of the prospective adopters.

4. Ekta wants to add audio to her presentation in such a way that it plays continuously in the background on all her slides. Also, she wants the audio symbol to be hidden. Which one of the checkboxes will she have to tick to meet her requirements?

   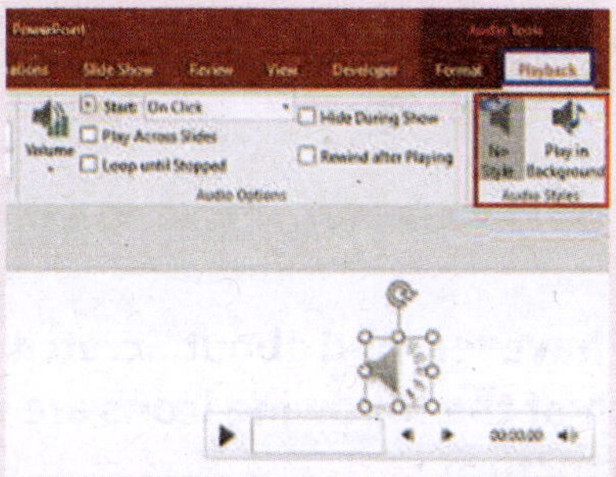

   If you want to use the slide transition of dissolving for 3 seconds, what steps will you use to enable this transition?

Group Activities

Collaboration

Form groups and create a presentation on one of the following topics:

a. Animal World

b. Global Pandemic

c. AI Used Today

d. The Universe

Make sure that the presentation includes multimedia and transitions.

One person from each group can present this in front of the class using the Slide Show view.

Chapter

6

Introduction to Game Creation-I

After reading this chapter, I will be able to:

- ✔ Add and delete sprites.
- ✔ Use the Looks blocks.
- ✔ Use the Motion blocks.
- ✔ Use the Sound blocks.
- ✔ Use a Pen extension.

Technology Literacy

Brainstorm and explore!

We have learned about Scratch platform in Class 5. Do you remember what each of the following icons are used? Write in the space provided alongside the picture.

1.  ______________________________

2.  ______________________________

3.  ______________________________

4.  ______________________________

The Scratch platform can be used to create games and animations. Let us recall what we learned about the scratch platform in Class 5. We will then learn more about Scratch blocks and how we can use them to create games.

Adding and Deleting Sprites

Let us revise how to add a new sprite. We can add a new sprite by using the **Choosing a Sprite** option in the **Sprite** area (Fig. 6.1). A new sprite will appear next to the current sprite. There is no restriction on the number of sprites one can add in a program. But remember, the more the sprites, the slower the program could get and the screen could look very crowded. Thus, add only a limited number of sprites.

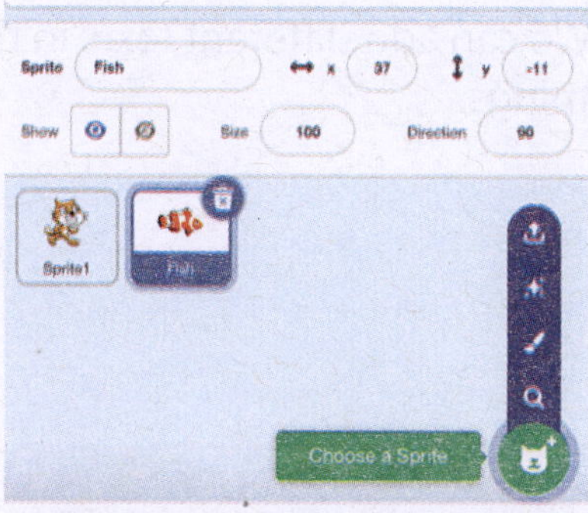

Fig. 6.1 | *Adding a new sprite*

Deleting a Sprite

Do you notice something weird in Fig. 6.1?

____

Fish live in water and cats live on land. So the cat and the fish should not be shown in the same frame. We should choose the characters carefully.

We can delete the cat and add a new sprite by following these steps:

1. Click the sprite that is to be deleted.
2. Click the dustbin icon that appears on top right.
3. The sprite disappears from the stage and the sprite area. Add another sprite as we need two characters for this (Fig. 6.2).

Fig. 6.2 | *Deleting a sprite*

Brush up!

What would be the output of this code?

____

____

____

____

The Looks Blocks

The looks blocks are represented by purple colour. These blocks are mostly used to change the appearance of the sprites or their costumes.

Think() and Say() Blocks

As the name suggests, the **Think** block is used to suggest that a sprite is thinking. The specified text is shown in the form of a thinking cloud, which is different from a speech cloud used in the **Say()** block.

We can add different texts in the white space of the block to make the sprite think or say different things.

Fig. 6.3 | *Steps to run a Think block*

Fig. 6.4 | *Different Think blocks*

There are two ways to add the think block:

1. **Think (Text) for (x) seconds**: This is used to run the block for a predefined time. Along with the text, we can also change the number of seconds we want the block to run. This is similar to the **say ( ) for** ( ) **seconds** block. For example, in Fig. 6.3, the cat will think "Hmm..." for two seconds.

2. **Think(text)**: This is used to run the block till the next command is to be executed. This is similar to the **say( )** block. The thought bubble stays active until:

   a. a speech block with its text is activated

   b. a thought block with its text is activated

   c. the **Stop** sign is pressed.

Soak up!

Try using the **Wait()** block, which is a **Control** block, when using two **Think()** blocks together, one after the other.

Clear up!

What block will you use to make the cat say "Nice weather today"?

Change Size by () and Set Size to ()

The change size by block is used to change the size of the sprite to the specified number of pixels (Fig. 6.5).

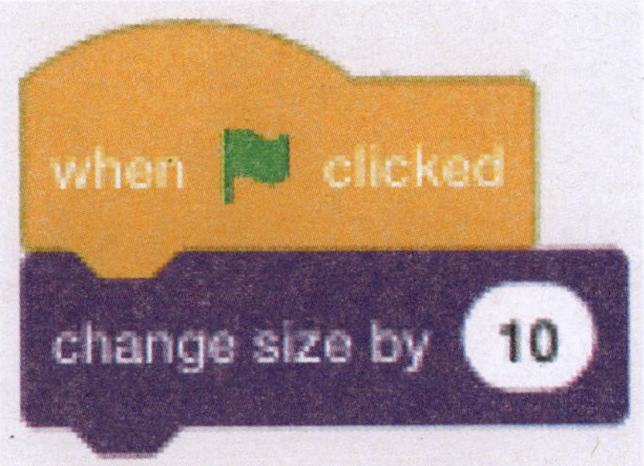

Fig. 6.5 | *Change size block*

The default size of a sprite is 100, which is mentioned in the **Sprite Lists** area as well.

This block can be used when one has to continuously increase or decrease the size of a sprite.

Set size changes the size of the sprite to the specified percentage. The default sprite size is 100%. Anything lower than it will decrease the size of the sprite on the stage, and anything above it will increase the size of the sprite on the stage (Fig. 6.6).

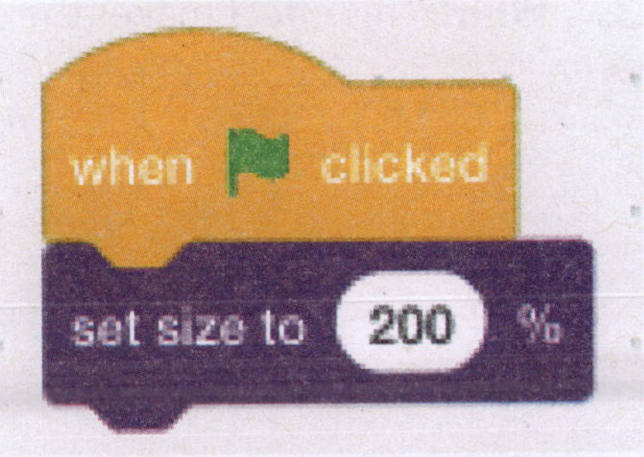

Fig. 6.6 | *Set size block used to double the actual size of the sprite*

The **set size** to block can, thus, be used to permanently change the size of the sprite. Unlike the **change size** block, it will not keep increasing the size every time one runs the program.

Brush up!

Can you tell where else can we change the size of the sprite?

Change ( ) Effect by ( )

The **Change ( ) Effect by ( )** block changes the specified graphic effect on its sprite by a certain amount (Fig. 6.7). There are seven different types of graphical effects—color, fisheye, whirl, pixelate, mosaic, brightness and ghost. Let us learn about these one by one:

Fig. 6.7 | *Change effect block*

1. **Color**: This effect changes the colour of the sprite from yellow to another colour, depending on the value specified (Fig. 6.7.1).

Fig. 6.7.1 | ***Change color*** *effect block*

2. **Fisheye**: This effect is used to make the sprite look as if it is in water (Fig. 6.7.2).

Fig. 6.7.2 | ***Change fisheye effect*** *block*

3. **Whirl**: This effect makes the sprite whirl or crooked (Fig. 6.7.3).

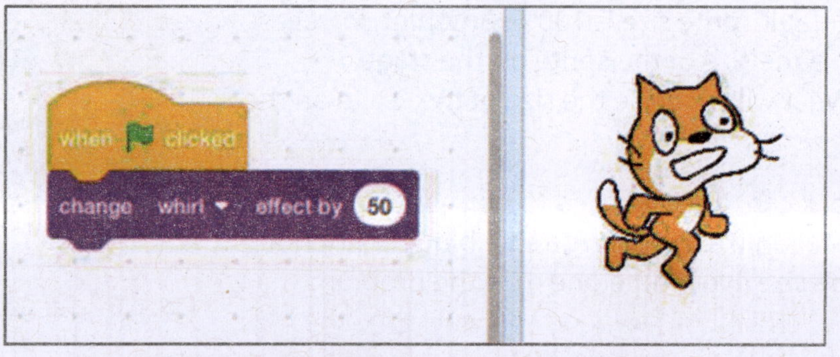

Fig. 6.7.3 | ***Change whirl effect*** *block*

4. **Pixelate**: This effect will give the sprite a pixel format (Fig. 6.7.4).

Fig. 6.7.4 | ***Change pixelate effect*** *block*

5. **Mosaic**: This effect will create the illusion of multiple sprites like mosaic tiles (Fig. 6.7.5).

Fig. 6.7.5 | ***Change mosaic effect*** *block*

6. **Brightness**: This effect will increase the brightness of the sprite (Fig. 6.7.6).

Fig. 6.7.6 | ***Change brightness effect*** *block*

7. **Ghost sprite**: This effect is used to make the sprite transparent and give it a ghost-like effect (Fig. 6.7.7). What do you think will happen if the effect is set to 100?

Fig. 6.7.7 | ***Change ghost effect*** *block*

Brush up!

1. The set color ▾ effect to (0) block is used similar to the **set size to ()** block. Write down its function if the effect is changed to 25.
2. Name the graphical effects available in it.

Hide and Show Block

As the name suggests, the **hide and show** block is meant for hiding or showing the sprite. This is one of the most used blocks in the **Looks** block. It is mostly used to hide a sprite, cover it with another sprite, or for preparing scenes.

A sprite added is by default shown on stage.

The **hide** block is used to hide it, especially when we want to introduce the character only after a certain period of time or after a certain action occurs.

The **show** block is used if the hidden sprite needs to be shown. If the sprite is already showing on the stage, nothing will change. Figure 6.8 shows that the sprite will hide after displaying the message.

Fig. 6.8 | ***Hide*** *block*

Clear up!

Make the sprite reappear with a different colour in Fig. 6.8. What blocks will you add?

Soak up!

Costumes are one of the many looks the sprite has. Every sprite has a minimum one costume designed from scratch.

Next Costume Block

The **next costume** block is used to change the costume of the sprite in between the program. When run, the **next costume** block displays the next available costume for the sprite.

For example, the shark sprite has two costumes in Scratch (Fig. 6.9.1). We can change the costume from one to another, once the shark comes near to the fish (Fig. 6.9.2).

Fig. 6.9.1 | *Costumes of shark sprite*

Fig. 6.9.2 | *Using* ***next costume*** *block*

Switch Costume to () Block

The **switch costume to ()** block changes its sprite's costume to a specified one.

It is used whenever a sprite must switch to a specific costume instead of the next costume block, which only switches to the next costume in the list.

Brush up!

What will happen when the following code is run?

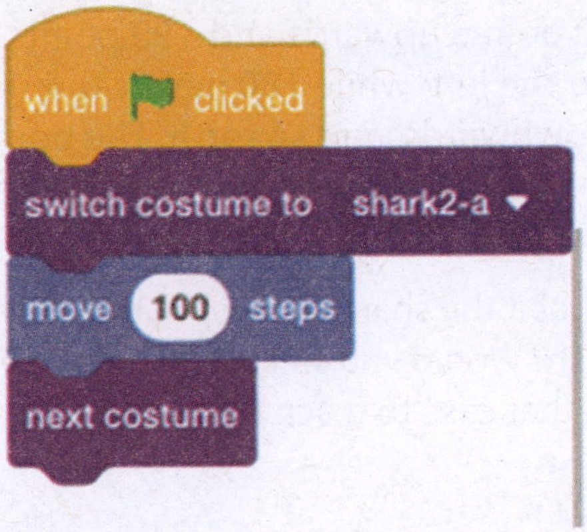

Next Backdrop Block

Lion King was filmed in a jungle but had different backgrounds for every new scene. The backdrop also had to be coded. Similar to the **next costume** block, the **next backdrop** block changes the stage to the next background image (Fig. 6.10). This is mostly used when one needs to change the background mid-story.

Fig. 6.10 | *Changing background*

Brush up!

What does the **switch backdrop to ()** block do?

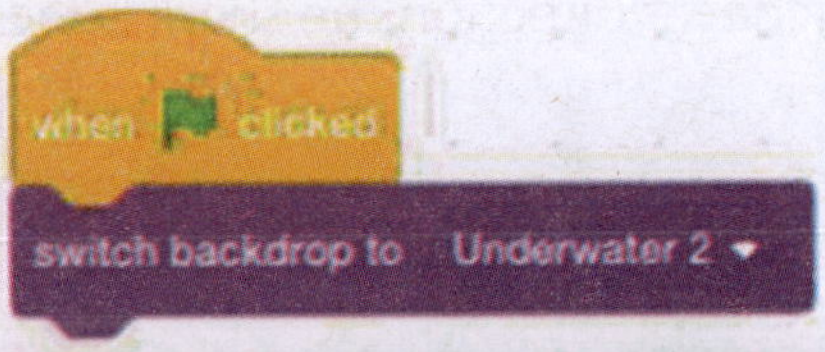

Soak up!

The backdrops can be coded as well. We can add effects such as fisheye and whirl, as well as use other blocks with it. The number of blocks used for the sprite and the backdrop vary slightly.

Clear up!

Add a ball sprite and change its colour and size every time the green flag is clicked.

Motion Blocks

Motion blocks are dark-blue blocks. They are very popular blocks used in game creation. By now, we know that the **move ()** block is used to move the sprite x number of steps. Let us look at some other motion blocks.

Point in Direction () Block

It is a **motion** block that points the sprite in the specified direction and accordingly rotates the sprite. The default value is 90, which points to the right. The block uses the circle, where 0 points upwards and –90 points the sprite to the left, while 180 makes the sprite point downwards, and so forth. The pointer can be used to move the sprite to the desired direction (Fig. 6.11.1).

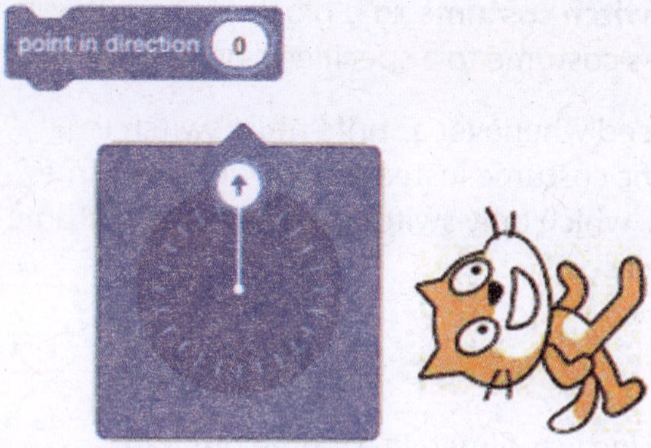

Fig. 6.11.1 | *Using point in direction(0)*

Now, what if the shark was not in the same line as the fish? Would you still use the **move()** steps block in that case to reach the fish?

Go to ()

The **go to** block directly takes the sprite to the specified position. It has three drop-down options (Fig. 6.11.1):

1. **Go to (Random position):** This takes the sprite to any random position.
2. **Go to (mouse pointer):** This takes the sprite to where the mouse pointer is placed.
3. **Go to (sprite_name):** This takes the sprite to where the other selected sprite is located on the stage.

To make the shark reach the fish, simply use the **Go to (fish)** block so that the fish will be moved to whichever direction the shark is facing (Fig. 6.11.2).

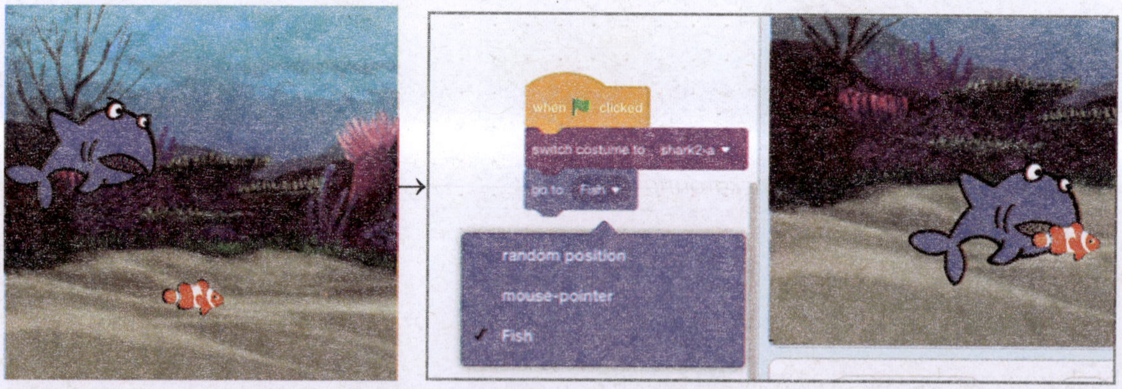

Fig. 6.11.2 | *Using* ***go to()*** *block*

Brush up!

Which of the go to options should be used in the following games?

1. Click on the object to keep it from falling.
2. Make the object fall randomly from the sky.

Glide () Seconds to ()

This block is similar to the **go to** block, except it glides to the end destination in the specified number of seconds, giving an animation effect. It has the same three drop-down options as the **go to** block.

For example, in the code shown in Fig. 6.12, the shark will move towards the fish and reach the end destination (the fish) in 3 seconds.

Fig. 6.12 | *Using **glide () seconds to ()** block*

Turn () Degrees

This motion block enables the sprite to turn to the specified number of degrees, clockwise or anticlockwise (depending on which block is used) (Fig. 6.13). This changes the direction the sprite is facing.

Fig. 6.13 | *Using turn (90) degrees clockwise*

Soak up!

The **go to X: () Y: ()** and **glide() seconds to X:() Y:()** are motion blocks used to set the sprite's X and Y positions to the specified amounts. The X and Y positions are visible in the sprite area on top-right end.

The **go to X: () Y: ()** command is usually used in the beginning, right below the **when green flag click** block to ensure that the program starts with the sprites in their respective positions.

Sound Block

Fig. 6.14 | *Sound blocks*

The **Sound** block enables us to add sound effects to our game. It has 8 blocks (Fig. 6.14):

1. **Play sound () until done**: This block plays a sound, waits for it to finish playing and then carries on with the next line in the script/code.
2. **Start sound ()**: This block plays the sound in the background, and at the same time runs the rest of the lines of the code.

3. **Stop all sounds**: This block cancels all the sounds currently playing.
4. **Set volume to ()%**: This block sets a sprite's volume to a certain percentage level.
5. **Change volume by ()**: This block changes a sprite's volume by the specified amount.

Steps to Add Sound to the Code

To add sound to the code, follow these steps:

1. Add the sound to the program from the **Sounds** tab (next to **Costumes tab**).
2. Add the **start sound ()** or the **play sound () until done** block and select the sound suitable for the backdrop. Add the sound to the program either by coding the backdrop or the sprite. The following code will play the "Ocean Wave" sound in the backdrop and the "Bite" sound in the end after changing the costume (Fig. 6.15).

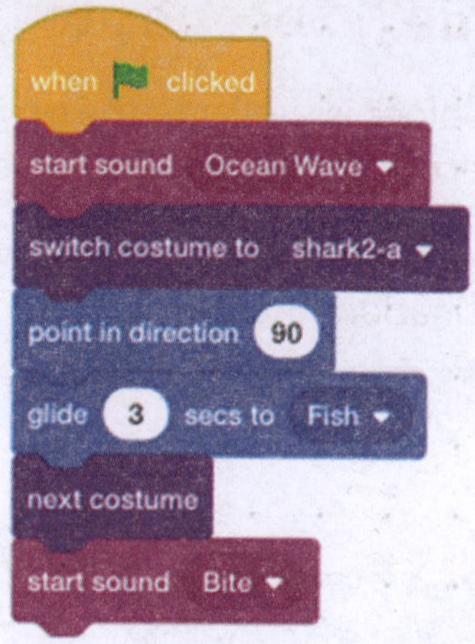

Fig. 6.15 | *Using start sound () block*

Brush up!

Code a program to make the tiny fish disappear once the shark eats it.

Today I learned!

- Look blocks are purple and consist of say, think, change size, set size, change effect, set effect, hide and show blocks, next costume, switch costume, next background and switch background blocks.
- The think block is used to suggest that a sprite is thinking.
- The change size block is used to change the size of the sprite to the specified number of pixels.
- The set size block changes the size of the sprite to the specified percentage.
- The change () effect by () block changes the specified graphic effect on the sprite.
- There are seven different types of graphical effects: colour, fisheye, whirl, pixelate, mosaic, brightness and ghost.
- The show and hide block is meant for hiding or showing the sprite.
- The next costume block is used to change the costume of the sprite in between the program, while the switch costume block changes the costume to the specified one.
- The next backdrop () and switch backdrop to () blocks in the Looks block are used to add a new backdrop to code.
- Motion blocks are dark blue and help sprites move, turn or go to certain positions.
- The point in direction () block is a motion block used to make the sprite turn and change its direction.
- The turn () degrees motion block helps in turning a sprite to the specified amount of degrees.
- Other motion blocks that help in moving the sprite to a specific location are the go to () and glide () seconds to () blocks.
- The Sound block enables us to add sound effects in our program. It has eight blocks.

Revise and polish!

1. Tick (✓) the correct answer.

a. Default colour of the flag is:

(i) Green ☐ (ii) Red ☐ (iii) Blue ☐ (iv) White ☐

b. Default size of a sprite is:

(i) 50 ☐ (ii) 100 ☐ (iii) 150 ☐ (iv) 200 ☐

c. ______________ transparency value hides the sprite completely.

(i) 100 ☐ (ii) 0 ☐ (iii) 250 ☐ (iv) 1 ☐

d. Which of these is not a Looks block?

(i) change pen size to () ☐ (ii) hide ☐

(iii) set effect () to () ☐ (iv) all of the above ☐

e. Which of the following blocks is used to make a sprite transparent?

(i) set (ghost) effect ☐ (ii) set transparency ☐

(iii) set pen (transparency) ☐ (iv) set (0) transparency ☐

f. Switch costume to () block is part of:

(i) Looks blocks ☐ (ii) Motion blocks ☐

(iii) Backdrops ☐ (iv) Events blocks ☐

g. Which of the following is a colour of Sound blocks?

(i) Dark blue ☐ (ii) Orange ☐ (iii) Pink ☐ (iv) Yellow ☐

h. The Sound block has ____________ blocks.

(i) 5 ☐ (ii) 6 ☐

(iii) 7 ☐ (iv) 8 ☐

i. Swami wants to change the action of the sprite he is using. Which block should he use?

(i) switch costumes to () block ☐ (ii) change the sprite ☐

(iii) change () effect by () block ☐ (iv) change () effect by (0) block ☐

2. What do the following blocks do?

a. think ()

b. turn ()

c. change (fisheye) by (25)

d. point in direction ()

e. change volume by (10)

f. move ()

3. Fill in the blanks.

a. The ____________________ icon needs to be clicked to delete the sprite.

b. Sound block has ____________________ blocks in it.

c. ____________________ is used to change volume of a sound by the specified amount.

d. ____________________ changes the costume of a sprite to the specified image.

e. The switch backdrop to () is a ____________________ block

4. State whether the following statements are true (T) or false (F).

a. The think block uses the speech cloud. ☐

b. The change (mosaic) effect is used to give an underwater effect. ☐

c. Red stop is clicked to stop the program. ☐

d. The default direction of a sprite is 0. ☐

e. Only 10 sprites can be added to the stage at a time. ☐

5. Match the following.

a.	Green flag	(i)	Pen extension
b.	point in direction	(ii)	Motion block
c.	erase all	(iii)	Events block
d.	set size ()	(iv)	Looks block
e.	start sound ()	(v)	Sound block

6. Answer the following questions.

a. What are the different sound blocks? Explain any four.

b. Write the steps to add sound to the background of a program.

c. Explain the difference between the next costume and switch costume blocks.

d. How many effects are available under the change ( ) effect by ( ) block? Explain three of them in detail.

e. Discuss any three blocks under the Looks block.

Experiential Learning

Lab Activities

1. Open a new Scratch program and do the following:
    a. Add a new sprite(s) using paint editor.
    b. Rename the program to "Second Scratch project."
    c. Save the project on the computer.
2. Sudha wants to create a new Scratch program, where she wants to create an animal kingdom and each sprite will describe itself on its own. Can you help her create it? Let the sprite describe itself using the say or think blocks.
    a. Add a minimum of 5 sprites.
    b. Make the animals make sounds as well while describing themselves.
3. Change the cat's (default sprite) colour to red and make it look like this:

   What did you do to change the colour? ______________________
4. Create a Scratch program and make sprites of your choice walk using the change costumes block as shown here.

5. Varsha drew the given image using the Scratch paint editor. But she is unable to complete the colouring inside the house. Can you replicate this on the Scratch paint editor and help her colour the house?

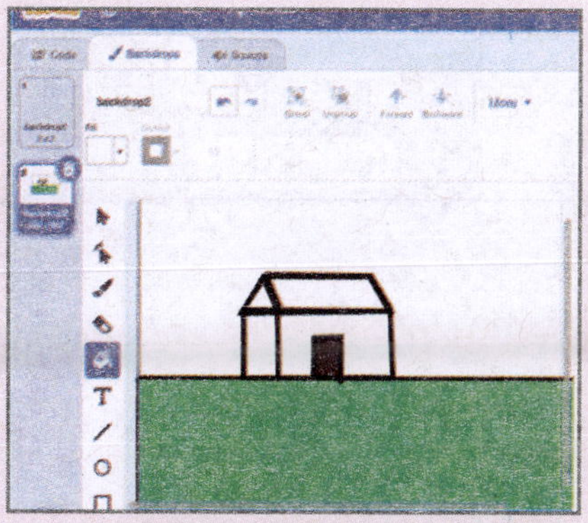

6. Draw a polygon as shown here:

7. Create an animation to give this output.

   Hint: Use the pen and motion blocks

Think and Answer

Problem-solving

Critical Thinking

1. Saloni wants to create a program to move the sprite only horizontally. Which of the two blocks should she use?

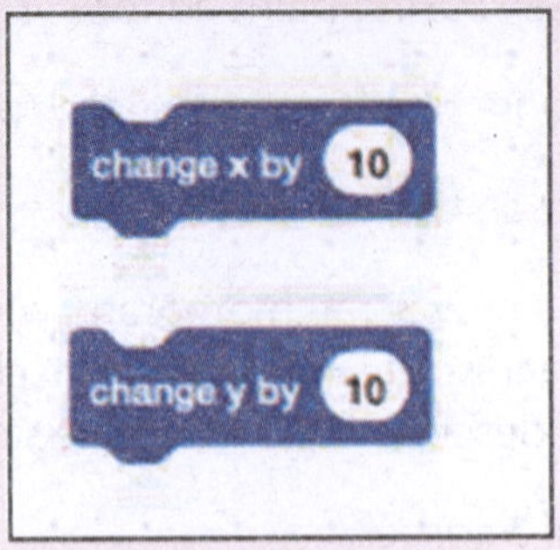

____

____

2. Ajinkya wants to draw his own background image and not copy it from the Internet or use the background images available in the Scratch library. Which options should he use while adding the background?

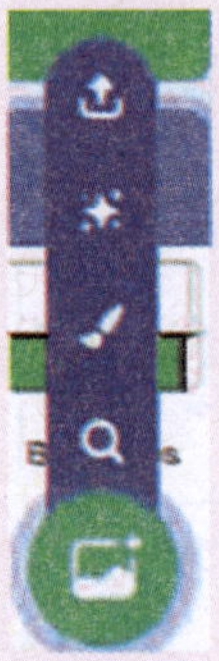

____

____

3. Which of these commands will say "Hello! How are you?"

____

____

Chapter

7

Introduction to Game Creation-II

After reading this chapter, I will be able to:

- ✔ Explain how to use Events blocks.
- ✔ Define and use Control blocks.
- ✔ Explain and use different Sensing blocks.
- ✔ Understand how to use variables in Scratch.
- ✔ Create a game using Scratch.

Brainstorm and explore!

Write functions of the following blocks.

1. 

____

2. 

____

3. 

____

4. 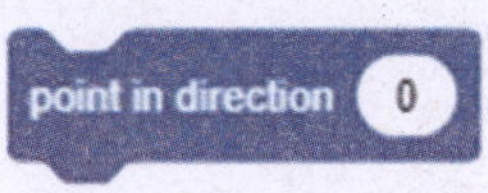

____

5. 

____

When programmers create a game, they write code for what will happen on the screen when a certain key is pressed. This is called an **event**. We have already learned about one such event in Scratch by using the "**When Green Flag is clicked** block." Let us learn about more such Scratch blocks in this chapter.

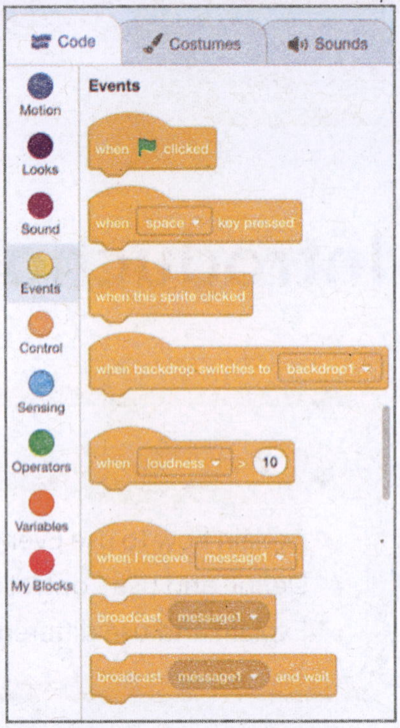

Fig. 7.1 | *Events blocks*

Events Blocks

There are eight Events blocks in Scratch (Fig. 7.1). They are represented in yellow. When the specific event occurs, it would trigger a line of script or code. They are mostly used to make the program run on its own.

Let us learn about these Events blocks one by one.

When () Key Pressed

The code placed underneath the **when () key pressed** block will be activated when the specified key is pressed. These are mostly keys on the keyboard such as alphabets (A–Z), numeric keys (0–9), spacebar and arrow keys.

Figure 7.2 shows the code to move the character to the right using the right arrow key.

Fig. 7.2 | *Using When() key pressed block*

Clear up!

Rani loves gaming. Can you help her program the sprite to move right, left, up and down by using the arrow keys? Write down the steps to do this.

When This Sprite Clicked

The code placed underneath the **when this sprite clicked** block is activated once the Sprite (that contains this code) is clicked. This is active only when that particular sprite is visible (shown) on stage. For backdrops, this block can be replaced by the **when stage clicked** block (Fig. 7.3).

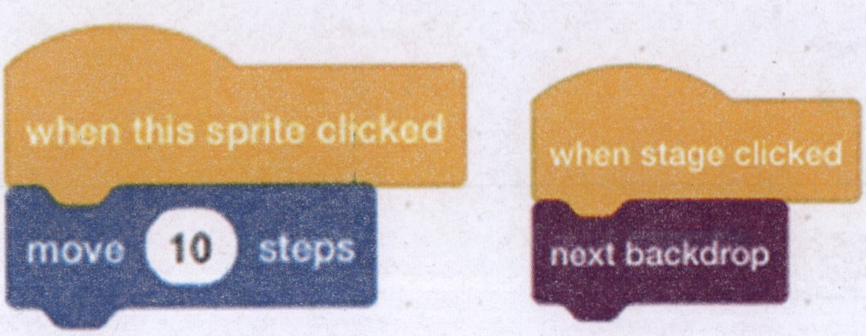

Fig. 7.3 | *Using **when this sprite clicked** and **when stage clicked** blocks*

When Backdrop Switches to ()

The code placed underneath the **when backdrop switches to ()** block is activated as soon as the background changes to the specified backdrop. This block is used when you want to show a new scene and add different characters to it. We can show the new sprites when the backdrop changes.

When ()>()

The **when ()>()** block starts the script below it when a value (loudness/timer) is greater than the specified numerical input. The code in Fig. 7.4 tells the sprite to move 10 steps only when the timer displays > 4, that is, after 4 seconds.

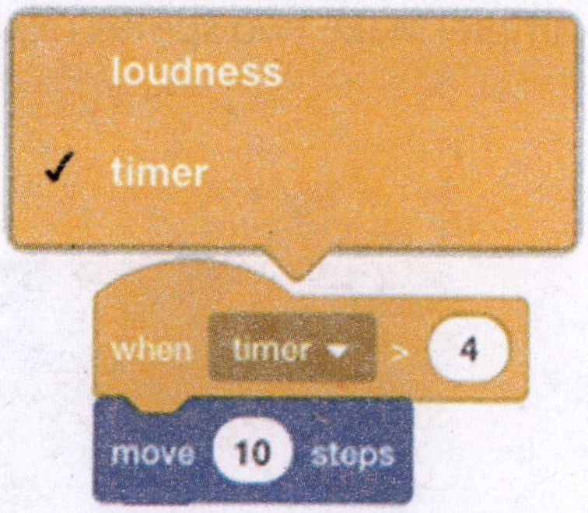

Fig. 7.4 | *Using* ***when ()>()*** *block*

Broadcast () and When I Receive ()

The **broadcast ()** block sends a broadcast/message throughout the Scratch program, whereas the **when I receive ()** block receives a broadcast and accordingly runs the required script. Both these blocks are always used together. **Broadcast ()** is used to start a new event. Any sprite or script that receives the specified broadcast message will activate the **when I receive ()** block (Fig. 7.5). In Fig. 7.5, the sprite will keep changing the costume as it is clicked, that is, once it receives the "message1."

Fig. 7.5 | *Using* ***broadcast*** *(message) and* ***when I receive*** *(message) blocks*

To change the message name in broadcast, click on the **New Message** option. A dialog box will appear. Add the new name as per your choice (Fig. 7.6).

Fig. 7.6 | *New message dialog box*

Broadcast () and Wait

This is similar to **broadcast message**, except this broadcast waits until the entire script activated by the broadcast ends. On the other hand, the **broadcast ()** block will restart the script in case it is activated again even before the script stops running.

Example: Make two sprites talk using the **broadcast** block (Figs. 7.7.1 and 7.7.2).

Fig. 7.7.1 | *Scratch code for the cat sprite*

Fig. 7.7.2 *Scratch code for the girl sprite*

When the Green Flag is clicked, the output will be as shown in Figs. 7.7.3 and 7.7.4.

Fig. 7.7.3 | *Output for the cat sprite*

Fig 7.7.4 | *Output for the girl sprite*

Brush up!

Write a program showing two friends arrive at a birthday party and wish the birthday boy. Make sure none of their conversations overlap.

Control Blocks

Control blocks are used to make the code more efficient. Using these blocks, we can add loops, conditions or pauses to our code. There are a total of 11 Control blocks and all are orange in colour (Fig. 7.8). Let us learn about some of the commonly used Control blocks.

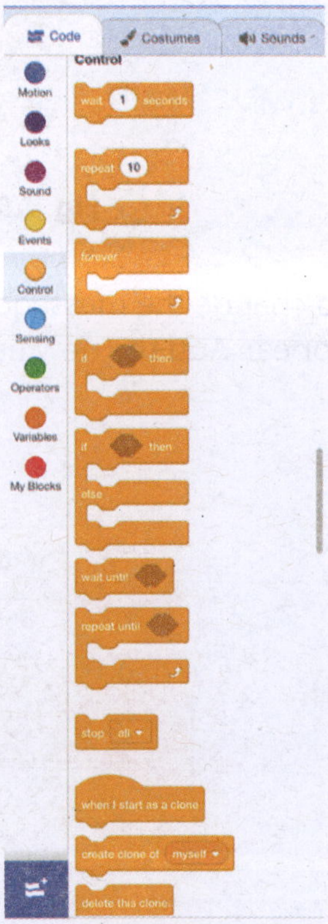

Fig. 7.8 | *Control blocks*

Wait () Seconds

The **wait () seconds** block pauses the script for the specified number of seconds. The seconds can also be written in decimals. This block is used when we need to pause the script for a short time. For example, when two or more sprites are having a conversation, we can use the **wait () seconds** block to avoid any overlap of conversations.

Brush up!

Which other block can we use to avoid an overlap of conversation between sprites?

Repeat ()

The blocks that are used within the **repeat ()** block are run in a loop for the specified number of times before moving to the next code block. For example, the code in Fig. 7.9 will change the colour of the sprite 10 times before saying "Hello!"

Clear up!

Can you try running the code in Fig. 7.9 by yourself in the lab?

Fig. 7.9 | *Using repeat block*

Forever

As the name suggests, the blocks within the **forever** block run infinitely. They do not stop unless someone uses the red **stop** sign or uses the **Stop all** block. Notice that this block has no bump (curve) at the bottom (Fig. 7.10).

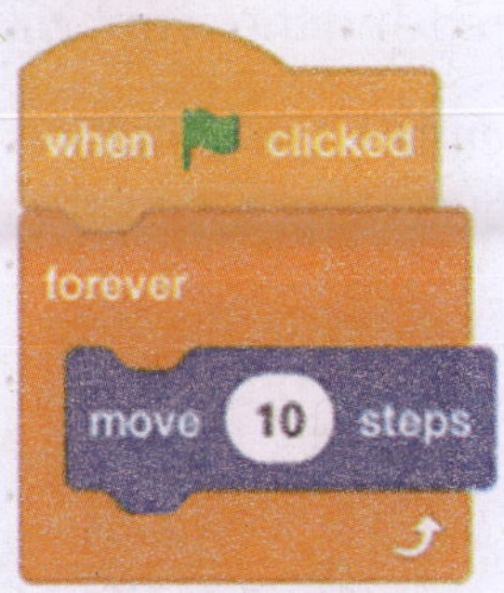

Fig. 7.10 | *Using the forever block*

Clear up!

What will be the output of this code?

____

____

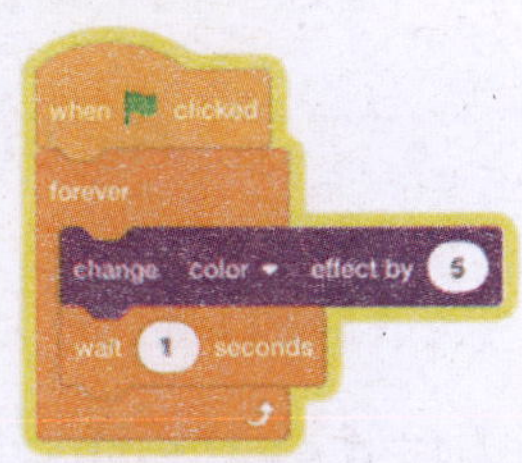

Stop ()

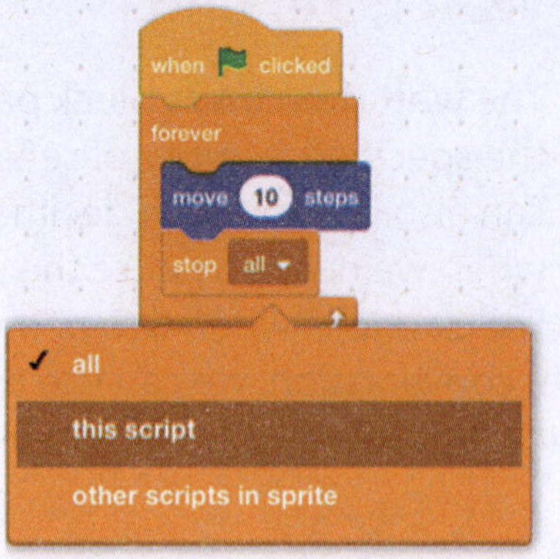

Fig. 7.11 | *Using the **stop ()** block*

The **stop** block is used to stop running the code. It is mostly used to stop the forever loop (Fig. 7.11) but can also be used outside it to end the project. It has 3 options that are used to either stop all scripts, one particular script or the other scripts running in that sprite.

The **stop** block is mostly used when we need to code a game. For example, to stop running the code once the number of lives are over or all the levels are complete.

Soak up!

Many **Control** blocks are used alongside ***Operators*** and ***Sensing*** blocks to make the code more efficient.

Sensing blocks shaped hexagonally are to be inserted in those **Control** blocks that have the hexagonal groove.

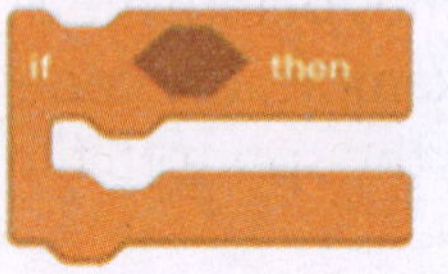

If <> Then Block

The **if <> then** block is used for comparing values, checking conditions, controlling keys, and so forth. This is another way to make the arrow keys work on Scratch (Fig. 7.12).

If the condition is true, the script inside the **if <> then** block will run first, and then, the script outside the block will continue. If the condition is false, the code inside the **if <> then** block will be ignored and the script will move on. The condition is specified using one of the **sensing** blocks.

Remember, the condition is checked only once. Thus, it is recommended to put this block in a forever loop, especially when it is meant to control keys.

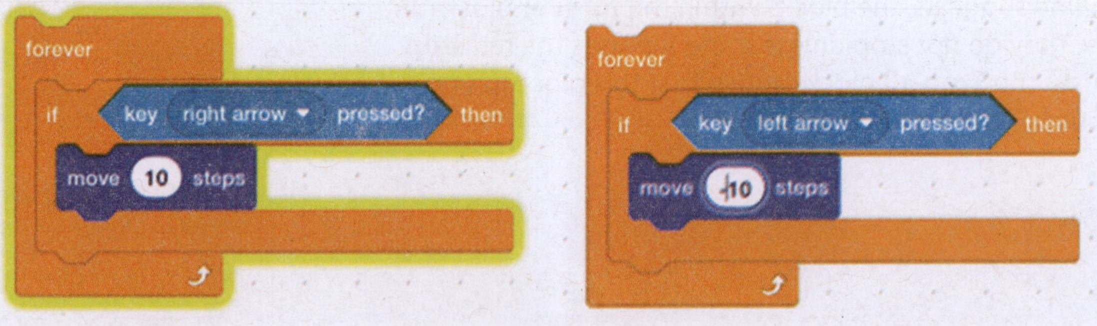

Fig: 7.12 | *Using the If <> then block to control the right and left arrow keys*

If <> Then Else Block

The first **if <> then** block is similar to the **if <> then** block. If the condition is true, the script inside the block will run first and then the script outside the block will continue. But, if the condition is false, the code inside the **else** block will run before moving to the script outside the block. For example, in Fig. 7.13 code, the sprite will say "I reached the end", if it is touching the edge of the stage. If it is not at the edge, it will move 20 steps (Here, "edge" could be any 4 sides of the stage area).

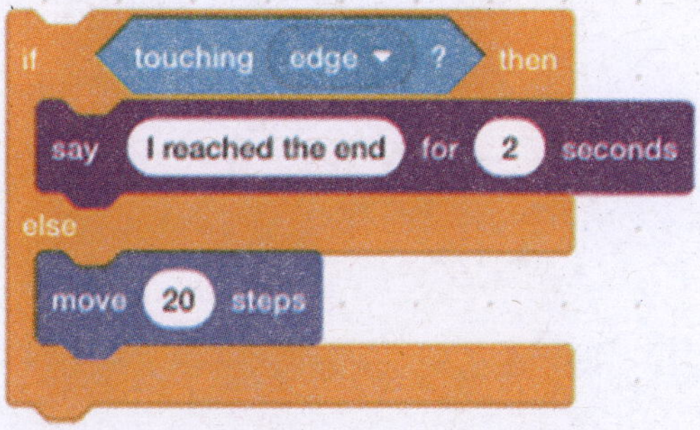

Fig. 7.13 | *Using the if <> then else block*

Brush up!

What output does this block give?

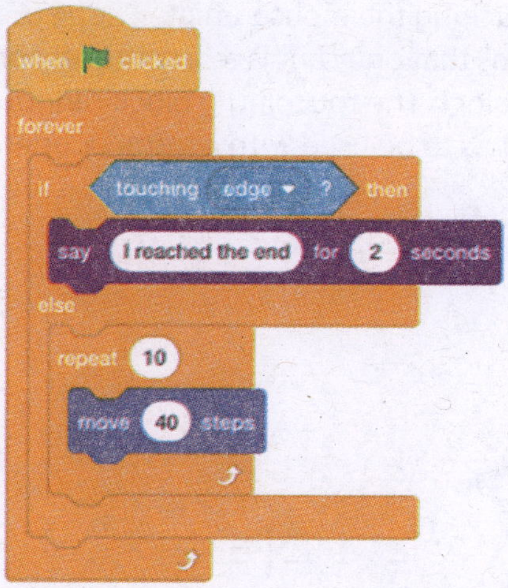

Repeat until <> Block

The script inside the **repeat until <>** block keeps running until a certain condition is met. It is used when we need to run a code under a certain condition.

For example, consider a scenario where a girl has to walk towards a tree. But, we do not know the exact number of steps she will have to cover, so cannot use the **move () steps** block. The **glide to ()** and **go to ()** blocks give an undesirable output (Fig. 7.14.1).

In such cases, we use the **repeat until <>** block (Fig. 7.14.2). This block will have to be accompanied with a sensing **"touching ()"** block to give the desired result.

Fig. 7.14.1 | *Using the **glide to** and **go to** blocks*

Fig. 7.14.2 | *Using the **repeat until** <> block*

Technology Literacy

Crank up!

Touching () block is a sensing block used to check if the sprite is touching the mouse pointer, edge or another sprite. This means that one can have a sprite respond to an action using this block. The touching () block cannot be used on its own and has to be used with control or operation blocks.

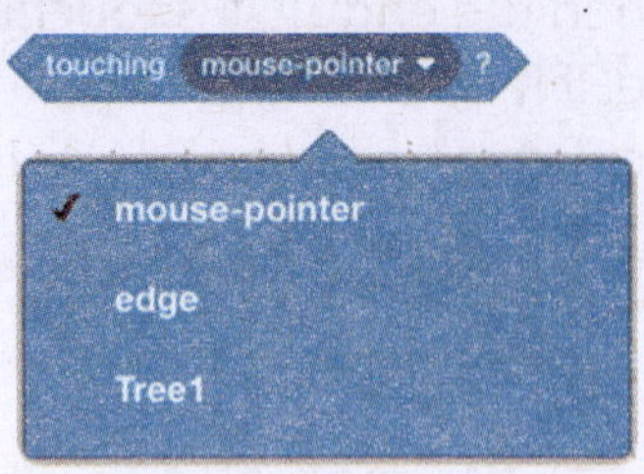

Clear up!

Use a **Control** block instead of a **motion** block to make the shark sprite reach the fish sprite. What differences do you observe between the two blocks?

Brush up!

Name your favourite online game.

- Does it have a scoreboard? ________
- Do you use keys to move around in the game? ________
- How does the scoring system work? ________
- How do you win the game? ________

Sensing Blocks

Sensing blocks are one of the categories of Scratch blocks. They are light-blue in colour (Fig. 7.15). They are used to detect objects. For example, they help a sprite detect when it collides with another sprite or touches the edge. Remember, **sensing** blocks are not standalone blocks and are mostly used inside a **Control** block.

Mostly, sensing blocks enable user interaction. For example, they are used to ask the user to reply or press a particular key or object. They detect the user input (which can be the click of the mouse, using the arrow keys on the keyboard, when a user types an answer into a question box and so forth) and accordingly, give output as coded.

Sensing blocks play a very important role in creating games using Scratch. Let us learn about the different uses of **sensing** blocks while coding.

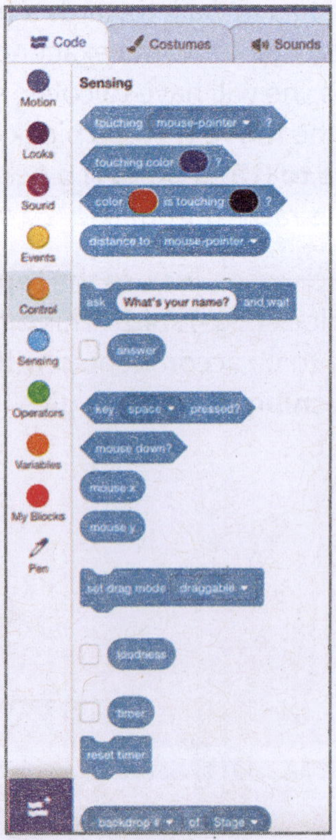

Fig. 7.15 | *Sensing blocks*

Sprites Collide with Each Other

Whenever we need to act upon when two sprites collide with each other, we can use any of the following blocks.

1. Touching Color ()?

This block is used when the sprite touches any object or another sprite of a particular colour. The script under this block will run if it touches the mentioned colour. We can choose the colour using the **color picker** to avoid any small colour differences (Fig. 7.16).

As shown in Fig. 7.17, if the sprite touches anything green, it will hide.

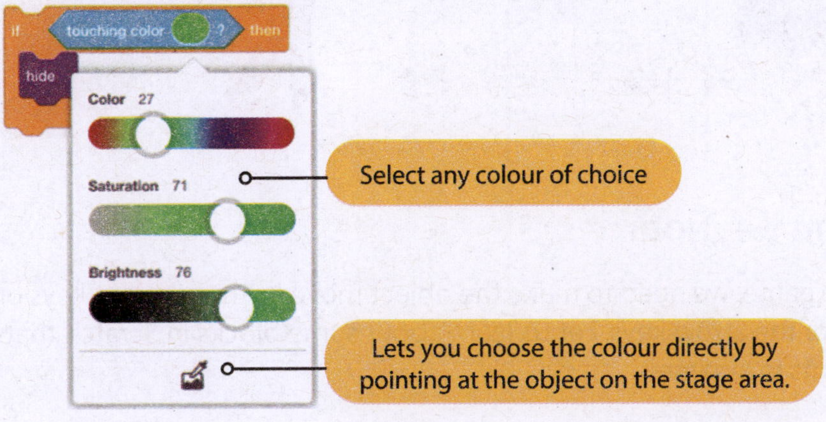

Fig. 7.16 | *Using touching () ? block*

2. Color () is Touching ()?

Using the **color () is touching ()?** block, we can set up a code to detect a collision, that is, for when any part of a sprite comes into contact with a specific colour on the stage. This is used to have a sprite detect and respond to contact with another sprite on the stage when one colour touches another colour. For example, in Fig. 7.17, we want the prince to hide only when the shoe (brown colour) touches the ball (green colour). As per the code, when the brown colour of the shoe touches the green colour anywhere on stage, the prince will hide.

Fig. 7.17 | *Using color () is touching ()*

Brush up!

Can you tell what this script is meant to do?

____

____

Using Keys on Keyboard

To play any online game, we need to make the object move or throw using keys on the keyboard, such as spacebar or the arrow keys. Let us learn about some blocks in Scratch that enable us to code for such events in a game.

Key () Pressed? Block

This block can be used to detect when the user presses a specific key on the keyboard. This is specifically used to enhance user interaction.

Fig. 7.18 | *Using key() pressed?*

Sprite Touching the Edge or Mouse Pointer

On touching the edge of the stage area or the mouse pointer, we can program the sprite to react accordingly. Let us learn how to do so.

Touching () Block

While using the **touching () ?** block, we have three options to choose in the drop-down—when it touches the mouse pointer (user interaction), the edge of the screen or another sprite (Fig. 7.19).

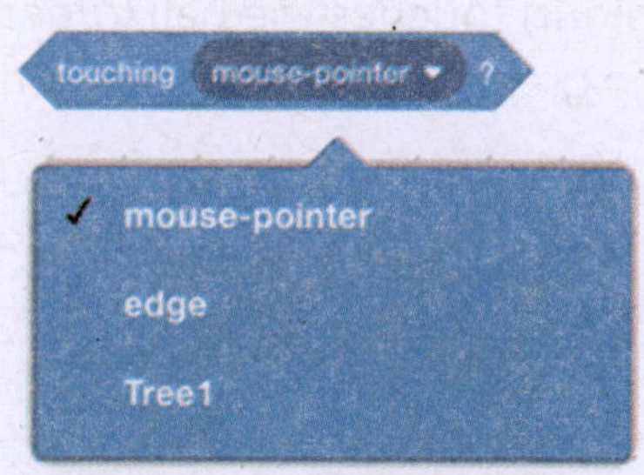

Fig 7.19 | *Using touching ()?*

Brush up!

Can you name a game you have played that could use the code given in Fig. 7.19?

____

Asking a Question

Another way to use sensing blocks is to directly ask a question to the user. Let us learn how to do that.

Ask () and Wait and Answer

The **ask** block allows us to ask a question on the screen and stores the keyboard input in the **answer** block (Fig. 7.20). On checking the **answer** block, it will appear in the stage area. The question appears in a callout on the screen, while the user can type the answer in the rectangle that appears below. The program waits till the user types in a response and presses the Enter key or clicks the check mark on the right (Fig. 7.21).

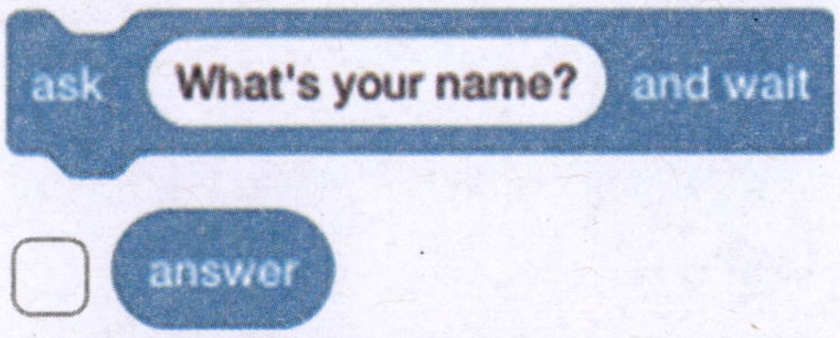

Fig. 7.20 | *Ask () and answer blocks*

Fig. 7.21 | *Using ask () block*

Clear up!

Create a program that asks "What is the capital of India?" If the answer is "New Delhi," you should hear the sound of claps.

Following the Mouse Pointer

Have you played games where the sprite follows the mouse pointer everywhere? Let us understand how this works.

Mouse *x* and Mouse *y* Blocks

The **mouse *x*** and **mouse *y*** blocks are used to give the *x* and *y* locations of the mouse pointer. They can be used with any of the blocks learned earlier, which have round empty blocks available. They let the mouse pointer control the movement of the sprite. In Fig. 7.22, the code will continuously have the sprite go to or follow the location of the mouse pointer, that is, the mouse's *x* and *y* coordinates. It has to be in the forever loop to make sure that the sprite always follows the mouse.

Soak up!

The sprite's location on the stage is based on *x* and *y* coordinates. These values are also shown in the sprite area where *x* is the horizontal axis and *y* is the vertical axis.

Clicking a Sprite

We have learned about the **when sprite clicked** block under the Events blocks. There is also a sensing block that can be used to detect if the sprite is clicked using a mouse. Let us know more about this.

Mouse Down?

As the name suggests, this block is activated when the mouse is down or clicked (Fig 7.22). As per the code in Fig. 7.22, the costume of the sprite changes each time, it is clicked. This block is used in games that use the mouse.

Fig. 7.22 | *Mouse down? block*

Soak up!

Operators blocks are one of the categories of Scratch blocks. They are colour-coded green and mostly used to code mathematical (addition, subtraction, multiplication and division) or logical (greater than, less than or equal to) operations. Like the **sensing** blocks, they are used along with the **Control** blocks.

Variables

Most of the games played online have a scoring system or a way to score points.

How can we add a scoreboard in Scratch?

To add a scoreboard to a game, we use **variables** in Scratch. A **Variables** block stores changeable values. At a time, it can hold only one value. Since the score keeps changing in a game, it is stored as a variable. Variables contain numbers as well as strings (i.e., alphabets or words). A variable has to be created first before we can use it. Variables can be created using the **make a variable** block. All the variables available in that project will be displayed below it. The default variable available on Scratch is "my variable" (Fig. 7.23).

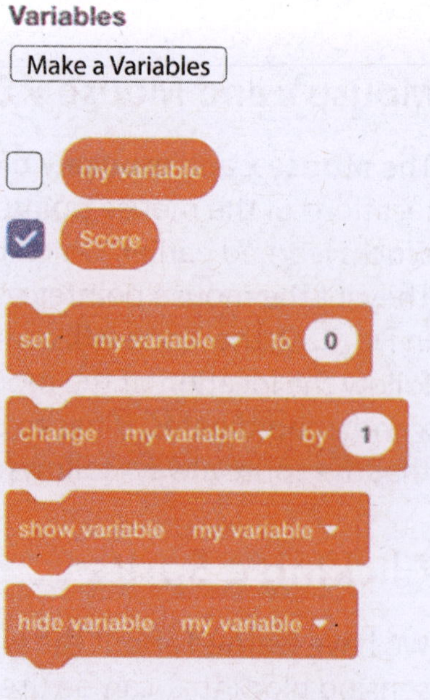

Fig. 7.23 | *Variables blocks*

1. **set variable_name to (value):** Gives a value to the variable. This could be a number or string.
2. **change (*variable_name*) to (numeric_value):** Updates the value of variable by the specified value.

3. **show variable (*variable_name*):** Displays the variable and its value on the stage area.
4. **hide variable (*variable_name*):** *Does not* display the variable on stage. This is also possible by unchecking the box where the variable_name is defined.

Figure 7.24 shows that every time the mouse is clicked, the variable (my variable) changes its value by 1, giving us the number of times the mouse is clicked or backdrop has been changed.

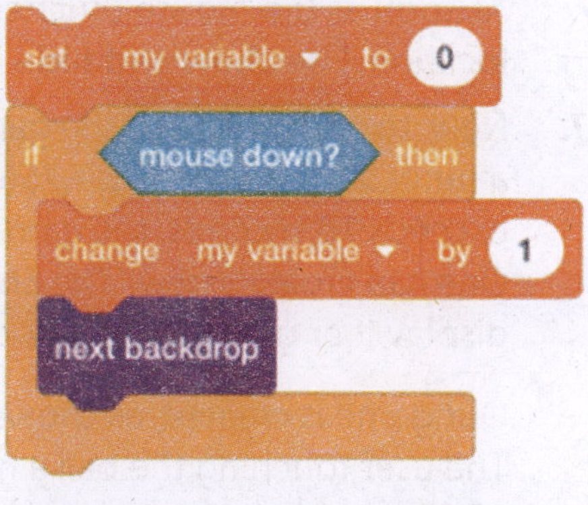

Fig. 7.24 | *Using Variables blocks*

Catch the Ball Game

Let us create our first Scratch game of catching the ball. For this, our sprite will be the ball.

Every time we touch the sprite, we should score a point. Follow these steps to create this game:

1. Add a sprite—ball.
2. When **Green Flag** is clicked, the ball should appear.
3. Create a variable name called "Score" by clicking on **Make a Variable** under the **Variables** block. Once you click OK, it will appear on the palette, as shown in Fig. 7.25(a).
4. Set Score to 0 in the beginning, as shown in Fig. 7.25(b).
5. Every time the mouse pointer touches the ball, it should add one point to our scoreboard **[Change (score) by (1)** block. A forever loop ensures that this is a continuous process, as shown in Fig. 7.25(c)].

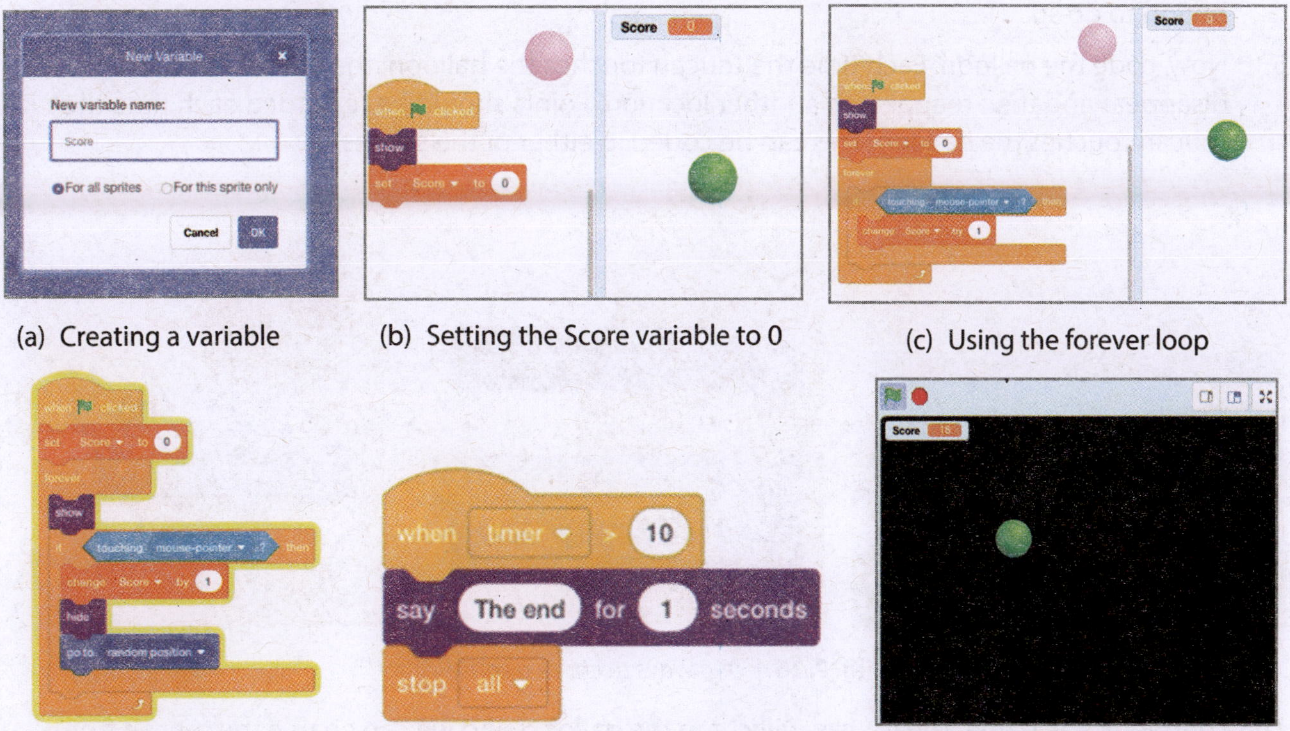

(a) Creating a variable (b) Setting the Score variable to 0 (c) Using the forever loop

(d) Using the show and hide blocks (e) Setting timer for the game (f) Catching the ball game

Fig. 7.25 | *Steps to create catch the ball game*

6. As soon as the mouse touches the ball, the ball should disappear and reappear in a new location. Use **show** and **hide** in the right locations, as shown in Fig. 7.25(d).
7. Now, to add an end to the game, let us set a timer, as shown in Fig. 7.25(e). If the timer exceeds 10 seconds, the game should end. One can create a new "The End" backdrop and display it or use the **say** block.

Our game is created, as shown in Fig. 7.25(f)! The user touching the ball a maximum number of times within 10 seconds wins!

Clear up!

1. Change the sprite's colour each time it hides and shows up again.
2. Make the ball disappear when you click on it instead of touching it.

Chase a Sprite Game

Now, let us create one more game. We will replace the ball with a balloon as a sprite. Add a new sprite, bird. Now, we need to make sure that each time the bird's beak touches the balloon, the balloon bursts, and accordingly, points are awarded.

Follow these steps to create this game (Fig. 7.26):

1. Add the two sprites—a balloon and a bird.
2. Change the background to sky.
3. Make the bird follow the mouse wherever it goes by using the **go to** block under **Motion** blocks.
4. The bird (toucan) should look like it is flapping its wings and flying. Use the **next costume** option to do so.
5. Now, code the balloon. Each time the toucan touches the balloon, the balloon should disappear and then reappear in another location. Points should be rewarded each time the toucan touches the balloon. This can be coded in either of the sprites.

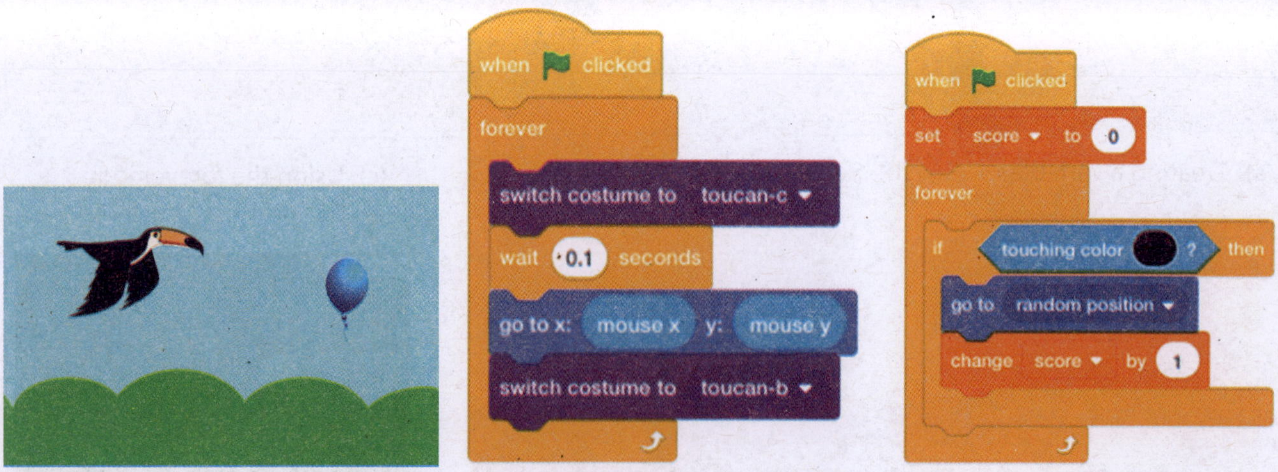

Fig. 7.26 | *Two ways to chase a sprite*

This completes the game. The toucan will chase the balloon, and we can enable the toucan from doing so by moving the mouse, as it follows the mouse position (using **go to**). If the toucan touches the balloon, a point will be awarded.

We can also use the arrow keys to control the toucan instead of the mouse pointer. We will just need to code the keys accordingly.

Clear up!

1. To get a "pop" sound whenever the beak touches the balloon, where should we place this block?

   `start sound Pop ▾`

2. Add a red balloon. Every time the toucan touches the red balloon, a minus point is rewarded.

Soak up!

Check the **tutorials** block on Scratch menu bar. We can learn about different types of games and animations through it.

Today I learned!

- There are 8 Events blocks. When the specific event occurs, an Events block would trigger a line of script or code.
- The different Events blocks are: when green flag clicked, when ( ) different event blocks key pressed, when this sprite clicked, when backdrop switches to ( ), when ( ) > ( ) • when i receive ( ), broadcast ( ), broadcast ( ) and wait.
- The different Control blocks are: wait ( ) secs, repeat ( ), forever, if ( ) then, if ( ) then, else, wait until ( ), repeat until ( ) and stop ( ).
- Sensing blocks are used to detect things.
- Sensing blocks detect the user input (which can be the click of the mouse, using the arrow keys on the keyboard, or when a user types an answer into a question box and so forth) and accordingly, give the output as coded.
- Sprites collision games can be created using the touch (color) or color ( ) is touching ( ) or touching (sprite_name) blocks.
- Games that involve user interaction using the keyboard use the key()pressed? block.
- Projects that involve touching the edge or mouse use the touching (edge) or touching (mouse-pointer) block.
- We can ask a question using the ask block and save the answer in the answer block in Scratch.
- A Variables block stores changeable values. At a time, it can hold only one value. Mostly, it is used to save the scoreboard.
- Set *variable_name* to (*value*), change (*variable_name*) to (numeric_value), show variable (*variable_name*), hide variable (*variable_name*) are a few Variables blocks.
- We can create a simple catch/chase the ball game by using Sensing, Events, Control and Variables blocks.

Revise and polish!

Learning Skills

1. Tick (✓) the correct answer.

a. Which of the following is not a Control block?

(i) repeat () ☐ (ii) if () then ☐

(iii) when key pressed ☐ (iv) rotate () ☐

b. Select the Events block from the following.

(i) broadcast () ☐ (ii) change (*variable_name*) ☐

(iii) move (10) steps ☐ (iv) turn (50) steps ☐

c. Which of the following is the colour of Variables blocks?

(i) Blue ☐ (ii) Orange ☐ (iii) Purple ☐ (iv) Pink ☐

d. There are __________ Events blocks.

(i) 7 ☐ (ii) 8 ☐ (iii) 9 ☐ (iv) 10 ☐

e. Which of the following blocks allows a user to type an answer?

(i) ask ☐ (ii) Broadcast ☐

(iii) broadcast () and wait ☐ (iv) Repeat ☐

f. Which of these blocks is used to create scoring system?

(i) Pen extension ☐ (ii) Variables ☐ (iii) Sensing ☐ (iv) Motion ☐

g. Which of the following blocks are yellow in colour?

(i) Events blocks ☐ (ii) Variables blocks ☐

(iii) Control blocks ☐ (iv) Pen blocks ☐

h. Which of the following blocks is used to add user interaction with the help of keyboard?

(i) stop() ☐ (ii) key () pressed ? ☐

(iii) is key () pressed ? ☐ (iv) both (ii) and (iii) ☐

2. Fill in the blanks.

a. Stop (__________) block will stop that particular script.

b. A sensing block has to be used with __________ blocks.

c. The __________ block sends a message throughout the Scratch program.

d. __________ is used to pause the script.

e. When () > () has two options for condition—__________ and timer.

3. State whether the following statements are true (T) or false (F).

a. All sensing blocks are used for user interaction. ☐

b. Variables can store only one value at a time. ☐

c. Repeat (10) blocks will run the code infinite times. ☐

d. The when i receive () block should always be used with a broadcast block. ☐

e. Repeat until <> keeps running until the stop button is clicked. ☐

4. Give the uses of the following blocks.

a. Color() is touching()

b. If() then, else

c. Stop()

d. When() key pressed

e. Mouse down?

5. Answer the following questions.

a. Explain the broadcast and when i receive () blocks with an example.

b. What are Control blocks?

c. What are the different Events blocks? Explain any three.

d. Write down the ways to detect one sprite colliding with another.

e. What are the different Variables blocks? Explain any three.

f. Which blocks will you use to create a quiz game?

6. What do these codes do?

a.

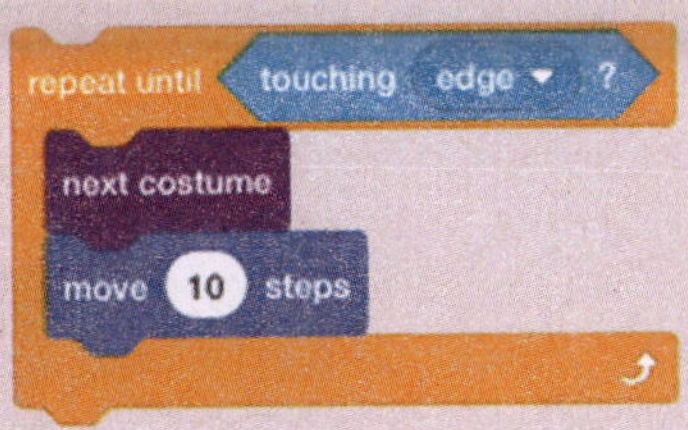

b.

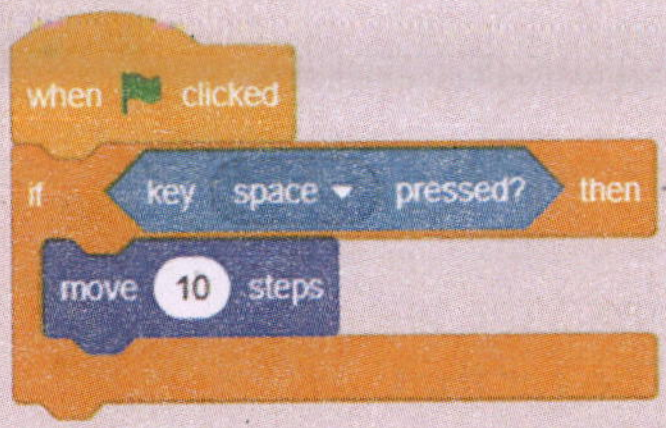

c.

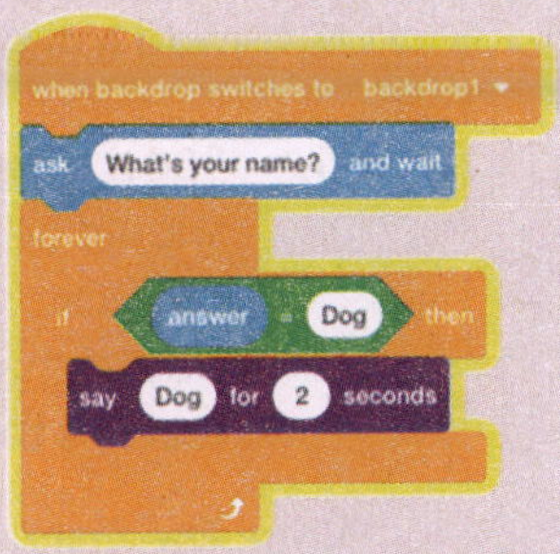

d.

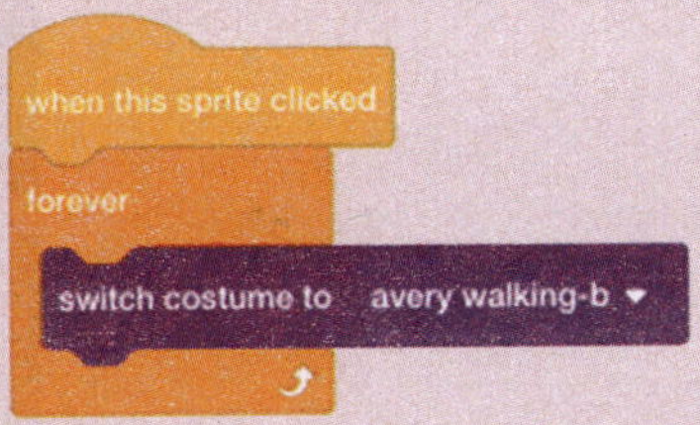

e.

Experiential Learning

Lab Activities

1. Sudha needs to create a chase game using two players—the shark and the fish.

   Arrow keys will be used as controls for player 1 (fish), and alphabet keys A, S, W and Z will be keys for player 2 (shark) to move around. Can you create this game for her?

2. Mrunal loves playing quizzes. Create a quiz for her on Scratch with a minimum of 10 questions.
   a. If the user gives the correct answer, the next question should appear. If they give the wrong answer, the quiz should end and the score should be displayed accordingly.
   b. Use variables for counting the score.
   c. Add music in the background.

3. Create a game to catch the ball.

   Make a ball appear on the screen and drop from top to bottom. The aim of the game is to click the ball the maximum number of times using the mouse. Ensure that the game is not too easy. You can add multiple balls or decrease the time the ball stays in its position.

   Keep score.

   If the ball touches the ground, the game should end.

4. Create a birthday game for a family member or your best friend. You can do this by adding an animation in the start, wishing them for their birthday, followed by a game quiz about this person. Make sure this is a multiple choice quiz like shown here.

   Add a minimum of three questions.

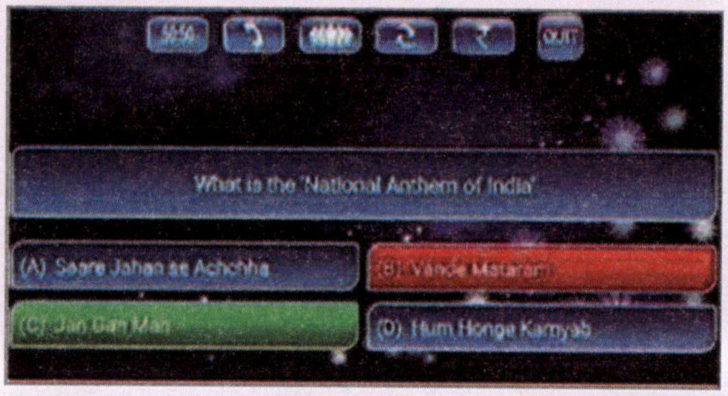

5. Show a car racing game. This should be a two-player game. Both cars will start from the left side of the screen. The car that reaches the finish line first will win.

Note: The first car will be controlled by the RIGHT arrow key to move right.

The second car will move right using the letter A.

The first car to reach the finish line should say "I Win!"

Problem-solving

Critical Thinking

Think and Answer

1. Which Events block should Khushbu use in her project to ensure that the game stops after the sound volume reaches 11?

2. Samarth wants to add background music for his entire project. The project is an animation that goes on for 10 minutes. Unfortunately, the music he is using is just 2-minute long. How can he ensure the same music runs again and again throughout the project?

3. Which block is used to take input from the user in Scratch?

4. Which block will be used while creating a ping pong game?

Hint: When the ball touches the *edge* of the screen, it should bounce back.

Chapter
8

Introduction to HTML

After reading this chapter, I will be able to:

- ✔ Define web page, website and web browser.
- ✔ Define HTML.
- ✔ List various features of HTML.
- ✔ Use various HTML tags.
- ✔ Design a web page.

Technology Literacy

Brainstorm and explore!

Have you seen these websites? What are they used for? Discuss their uses with your classmates.

1. 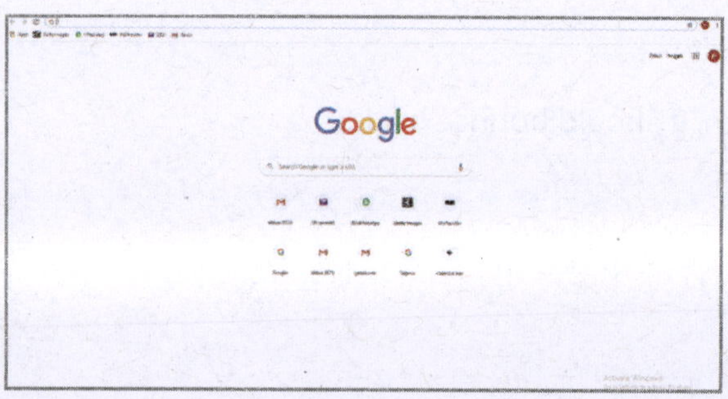

2. 

3. 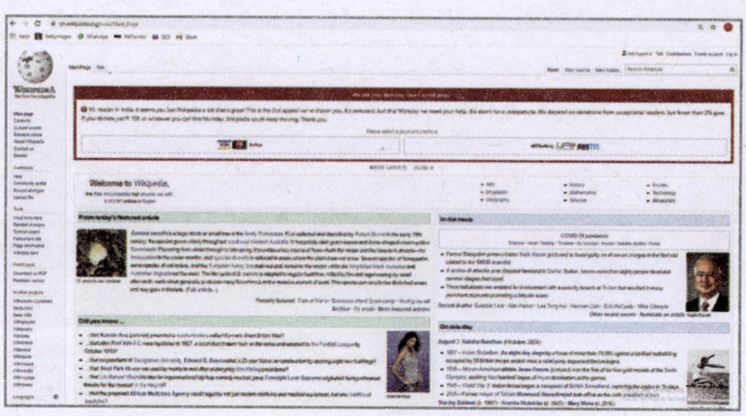

We all access different websites all the time for school work, to watch movies, listen to music, read news, play games or simply browse.

A **web page** is a document with specific information that is connected to the internet. Thus, it can be used by millions of users across the world.

A **website** is a location that contains more than one web page linked together by using a hyperlink.

Fig. 8.1 | *A website*

> A website is a collection of linked web pages that contain specific information about a topic.

hyperlink: a special text or image that takes us from one document to another by simply clicking on it

Software applications that are used to access websites are called **web browsers**. Websites or web pages are written using computer languages such as HTML, JavaScript and CSS. These programs are translated by a browser, which makes the website available to the user through its window. Commonly used web browsers are Microsoft Edge, Google Chrome, Safari, Mozilla Firefox and Netscape Navigator.

Today, the internet consists of billions of websites created by billions of people. Websites can be created for many purposes. For example, to sell products, to entertain, to educate, etc. We can also create a website on the internet. Ever wondered which language is used for this purpose?

Soak up!

The first website was built by Tim Berners-Lee and launched on 6 August, 1991. As of 1 January, 2020, there are 1,744,517,326 websites.

What is HTML?

HyperText Markup Language (HTML) is used to create websites or web pages. With the help of HTML, the user can insert and display text, images, audios and videos through a web page. Here, in HTML:

- **HyperText** is a way to move around on the web, using hyperlinks that take us to the next page.
- **Markup** are special short codes or elements, called HTML tags.
- **Language** as it has code words and syntax like any other language.

HTML is simple to learn and is continuously being improved under the direction of World Wide Web Consortium (W3C). We will be learning about HTML 5.2 in this chapter. It was released in 2017 on W3C recommendation.

Features of HTML

Some important features of HTML are given below:

- HTML can be used to add text, images, videos and audio to a web page.
- HTML is easy-to-learn, edit and use.
- HTML is not case-sensitive.
- HTML supports all web browsers.

HTML Editors

An HTML editor is a tool used for creating and editing HTML code. Once the code is created, a browser is used to view it. There are two types of HTML editors—text-based editors and WYSIWYG editors.

Text-based Editors

Text-based editors or text editors allow the source code to be edited directly. Some commonly used text editors are Notepad, WordPad and TextEdit.

Advantages

- There is a lot more freedom to code and add personalized options.
- Users can optimize a page better for search engines.

Disadvantages

- A person needs to have an HTML background and know how to use HTML tags to use these editors. Therefore, not everyone can use them.
- These editors are slow and not easy to use.

WYSIWYG Editors

WYSIWYG stands for *What You See Is What You Get*. WYSIWYG editors show the document to be edited in the way it is displayed as a website on the browser. You need not have a coding experience to start working on these. SiteSpinner and NVU are some examples of WYSIWYG editors.

Advantages

- Using these editors require very little knowledge of HTML. Therefore, they are easier to learn.
- Working on these editors is faster than on text-based editors.

Disadvantages

- Some WYSIWYG editors give restricted access while creating websites.
- Sometimes, websites created using these editors may look different in different browsers.

Soak up!

A few new text editors make it easier for the coder to code, as they provide autocomplete and error detection functions. For example, Microsoft Expression Web, Google Web Designer, Adobe Dreamweaver CC, etc., can be used both as WYSIWYG and text-based editors.

Brush up!

Give the full forms of the following.

1. HTML ____________________

2. W3C ____________________

3. WYSIWYG ____________________

HTML Tags

Tags are short codes required to create an HTML code. Tags are used to mark certain sections of the text, depending on their function. For example, tags can make a particular text bold or can structure the document by mentioning the different parts of web pages, such as the header, title, main body and footer. Some features of the HTML tags are listed below:

a. A tag name is a keyword surrounded by angular brackets (< and >).

b. Generally, tags come in pairs. The tag starts with the **ON** tag or the **Opening** tag and ends with the **OFF** tag or the **Closing** tag. The OFF tag is preceded by a forward slash (/) before its name. For example, <ON Tag> Content </OFF Tag>.

c. Tags are not case sensitive but are universally written in lowercase.

d. Different tags perform different functions.

e. The tags will not be visible on the website. However, only the content within the open and close tag will be displayed, along with the effect the tag is trying to achieve.

f. When there are tags added within a tag, the inner tags need to be closed before the outer tags.

   For example,

```
<h1> <i>
  Correct way of closing the tags.
</i> </h1>
```

```
<h1> <i>
  Incorrect way of closing the tags
</h1></i>
```

g. There should be no spacing between angular brackets (<, >) and the tag name.

HTML Elements

Text written between an HTML tag is called HTML element. For example:

> Text written between an HTML tag is called HTML element.

```
<ON Tag> This is an element. </OFF Tag>
```

An HTML element comprises a starting tag, content and an end tag. The two types of HTML elements are discussed below:

Basic Elements

HTML has a basic page structure that consists of various start and end tags. Some basic HTML elements are discussed in Table 8.1.

Table 8.1 | *Basic elements*

Tag	Description
<html> … </html>	It represents the start and end of an HTML program.
<head> … </head>	It defines the metadata, that is, the data about the HTML document. It comprises page title, styling, etc.
<title> … </title>	It defines the page title for the document.
<body> … </body>	It defines the part of the HTML document that is visible on the web page.
 	It inserts a line break and takes the cursor to the next line.
<hr>	It is used to insert a horizontal line across the page.
<p>	It defines a paragraph.
<h1>, <h2>, …, <h6>	It represents headings, where <h1> defines the most important heading and <h6> defines the least important heading.

Formatting Elements

A few HTML tags are used for beautifying or formatting HTML text. All of them have an end tag. Some basic formatting elements are discussed below in Table 8.2.

Table 8.2 | *Formatting elements*

Tag	Description
<b> … </b>	It defines bold text.
<i> … </i>	It defines the text in italic.
<u> … </u>	It defines the text with an underline.
_…	It defines subscript text.
[…]	It defines superscript text.
<mark> … </mark>	It defines the text that should be marked or highlighted.

Based on the opening and closing tags, there are two types of HTML elements:

1. **Container elements**: The elements having both an opening and a closing tag. Examples of container elements are <title> … </title>, <b>...</b>, etc.
2. **Empty elements**: The elements having an opening tag but no closing tag. Examples of empty elements are <br>, <p>, etc.

Soak up!

Heading tags are just a combination of <br> and <b> tags, as they set the desired text in bold and also take the cursor to the next line.

Soak up!

Subscript text appears half a character below the normal line and is sometimes rendered in a smaller font. For example, a subscript can be used to display chemical formulas, such as H_2O.

Superscript text appears half a character above the normal line and is sometimes rendered in a larger font. For example, a superscript can be used to display ranks, such as 2nd and 5th.

HTML Attributes

A tag may have attributes, which are special words used inside the opening tag to control the behaviour of an element. Multiple attributes can be used with one tag. For example, align is an attribute of the <p> tag that specifies the alignment of the text within a paragraph.

Attributes are special words used inside the opening tag to control the behaviour of an element.

Syntax:

```
<p align="center">This is some text in a paragraph. </p>
```

Here, center specifies that the text will be center-aligned. Here, center is called the **value** of an attribute. Other values for this attribute are: left, right and justify.

bgcolor is an attribute of the <body> tag. It is used to specify the background colour of the text.

Syntax:

```
<body bgcolor="red">
```

Here, red is the value of attribute bgcolor. Thus, it changes the background colour of the webpage to red.

Note: The attribute bgcolor is now obsolete and is not supported in HTML5. Let us discuss few more HTML tags below.

The <font> Tag

This tag is used to define the font style for the text given within it. It is a container tag. It has three attributes as discussed below:

- **face**: It is used to specify the typeface of the text.
- **size**: It is used to specify the size of the text.
- **color**: It is used to specify the colour of the text.

Syntax:

```
<font size="12" face="Arial" color="blue">
```

This can also be written as

```
<font size ="12">
<font face ="arial">
<font color="blue">
```

Note: This tag is now obsolete and is not supported in HTML5.

A sample program using the <font> tag is given here:

```
<html>
<body>
    <font size="3" color="green">Hello</font> <br>
    <font size="5" color="red">Hello</font> <br>
    <font size="7" color="yellow">Hello</font> <br>
    <font size="9" color="blue">Hello</font> <br>
</body>
</html>
```

Soak up!

Today, to change the background colour and font of a webpage, CSS is used by most programmers. CSS or cascading style sheets is another markup language used to design the webpage.

Clear up!

How will you change the background colour of a webpage?

Structure of an HTML Document

The basic structure of an HTML document, using Notepad, is shown in Fig. 8.2. Notice the indentation while starting a new tag in the HTML program. It is not compulsory but is a good practice to use.

```
*Untitled - Notepad
File  Edit  Format  View  Help
<html>
        <head>
                <title> Page title goes here </title>
        </head>
        <body>
        Entire website content will come here including the other HTML tags
.
.
.
.
        </body>
</html>
```

Fig. 8.2 | *Structure of an HTML document*

indentation: the space at the beginning of a line of writing when it starts further away from the edge of the paper than all the other lines

Creating and Viewing an HTML Document

As discussed earlier, we need an HTML editor to write a program. In this chapter, we will use the Notepad application to write all the programs. The steps to create and view an HTML document are given below:

1. Open Notepad on your computer and start typing the program.

```
Untitled - Notepad
File  Edit  Format  View  Help
<html>
        <head>
                <title> My profile </title>
        </head>
        <body>
                <h1>This is my profile </h1>
                <h2> I love computers </h2>
                <i> Computers are future! </i>
                And thus very exciting as a subject. <br>
                <b> Charles Babbage </b> invented computers.
                They were created to calculate a series of values
                automatically.
        </body>
</html>

Windows (CRLF   Ln 15, Col 1   100%
```

Fig. 8.3 | *Using Notepad as a text editor*

Clear up!

Write the program to change the background colour of a webpage.

2. After typing the program, click on **File** and then select the **Save** option. A dialog box will open, as shown in Fig. 8.4. Enter the File name and save it with the extension **.html**. Also, change the field **Save as type**: to **All Files**. Then, click on the **Save** button.

3. Go to the file location (Fig. 8.5). You will notice that the file icon is similar to your default browser. Here, it is Microsoft Edge. Double-click on the file to open.

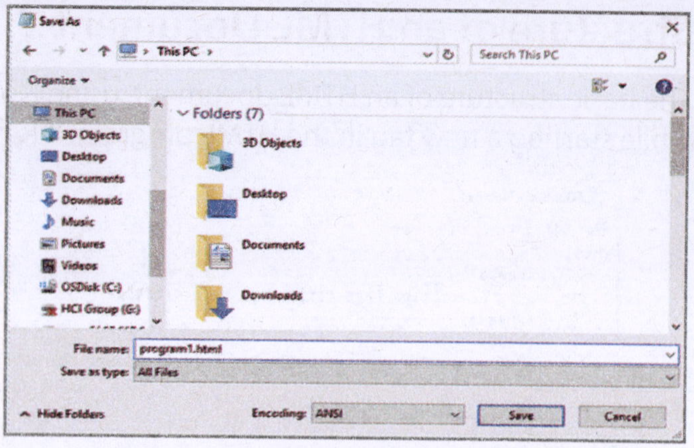

Fig. 8.4 | *Saving the HTML document*

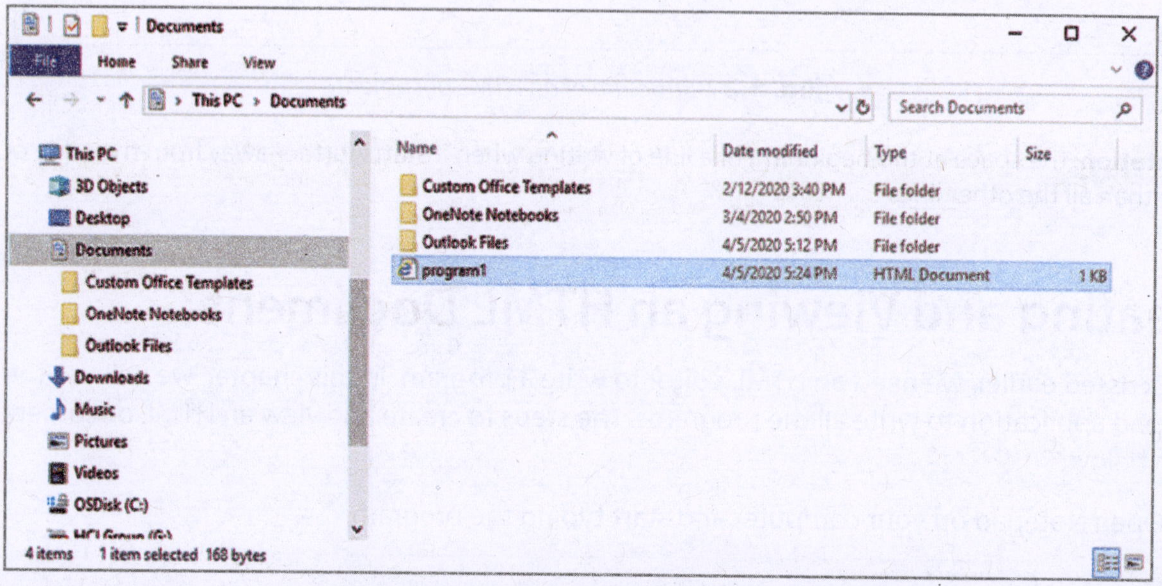

Fig. 8.5 | *Go to the location where the file is saved*

4. The file will be opened in Microsoft Edge, as shown in Fig. 8.6.

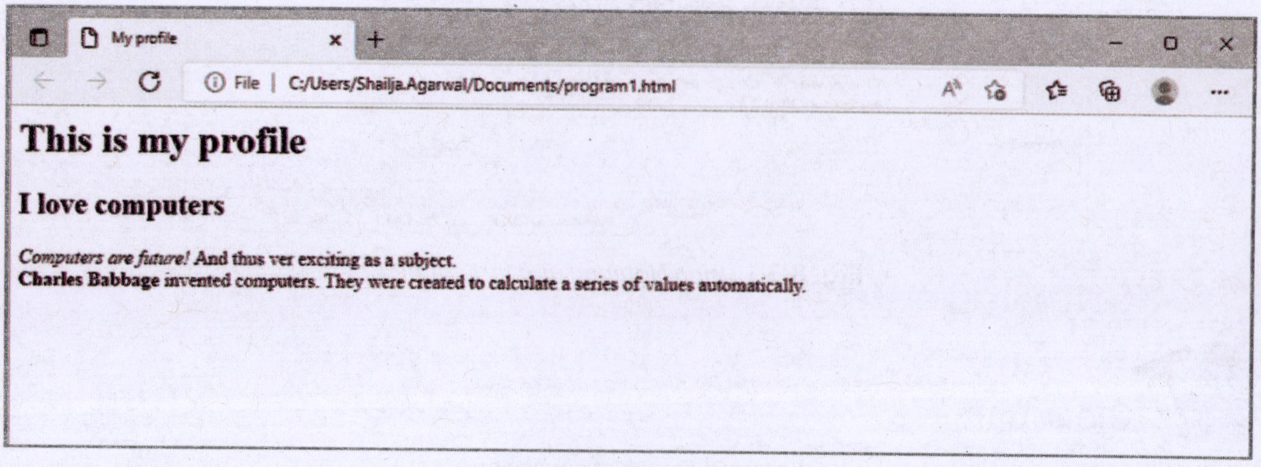

Fig. 8.6 | *The output*

Soak up!

A browser interprets the HTML code and converts the text into a visual form, giving us the website we intend to see.

Clear up!

Create an HTML page which has the following elements:

1. <p> tag with the text 'My first program'. Inside it, add the heading tags.
2. <h1> tag with the text 'I am the strongest!'
3. <h2> tag with the text 'I am stronger!'
4. <h6> tag with the text 'I am strong!'
5. Bold text 'I am not that strong!'
6. <i> tag with the text 'I am not that weak!'

Today I learned!

- A website is a location that contains more than one web page linked together by using a hyperlink.
- Hypertext markup language (HTML) is used to create web pages.
- HTML can be used to add text, images, videos and audio to a webpage.
- HTML is easy to learn, edit and use.
- HTML is not case-sensitive.
- HTML supports all web browsers.
- HTML editors are of two types: text-based editors and WYSIWYG editors.
- Tags are special codes used in HTML represented by angular brackets.
- Text written between an HTML tag is called HTML element. The two types of HTML elements are: basic elements and formatting elements.
- Attributes are special words used inside the opening tag to control the behaviour of an element.
- The <html> tag is the first tag used in the HTML code, followed by <head>, <title> and <body> tags in an HTML program. They all have an opening and a closing tag.

Revise and polish!

1. Tick (✓) the correct answer.

a. A __________ is a document with specific information that is connected to the internet.

(i) web page ☐ (ii) hyperlink ☐ (iii) website ☐ (iv) tag ☐

b. __________ tag is used to bring text to the center.

(i) <hr> ☐ (ii) <center> ☐ (iii) <p> ☐ (iv) <c> ☐

c. Different HTML tags perform __________ functions.

(i) different ☐ (ii) similar ☐ (iii) common ☐ (iv) cross ☐

d. Which of the following is true about HTML tags?

(i) All tags in HTML need a closing tag. ☐

(ii) Tags may or may not be used with attributes. ☐

(iii) Best to be written in capital letters as per W3C. ☐

(iv) Tags are very difficult to use. ☐

e. The bgcolor attribute is used to ____________________.

(i) change the background colour ☐ (ii) change the font colour ☐

(iii) change the image colour ☐ (iv) change the colour of video ☐

f. Which tag is used to make text bold?

(i) <bold> ☐ (ii) <b> ☐ (iii) <big> ☐ (iv) <bf> ☐

g. Which tag will be used to display the following equation:
'$a^2 + b^2 = c^2$'?

(i) <sub> ☐ (ii) <sup> ☐ (iii) <square> ☐ (iv) <centre> ☐

h. Full-form of W3C is:

(i) World wide web concert ☐ (ii) World wide web consortium ☐

(iii) World web wide consortium ☐ (iv) World wide web corner ☐

i. Which of the following is not an example of a WYSIWYG editor?

(i) Adobe dreamweaver CC ☐ (ii) Notepad ☐

(iii) Sitespinner ☐ (iv) All of the above ☐

j. Special words used inside the opening tag to control the behaviour of an element are called __________.

(i) attributes ☐ (ii) HTML tags ☐

(iii) container tags ☐ (iv) empty tags ☐

2. Fill in the blanks.

a. HTML is a __________ language.

b. __________ is a text-based editors editor.

c. Website is a collection of __________.

d. The __________ tag inserts line break

e. SiteSpinner and NVU are the examples of __________ editors.

3. State whether the following statements are true (T) or false (F).

a. <small> is a formatting element. [ ]

b. HTML is a programming language. [ ]

c.
 is an empty tag. [ ]

d. Microsoft Edge is an HTML text editor. [ ]

e. Tags are not visible on the web browser. [ ]

4. Underline the errors in the following code. Rewrite the correct code in your notebook.

```
<html>
<title>Video games</title>
<body>
<h1>Video Games<hr>
   Research has shown that video games can have positive effects on
   behavioural and cognitive skills. But, one must also accept the
   detrimental effects that can potentially arise in children being
   over exposed to video games.
   It has been shown that playing pro-social games led to a more
   'helping' behaviour, but it was also seen that playing a violent
   game led to a more 'harming' behaviour.</p>
   Other difficulties also arise through prolonged periods of gaming,
   or when <i> "addiction"</i> creeps in; indeed, excessive internet
   use or gameplay can lead to adverse consequences on behaviour, such
   as <i> social withdrawal, loneliness, depression, or even heightened
   irritation and trouble focusing on less stimulating work or in less
   rewarding social environments.</i>
   <Conclusion>Moderation is the key, and a child who is able
   to control himself, properly manage his time and balance
   responsibility & necessity with leisure, will learn to uphold the
   necessary etiquette for living a balanced life.
</html>
```

5. Answer the following questions.

a. Explain HTML formatting tags.

b. What are HTML tags?

c. Discuss the two types of HTML elements with examples.

d. What is the basic structure of an HTML document?

e. Differentiate between web browser, website and webpage.

6. Give the output of the following HTML tags.

a. <b> HTML is an easy language </b>

b. <h1> Coding is a 21st century skill</h1>

c. <p> full form of HTML is <u> HyperText Markup Language </u> </p>

d. H ₂ O

e. <p> I came 2 nd in the class </p>

Experiential Learning

Lab Activities

1. Write an HTML program describing your hobbies. Use at least four formatting tags.

2. Sneha loves to read. She wants to create an HTML page that gives a review of the books she reads. Can you help her create that?

Critical Thinking

Problem-solving

Think and Answer

1. If a web page has a red coloured background and black coloured text. What HTML tags do you think are used?

____

____

2. While opening a website, Shreya wants the heading to be present in the centre of the web page. However, rest of the text should be starting from the left.

Can you help her by giving the steps to do so?

____

____

Chapter
9

Email and Cloud Storage

After reading this chapter, I will be able to:

- ✔ Demonstrate how to use email effectively.
- ✔ Practice responsible behaviour on the internet—Netiquettes.
- ✔ Describe the uses of cloud storage using the example of Google Drive.

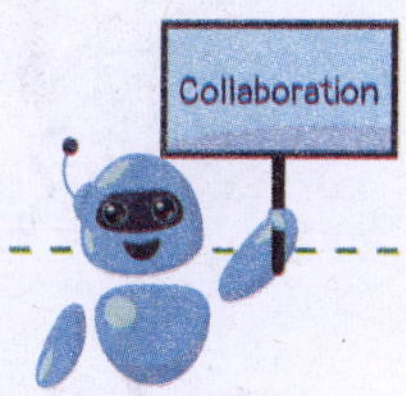

Brainstorm and explore!

The internet has connected computers across the globe. People of all ages use the internet via a computer, laptop or a smartphone. What are the top three sites you visit as a student and what is their purpose? Also, discuss with your teacher and parents/elders about their internet usage and list down the three sites they visit the most.

You	Teacher	An elder at home
1. ____________	1. ____________	1. ____________
2. ____________	2. ____________	2. ____________
3. ____________	3. ____________	3. ____________

Notice how the sites they visit and their purposes are vastly different from yours. This shows that the internet caters to the needs of a diverse audience. There are many websites and online platforms catering to these diverse needs. One of the commonest uses of the internet is connecting to other people. Writing emails, using social media, writing blogs, uploading podcasts—all these are ways in which we connect to other people. We will learn more about the effective use of emails in this chapter.

Email

For most of the part of communication in history, people used to write letters to each other. Sometimes, they would enclose pictures with the letters, which had to be posted. These letters would take days, and sometimes weeks, to reach the recipient.

With the advent of technology and consistent access to the internet, it has become easy for people to stay in touch with each other. Instant messaging, video calling and emailing are some of the ways people can stay in touch. To send and receive emails, both the sender and the **recipient** need to have a device that is connected to the internet and an email address. There are dedicated e-mail service providers that can be used to set up an email account and get an email address.

Electronic mail is the system of sending and receiving messages across the internet.

recipient: the person who receives something

Email services are provided by various companies, such as Google (Gmail), Microsoft (MS Outlook), Yahoo (Yahoo mail), Rediff (Rediffmail), Apple (Apple Mail), and so on. Emails can be accessed on personal computers, as well as smartphones and tablets.

Fig. 9.1 | *Email from a laptop*

Fig. 9.2 | *Apple Mail on different devices*

Soak up!

Before the invention of the internet, a system called ARPANET was used, which enabled computers to communicate with each other in a closed network. Ray Tomlinson, an engineer, invented the email program in 1971. He sent a message to himself from one computer and received it on another that was right next to him!

Brush up!

What is the difference between Gmail and email?

Using an Email Account

An email account needs to be created in order to send and receive emails. Most email service providers allow us to create an account without any cost. For children younger than 13 years of age, the email account needs to be created under the supervision of an adult. To login to your email account, enter the email address in the URL of your browser. Enter the email address and password and click on **Sign In**.

Components of an Email Account

Figure 9.3 shows components of a Gmail account.

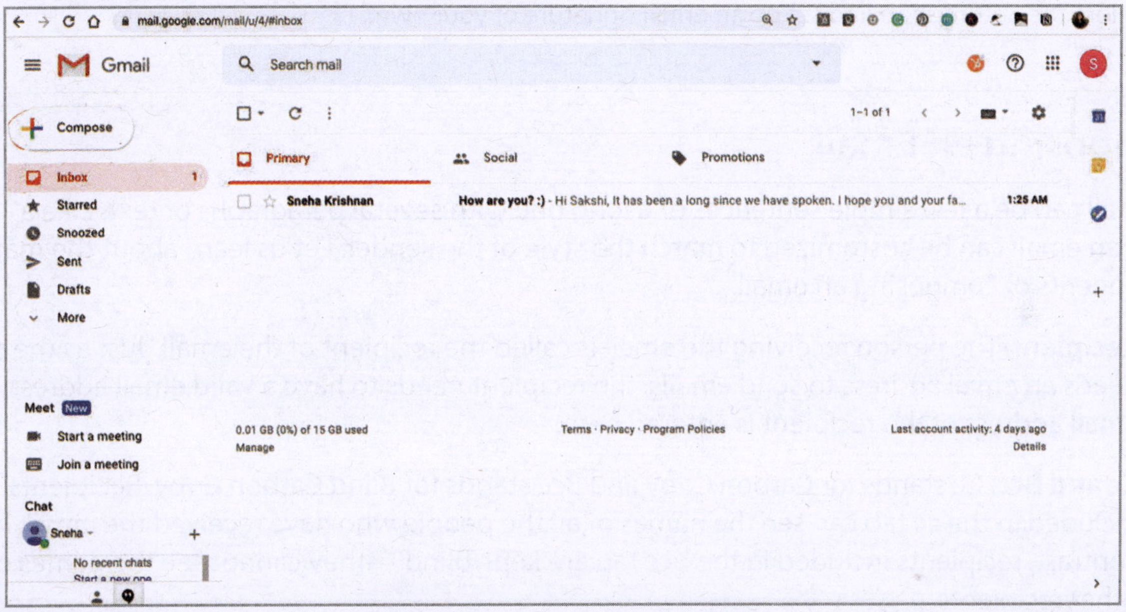

Fig. 9.3 | *Inside an email account*

Let us discuss these components in detail.

a. **Inbox**: It contains all the emails you have received. Unread emails are highlighted for easy identification. Generally, inbox messages are displayed when you sign in. You can search for a specific email using different search criteria, such as date and sender.

b. **Sent Mail**: It contains all the emails you have sent to others.

c. **Drafts**: Sometimes, while writing a mail, it is not entirely complete in one go. Such messages get automatically saved in Drafts for future use. Once a draft message is opened, you can pick up from where you left.

d. **Trash**: As the name suggests, it contains deleted emails. These emails remain in the Trash for a particular amount of time before they get permanently deleted.

e. **Compose**: Clicking on Compose opens a window that contains the options for writing an email.

f. **Settings**: The Settings tab contains many options, such as modifying how the inbox looks as well as changing your password, which allow you to personalize your email account.

Technology Literacy

Crank up!

An email signature is a fixed text at the end of the email, mentioning the name of the sender with the information they wish to include. Examples of email signatures are:

Regards, Sneha K	Manasi K Co-founder, MindChamp Mumbai, India	Best wishes, Sakshi Gupta

Explore the Settings tab and set up an email signature of your own.

Composing an Email

An email can be a few simple sentences or a long one with several paragraphs of text. Like a letter, an email can be customized to match the style of the sender. Let us learn about the major components of composing an email.

1. **Recipient**: The person receiving the email is called the recipient of the email. Just as the sender needs an email address to send emails, the recipient needs to have a valid email address. The email address of the recipient is entered here.

2. **Cc and Bcc**: Cc stands for Carbon Copy and Bcc stands for Blind Carbon Copy. Recipients included in the cc tab can see the names of all the people who have received the email. In contrast, recipients included in the bcc tab are kept 'blind'—they cannot see the names of the other recipients.

Technology Literacy

Crank up!

Often, when people send work emails or other important emails, the recipient is required to act based on the email. But, there may be other people who need to know about the contents of the email. For example, if your teacher emails you all the details of your science project, she will keep your email id in the To tab. She will also include your parents' email addresses in the cc tab. This way your parents will come to know about your science project as well.

3. **Subject Line**: In the inbox, the text, that is, displayed with the sender's name is known as the Subject Line (Fig. 9.4). It gives the recipient an idea of what the email is about.

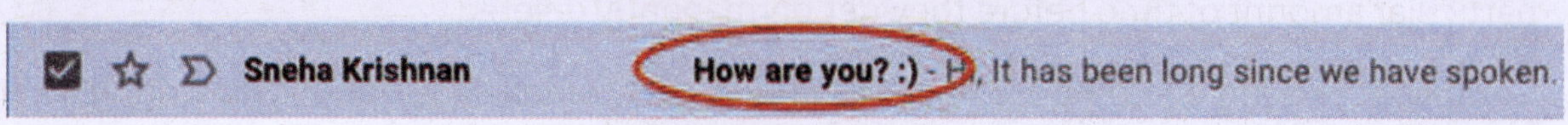

Fig. 9.4 | *Subject line*

4. **Email body**: This is where the contents of the email are typed. It could be text a well as images.

5. **Formatting the text**: We have learned about text formatting in MS Word. Some similar options are available for formatting the text in an email, too (Fig. 9.5).
6. **Attachments**: Attachments such as pictures, video and audio files can be sent with the email text.

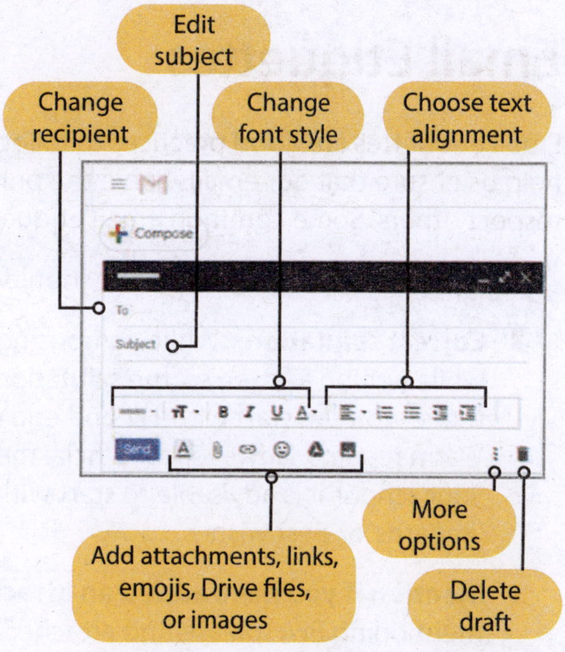

Fig. 9.5 | *Formatting options in emails*

Soak up!

The options that appear while replying to an email are similar to the ones in the Compose window. If one or more than one person is copies on the email, an extra option called Reply All is displayed, which allows the reply to be sent to all in the email thread.

Clear up!

If your name was in the Bcc tab of an email sent to many people, will you be able to see the details of the other recipients of the email when you click on Reply All?

Crank up!

Technology Literacy

Email Acronyms

Billions of emails are exchanged throughout the world. There are some commonly used phrases that have short forms and are understood by the sender and the recipient. Some of them are as follows:

PFA: Please Find Attachment

"My birthday was awesome! PFA the pictures".

ASAP: As Soon As Possible

"Let me know the update on the assignment ASAP".

EOD: End of Day

"Please send the pictures for the project by EOD".

EOM: End of Month

"The timetable for exams will be out by EOM".

FYI: For Your Information

"FYI, I have completed the revision".

Email Etiquettes

Email etiquettes are good practices to follow while sending and receiving emails. These practices help us ensure that our emails serve the purpose they are intended to. It also conveys that we respect others. Some common email etiquettes are:

- **Use a relevant subject line**: It should be crisp and describe the content of the email correctly.
- **Correct salutations**: While composing an email, follow all the guidelines that you would while writing a letter; so, the salutations should be appropriate. If the email is addressed to a friend, you can start with 'Hi!' and end with an informal closure like Cheers!, Affectionately! or Warm regards. However, for official mails, such as the one to your teacher or to the principal of your school, it is advisable to start with something like 'Respected Ma'am/Sir' and close with 'Regards' or 'Best wishes'.
- **Mention if you have added an attachment**: Attachments tend to get missed out and mentioning PFA (please find attached) would help avoid any confusion.
- **Do not overload**: It is important to send only the necessary attachments so that it does not cause trouble while downloading or problems with their computer memory. At the same time, avoid sending unwanted emails or forwarding messages.
- **Use respectful language**: Just as in real life, emails should be polite. If anyone is being impolite to you, do not respond hastily or immediately. Let parents/teachers know.
- **Use acronyms smartly**: "HRU, CU ASAP" might not be the best way to communicate. Use acronyms along with the proper context.
- **Re-check before sending**: Re-read the email before sending to make sure that the email addresses are correct, the mail is free of typos and grammatical errors, the attachments are included (if any), and nothing is missed out.

Fun with AI

Of the several tabs you see on your email, there is one labelled Spam. Spam is nothing but unwanted mail, that is, sent to multiple people. The contents of an email labelled Spam are often inappropriate. In contrast, Junk mail simply refers to unsolicited/unwanted advertising or promotional emails. Your email service provider uses artificial intelligence/ machine learning to identify Spam and Junk emails. These ML techniques have the capacity to identify spam mails and phishing messages by analysing loads of such messages throughout a vast collection of computers. Since machine learning has the capacity to adapt to varying conditions, Gmail and Yahoo mail spam filters do more than just checking junk emails using the pre-existing rules. They generate new rules themselves based on what they have learned as they continue in their spam filtering operation. The machine learning model used by Google has now advanced to the point where it can detect and filter out spam and phishing emails with about 99.9 per cent accuracy.

Cloud Storage

When we search for a video on YouTube, a list of videos related to our search term appears. Have you ever wondered where these videos are actually stored? On the cloud!

Cloud storage refers to a model of storage where data is stored in the cloud, that is, an external data server that can be accessed via the internet.

A computer's primary functions include storing and processing data. Traditionally, both storage and processing used to place in the same physical location—the computer itself. The computer itself is maintained by the owner, be it individuals or in offices. Over time, the amount of data that needs to be stored by individuals and offices has increased significantly. Hence, the need for increased storage has led to the development of cloud storage. The term 'cloud' refers to the huge data servers, often maintained by specialist service providers, that are capable of storing large amounts of data. This space on the server is rented out to the users for a fee. This is similar to renting a flat in an apartment complex.

Fig. 9.6 | *Cloud storage*

At times, the same servers can be used for data processing. This is called cloud computing. Cloud storage refers to storing files on the cloud, whereas cloud computing refers to the use of the resources of an external server for processing data. The advantages of cloud storage are:

- Files can be accessed anytime, anywhere
- Large storage capacity
- Speedy access
- Easy data backup
- Lesser risk of losing data from physical damage to the storage device

Google Drive is one of the most widely used storage services on the cloud. Other cloud storage services include Microsoft OneDrive and Dropbox.

Features of Google Drive

The features of Google Drive include:

- **Storage capacity**: Google Drive provides 15 GB of free storage for personal users. The storage capacity can be expanded by paying a fee.
- **Desktop and mobile apps**: Google Drive is available on the browser and can be accessed with the URL www.drive.google.com. The mobile app version is available on PlayStore on Android devices and App Store on iOS devices.

- **File formats**: Google Drive supports a wide range of file formats, such as documents, spreadsheets and presentations. One can create and edit files on the web with the help of Google Drive.
  - Google Docs https://docs.google.com/document : Word Documents
  - Google Spreadsheets https://docs.google.com/spreadsheets : Spreadsheets
  - Google Slides https://docs.google.com/presentation/ : Presentations
  - Google Forms https://docs.google.com/forms/: Forms and Surveys
- **Access control**: If a user creates a file on Google Drive, he/she can share it with others. Users can also control what level of permissions can be given to others, which include (Fig. 9.7):
  - Viewer: The person with whom the file is shared can only view the file
  - Commenter: The person with whom the file is shared can only view the file and add comments.
  - Editor: One can add single or multiple people to collaborate on a document. For example, if you are doing a group project, the members of the group can be added as editors.

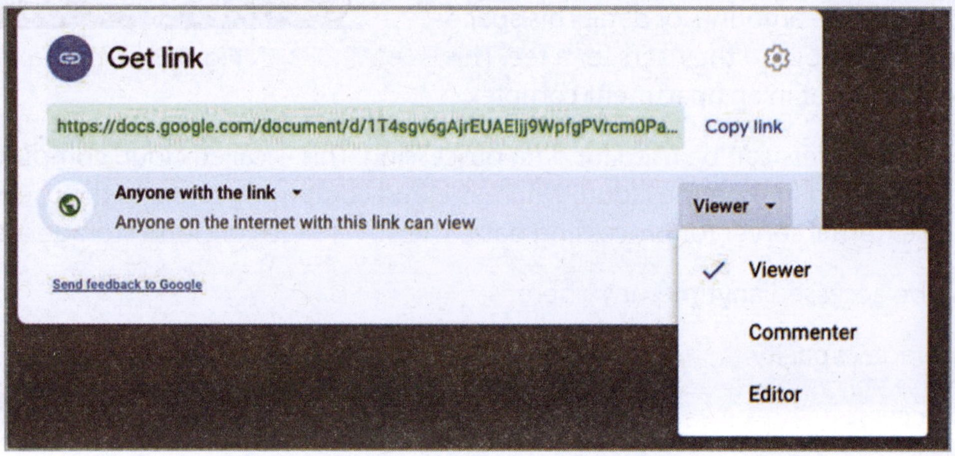

Fig. 9.7 | *Access control on Google Drive*

- **Anywhere access from any device**: As long as the device is connected to the internet and has a browser such as Safari, Mozilla Firefox, Google Chrome or Microsoft Edge, Google Drive can be opened and used.

Soak up!

Google Forms can be used to create surveys and send the link of the questionnaire. Explore the Google Forms option in Google Drive.

We have learned about MS Office in previous classes, in which documents, spreadsheets and presentations can be edited on a software **installed** in the computer. The same functionality is available on Microsoft OneDrive, which can be referred to as the cloud version of MS Office.

Using Google Drive

Let us learn how to use Google Drive.

Logging In

Google Drive can be accessed via a Gmail account. After creating a Gmail ID, the steps to access Google Drive are as follows:

1. Navigate to the URL www.drive.google.com.
2. Enter your Gmail account user name and password.
3. Click on **Sign In**.

Alternatively, if you are already logged into Gmail, click on the options icon on the top right corner of the inbox screen (Fig. 9.8). Click on the Drive icon.

Fig. 9.8 | *Google services option via the inbox*

Creating and Uploading Files and Folder

Follow these steps to create a new file on Google Drive:

1. Sign in to Google Drive.
2. Click on the + **New** button on the top left corner of the screen (Fig. 9.9).
3. Depending on the type of file you want to create, select from a Blank file or a preset template (Fig. 9.10).

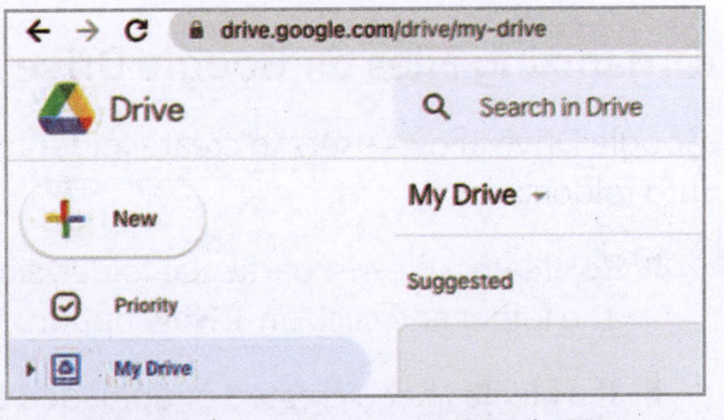

Fig. 9.9 | *New button on Google Drive*

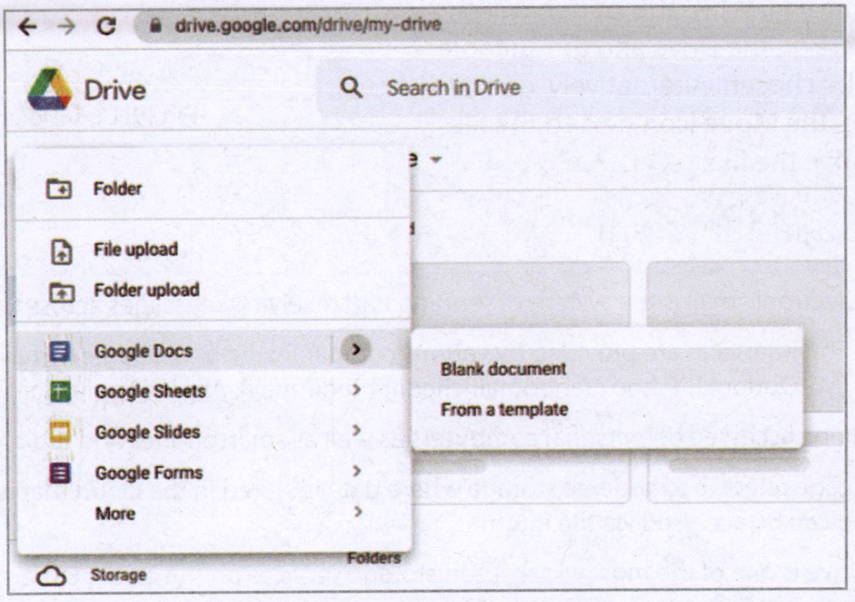

Fig. 9.10 | *Creating a new file*

Uploading a File

Google Drive offers a cloud storage service. Therefore, it allows us to upload individual files as well as folders. The steps to upload a file on Google Drive are given here:

1. Sign in to Google Drive
2. Click on the + **New** button on the top left corner of the screen.
3. Click on **File Upload**. It will open a window to select the file to be uploaded.
4. Select the respective file and click on **Upload**.

Brush up!

We have learned how to upload a file on Google Drive. Explore and note down the steps to upload a folder on Google Drive.

____

____

Organizing Files on Google Drive

Google Drive allows users to create folders to organize files. These are the options to organize files into folders:

- To create a file in a particular folder, simply open the folder and click on + **New** option.
- If a file has been created or uploaded and needs to be moved to a particular folder, select **File** → **Move** (Fig. 9.11). This option will show all the folders on the Drive and the suitable folder can be chosen. Alternatively, one can also click on the **Move** Icon next to the file name to move the file.

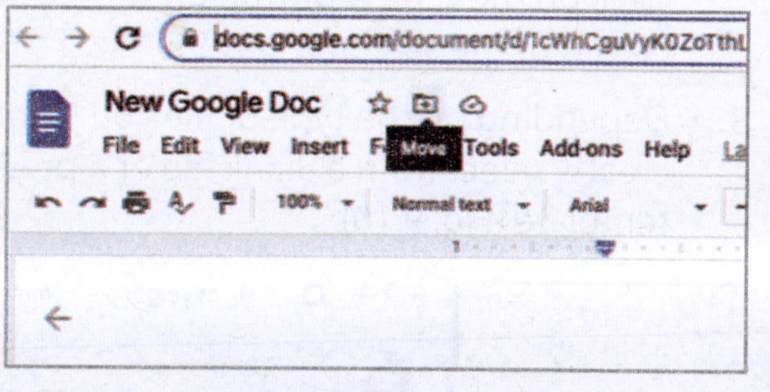

Fig. 9.11 | *Move button*

Today I learned!

- Electronic mail is the system of sending and receiving messages across the internet.
- Email services are provided by various companies such as Google (Gmail), Microsoft (MS Outlook), Yahoo (Yahoomail), Rediff (Rediffmail), Apple (Apple Mail) and so on.
- Emails can be accessed on personal computers as well as smartphones and tablets.
- Cloud storage refers to a model of storage where data is stored in the cloud that is an external server and can be accessed via the internet.
- Google Drive is one of the most widely used storage services on the cloud. Other cloud storage services include Microsoft OneDrive and Dropbox.

Revise and polish!

Learning Skills

1. Tick (✓) the correct answer.

a. Which of the following services is not powered by the internet?

(i) Email ☐ (ii) Wi-Fi ☐
(iii) Blogging ☐ (iv) Social media ☐

b. What are files stored on an external server that can be accessed through the internet called?

(i) Rainbow ☐ (ii) Trees ☐ (iii) Cloud ☐ (iv) Air ☐

c. Which of the following displays all the emails received by a user?

(i) Inbox ☐ (ii) Outbox ☐ (iii) Postbox ☐ (iv) Spam ☐

d. Which of the following are the names of cloud storage service?

(i) Google Drive ☐ (ii) Dropbox ☐
(iii) Microsoft OneDrive ☐ (iv) All of the above ☐

e. Which of the following devices can be used to access emails?

(i) Smartphone ☐ (ii) Tablet ☐
(iii) Personal computer ☐ (iv) All of the above ☐

f. Which of the following buttons is used to create a new email on Gmail?

(i) Create ☐ (ii) New ☐ (iii) Compose ☐ (iv) Write ☐

g. Which of the following is used to create surveys?

(i) Google Forms ☐ (ii) Google Slides ☐
(iii) Google Docs ☐ (iv) Google Photos ☐

h. What is a file that can be sent along with an email called?

(i) Email file ☐ (ii) Document ☐
(iii) Attachment ☐ (iv) Sample ☐

i. Which of the following options is available to share a document with another user on Google Docs?

(i) View ☐ (ii) Comment ☐ (iii) Edit ☐ (iv) Review ☐

j. Which of the following is an advantage of cloud storage?

(i) Files cannot be accessed anytime, anywhere ☐
(ii) Limited storage capacity ☐
(iii) Slow access ☐
(iv) All of the above ☐

2. Fill in the blanks.

a. Services and facilities provided by the internet are called ____________.

b. ____________ is the email service by Google.

c. ____________ refer to files that can be sent with emails.

d. Google Drive allows users to upload files as well as ____________.

e. In cloud storage service, data is stored in ____________ and accessed via the internet.

3. Match the following.

a.	Google Docs	(i)	Presentations
b.	Google Spreadsheets	(ii)	Word documents
c.	Google Slides	(iii)	Forms and surveys
d.	Google Forms	(iv)	Spreadsheets

4. Which Google Drive service would you use for the following purposes?

a. Help the teacher create a list of all students according to their roll numbers and height

____

b. Create a presentation on the actionable steps one can take to tackle climate change

____

c. Write an essay on the most important trait of a famous personality that inspires you

____

d. Maintain subject-wise record of all your grades

____

e. Create a picture gallery of a class trip to the zoo

____

5. Answer the following questions.

a. What are the components of an email inbox?

b. Explain cloud storage in your own words with the help of a diagram.

c. What are the features of Google Drive?

d. Mention any three email etiquettes.

e. Mention any three uses of Google Drive in the classroom.

6. **Look at the following email. Is this an example of a well-written email? Highlight all the problems you notice in this email.**

> To: science_teacer@xxxxx.com
>
> CC: class_teacher6A.@xxxx.com
>
> Subject: Science project
>
> Dear Kanikar Miss,
>
> I have been trying to finish my science projects timely. But I am not getting all the materials. Can you please give me extension till Monday?
>
> Cheerys!
>
> Manok J.
>
> **Attachments**: project.jpg (20 MB), project2.jpg (17 MB), project5.jpg (15 MB)

Lab Activities

Compose an email for the following situations:

a. An email to the Principal of your school informing of your first place in the inter-school chess competition.

b. An email to your project group about the research you have done on the project.

c. An email to your class teacher requesting for a 5-day leave of absence for a fam[illegible] function.

d. An email to your cousins in a different city describing the last vacation.

e. An email to your grandparents appreciating them for their time and care.

Chapter

10

E-Commerce, Blogging and Podcasting

After reading this chapter, I will be able to:

- ✔ Describe the concept of e-commerce.
- ✔ Describe how online payments are sent and received.
- ✔ Describe the meaning and uses of blogging and podcasting.

Brainstorm and explore!

Which of the following names is familiar to you? Tell the class what you know about each. Write about it in the space given.

1. Amazon: ____________________
2. Flipkart: ____________________
3. BigBasket: ____________________
4. Zepto: ____________________
5. Fresh2Home: ____________________
6. golbibo: ____________________
7. MakeMyTrip: ____________________

All these are the names of companies from which you can buy various items you want. Using the internet, buyers can place their orders and pay. The companies then deliver the goods bought as per the promised delivery time. Anyone purchasing anything from these companies is using e-commerce.

E-Commerce

The word *commerce* originates from the 16th century French word *commercium*, which is a combination of *com-* (together) and *merx* (merchandise). Commerce implies the trade of goods and services. E-commerce means electronic commerce, that is, the exchange of goods and services over an electronic network such as the internet. The first electronic network in the world is believed to be the Boston Computer Exchange, established in 1982 in the United States. The first e-commerce company in India was Fabmart, established in 1999.

Fig. 10.1 | *Online shopping*

E-commerce has several advantages. Here are some of them:

- **Sell anywhere**: E-commerce allows traders and/or organizations to sell their products anywhere in the world. Since potential buyers can discover about their products from anywhere in the world, e-commerce opens up many possibilities.
- **Buy anytime**: Unlike traditional stores that are open only for a certain period of time every day, buyers can shop online anytime from anywhere.
- **Online payments**: Payments can be made at the click of a button.
- **Reviews**: While physical stores have a smaller number of customers who can provide feedback, online shopping affords users the opportunity to read reviews from a wide range of users and make an informed decision.

Link up!

The precursor of online shopping was teleshopping, where products were advertised on TV and users could call a telephone number and place order for the products they needed.

Modes of E-Commerce

Depending on who is selling to whom, here are the different modes of e-commerce:

- **Business-to-Business**: Business-to-Business, also called B2B, refers to the buying and selling of goods over the internet between businesses. For example, a manufacturer of inks could sell his goods to different pen-making companies over the internet.
- **Business-to-Consumer**: Business-to-Consumer, also called B2C, refers to the selling of goods by businesses (companies) directly to consumers over the internet. This mode is quite prevalent in today's times. Examples include Lenskart, which sells spectacles and sunglasses. Marketplaces are another variation of B2C e-commerce. In sites such as Amazon and Flipkart, sellers (businesses) can list their products and consumers can browse the products and buy them.

- **Consumer-to-Consumer**: As the name suggests, consumers can list products they want to sell to other buyers. An interesting application of C2C sites is the selling of unused/lightly used clothes on the internet. Websites allow users to list their clothes along with an expected price. Others can browse the site and buy their choice of clothing. This way, unused clothes are not discarded and they do not crowd landfills. This is an example of using e-commerce as a tool to solve the environmental concern of creating and dumping huge amounts of waste.

- **Consumer-to-Business**: In this mode, customers trade data or their work with a business for a fee. Popular examples include photosharing websites, such as Freepik and Shutterstock. Bloggers and influencers also come under this category.

Apart from the categories mentioned here, there are G2C (Government-to-Citizens) sites that enable easier access to government services for the citizens. The Income Tax filing website is an example of G2C.

Fun with AI

Many e-commerce websites use AI-driven algorithms to suggest related products.

Brush up!

Research the internet and write down examples of real companies for each mode of e-commerce.

____

____

Online Payments

The basis of all commerce today is the exchange of goods or services for money. In the earliest days of civilization, people used to barter, that is, exchange goods or services for goods or services. Money or currency developed when there came about a need for determining a common value. Today, since trade can be carried out from anywhere across the world, payments also can be made with the help of the internet. The benefits of online payments are as follows:

1. **Cannot be physically stolen**: Carrying cash physically possesses the risk of being stolen. With online payments, these thefts can be avoided.
2. **Convenient**: One does not have to physically withdraw cash from the bank or the ATM.
3. **Quick and simple**: With a few steps, one can transfer money to anyone.

Modes of Online Payments

The first step to carrying out any online payment is to have a bank account. Most banks today provide internet banking services. Some of the ways to make payments digitally are discussed below:

Cards

Credit cards and debit cards are used for online payments. POS machines (Point-Of-Sale machines) are the devices that accept payments from debit or credit cards, provide a receipt and store transactions. POS machines are usually operated by businesses, such as restaurants, grocery stores, clothing shops and the likes. The card of the user can be either swiped or tapped. The user can then enter a secret pin that authenticates the transaction.

Fig. 10.2 | *POS machine*

Internet Banking

The bank in which a person holds an account activates the internet banking facility. As the name suggests, most banking features can be accessed with the help of internet banking. The bank provides an internet banking ID and password. Once logged in, the user can check account balance, transfer money, view past transactions and so on.

Soak up!

The Society for Worldwide Interbank Financial Telecommunication (SWIFT) simplifies international payments by helping banks across different countries communicate with each other.

Digital Wallets

A digital wallet (or e-wallet) allows users to make transactions over the internet. Most digital wallets today exist in the form of apps—Phone-Pe, Google Pay and Paytm. Businesses such as Amazon and Ola also have wallets of their own, known as Amazon Pay and OlaMoney, respectively. Wallets are integrated to a bank account. The Unified Payments Interface (UPI) enables various banking features to be accessed via an app with the help of the UPI ID and pin.

Fig. 10.3 | *Scanner on a payment app*

Payment Gateways

A payment gateway refers to a service used by online businesses to accept payments on their website. Users can add their purchases to a cart and then checkout. After filling information such as mobile number and address, they are taken to the payment gateway. Customers can choose to pay via Cards, Internet Banking, Wallets, etc. Some of the prominent payment gateway services are PayUMoney, CCAvenue, Paypal and Instamojo.

Figure 10.4 shows information flow between all stakeholders while making an online payment.

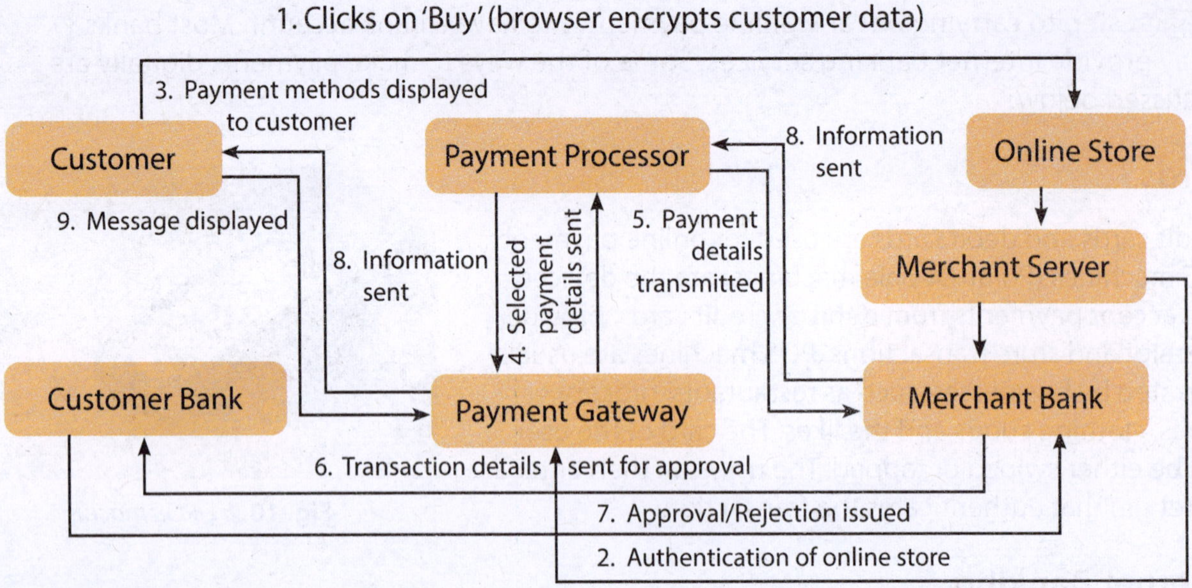

Important Entities

1. Customer and Customer Bank (Buyer)
2. Merchant Server and Merchant Bank (Seller)
3. Payment Processor and Payment Gateway (Mediators)

Fig. 10.4 | *Information flow between all stakeholders while making an online payment*

Soak up!

Internet and smartphones have opened up a world of possibilities in terms of e-commerce. Among all the countries in the world, India has one of the highest smartphone penetrations, with 54% of its population having a smartphone in 2020. This has enabled a wide range of businesses to participate in the digital economy.

Mini Scientist

Working in groups of four, gather information from the adults around you to understand the impact of e-commerce on our lives. To do this, discuss within your group and create a list of questions that you want to ask. Each member of the group should put these questions to at least three adults and note down their response. As a group, collate the response of all twelve adults. Create a PowerPoint presentation or a poster describing your findings. Do not forget to add your thoughts to the PowerPoint presentation.

Blogging

A blog, an abbreviation of the word *weblog*, is an informational site where an individual, a group of people, or a business can write on a topic, activities, thoughts or beliefs in the textual format, with or without pictures. A blog features diary-type commentary and links to articles on other websites, usually presented as a list of entries in the reverse chronological order. Here are some of the components of a blog:

- **Dated posts**: Posts are arranged in the reverse chronological with the latest one first.
- **Images and embedded videos**: Blogs are made more interesting and engaging by including images and videos. Videos are typically embedded, meaning they are linked to YouTube or a similar platform but are displayed on the blog.
- **Comments**: People who read the blog can add comments if the comments feature has been enabled by the creator of the blog.
- **Tags**: Tags are nothing but keywords that help Google find the blog on the internet. For example, the tags for a cricket blog would include sports, IPL, T20, ODI and the likes. When people search for ODI on Google, having tags on the blog increases the chance of getting listed on Google's first page.
- **Subscribe option**: If readers like the content on a blog, they can click on the Subscribe option and enter their email ID. The next time a new blog is published, they would get an email with a link to the blog in their email inbox.

WordPress and Wix are some of the most popular blog creation platforms. Once can choose to create a blog from scratch or use templates already present on these sites. In appearance, a blog is similar to a website. However, there are some key differences, as summarized in Table 10.1.

Table 10.1 | *Differences between a website and a blog*

Website	Blog
A website contains detailed information about a person or an organization, including unique features, past work, contact details, etc.	A blog contains a collection of posts in the textual format, which is often accompanied with images or texts
A website is an independent entity on the world wide web	A blog can or cannot be a part of a parent website
A website is updated infrequently	A blog gets updated with new content as and when the creator decides to share it

Fun with AI

Artificial intelligence-powered applications can be used to write blogs, stories, or even the script for a podcast. An AI story generator is an artificial intelligence-powered tool that helps story creators to come up with ideas for stories and create stories, novels, etc. It works by analysing data from previous stories and using it to generate new story concepts. AI story generators use machine language, artificial intelligence and other algorithms that convert written input into longer text such as stories, novels, etc. Few AI writing tools use natural language processing to analyse a body of text and then generate a story based on the data. Researchers have successfully used these tools to write horror stories too! Basically, you need to provide some inputs relevant to the story you want to write about. Then, the AI story generators will generate the relevant text or story for you. The output of your stories totally depends on the tools you use and the input you provide. Jasper, Rytr and CopyAI are some commonly available tools that you can use.

Podcasts

A podcast is a series of audio files on a topic that you can listen to or download from the internet. You could listen to a podcast on your phone through an app or through any internet-enabled device like a laptop. The word podcast is a combination of *iPod* and *broadcast*, which imply broadcasting for iPods (in the audio format). Just as one can subscribe to a blog, one can subscribe to a podcast as well. Podcasts can be of different types:

- A single person speaking on a topic or area of interest.
- An interview or conversation among two or more people.
- A mix of the above.

Podcasts have become increasingly popular in the last few years. The process of creating and releasing podcasts is called Podcasting.

It is important to note that audiobooks and podcasts are different from one another. A single podcast is typically called an episode and can be up to an hour long. While an audiobook is the audio version of a book, a podcast is a series of episodes released at regular intervals. Here are some of the apps on which one can listen to podcasts:

- Apple Podcasts
- Spotify
- SoundCloud

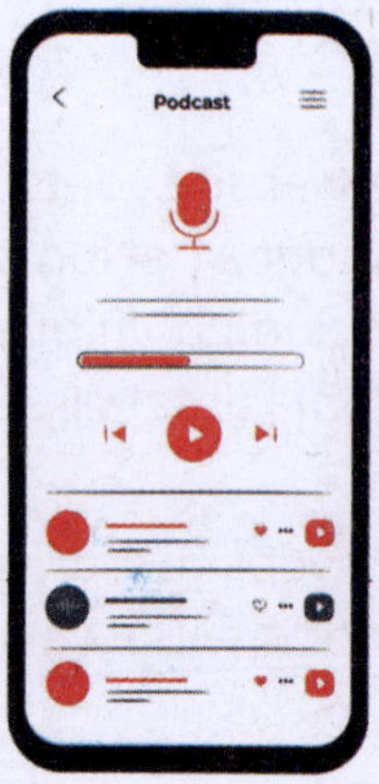

Fig. 10.5 | *Podcast screen on an app*

Some of the platforms to create podcasts include Buzzsprout, Podbean and Soundcloud.

Getting Started

Both blogs and podcasts are platforms where anyone and everyone can start creating content free of cost. They can be created for educational, entertainment, news, as well as for hobby purposes. Whether you are starting a blog or a podcast, here are some of the factors to think ahead of time:

- What interests me?
- What do I want to share?
- How will I share my thoughts with others—blog (writing) or Podcast (speaking)?
- Who will read/listen to my content?
- How frequently do I want to write/speak?

Table 10.2 gives some examples on approaches to creating content.

Table 10.2 | *Sample approaches to creating content*

Category	People who create content and consume	Blog or Podcast on:	Blog/Podcast name examples
Food	Restaurant owners, food lovers and home chefs	▪ Recipes ▪ Farming—how food is produced ▪ About a type of food	▪ Recipes of Indian Foods ▪ All About Fruits ▪ Vegetables in a home garden
Sports	Sports fans, turfs and sportspersons	▪ Different football clubs ▪ History of sports ▪ Performance in matches	▪ Top Football clubs in the world ▪ History of cricket in India ▪ Basketball matches of all time

Soak up!

Since the internet has enabled people to create content in the form of videos, blogs and podcasts, a new way of earning has emerged. The content created can be used to earn money. This mode of earning with the help of content created is popularly known as creator economy.

Today I learned!

- Electronic commerce refers to the exchange of goods and services over the internet.
- There are several modes of e-commerce.
- Online payments allow individuals to send and receive money electronically via cards, internet banking and e-wallets.
- A blog is an informational site where an individual, groups or business can write on a topic in the textual format.
- A podcast is an informational site where an individual, groups or business can speak on a topic in the audio format and release regular content.

Revise and polish!

1. Tick (✓) the correct answer.

a. Cards can be swiped in shops for processing a transaction with the help of a device called the:

(i) Payment gateway (ii) POS machine
(iii) UPI (iv) Bank

b. Which of the following formats is used to create blogs?

(i) Video (ii) Images (iii) Text (iv) App

c. A single podcast is typically called:

(i) Episode (ii) Meta (iii) Unity (iv) Paragraph

d. WordPress and Wix contain which of the following to create blogs?

(i) Pages (ii) Accounts (iii) Templates (iv) Bases

e. Which of the following is a service used by online businesses to accept payments on their website?

(i) WhatsApp (ii) YouTube
(iii) Payment Gateway (iv) Facebook

f. What is the first step to carry out an online transfer of money?

(i) Owning a credit/debit card
(ii) Getting internet banking enabled for your bank account
(iii) Getting a UPI ID
(iv) All of these

g. Which of the following modes of e-commerce involves businesses selling directly to customers?

(i) B2B (ii) B2C (iii) C2C (iv) C2B

h. E-commerce can be carried out throughout the:

(i) City (ii) State (iii) Country (iv) Anywhere

i. Which of the following is an advantage of e-commerce for buyers?

(i) Can touch and feel the products (ii) Near to one's home
(iii) Can shop anytime, anywhere (iv) All of the above

j. Through a payment gateway, one can choose to pay via:

(i) Credit card (ii) Internet banking
(iii) e-wallet (iv) All of the above

2. **Fill in the blanks.**

a. E-commerce is the exchange of goods and services over the ___________.

b. In B2B e-commerce, businesses carry out trade online with other ___________.

c. The ___________ enables features of banking on a e-wallet.

d. A blog contains content in the ___________ format.

e. A podcast contains content in the ___________ format.

3. **Match the following.**

a.	B2C e-commerce	(i)	POS machines
b.	Credit cards	(ii)	Flipkart
c.	Podcasts	(iii)	Episodes
d.	e-wallets	(iv)	PhonePe, Google Pay

4. **Categorize the following features of stores into online and offline features or in both, if applicable:**

a. Can touch and feel the product

b. Pay via credit card

c. Read reviews from many customers

d. Speak to the salesperson

e. 24×7 availability

Online	Offline	Both

5. **Brainstorm with your classmates and write down how each of these modes of e-commerce can be used for benefit of the society or a particular group of people.**

a. B2C e-commerce

____

____

b. C2C e-commerce

____

____

6. **Research the internet and write down the aspects of a blog you find most appealing.**

____

____

7. **Answer the following.**

   a. What are the advantages of e-commerce?

   b. What are the different modes of online payments?

   c. What are the components of a blog?

   d. Write a note on podcasts.

   e. List the similarities between a blog and a podcast.

   f. What are the differences between a website and a blog?

Project

We have learned that a large number of Indians have a smartphone and connectivity to the internet. Imagine you are the District Collector in an area where there are many small villages. How will you use the power of the internet to improve their lives?

(**Hint**: *Think along the lines of water supply, electricity, basic education, roads, etc.*)

Worksheet 1 (Chapters 1, 2 and 3)

1. **All applications and websites are created using different programming languages. Using the internet, find out the languages used to create the following applications/websites:**

a.	Netflix __________________	b.	WhatsApp __________________
c.	YouTube __________________	d.	Wikipedia __________________

Did you find something common between the languages used to create these websites?

____

2. **Embedded systems consist of a software component that serves a specific function embedded on the hardware of the device. In a classroom, a teacher manages more than 30 students at a time. If you had to build a smart assistant for teachers in the form of an embedded system placed in the classroom, what would it look like? What would be the problems that the system will solve for teachers and students? Draw the system and write down its features.**

3. **Files stored on computers are representations or records of the real world. For the following situations, what type of file would you record/create and store on the computer? For each type of file, mention the format(s) in which it could be stored on the computer. One has been done for you.**

	Real world scenario	Type of data	Format
a.	Akshay has learned a new tune in the music class.	Record my voice in an audio file.	.mp3
b.	Sonia has to save her dance performance from the Republic Day celebrations.		
c.	Raman wants to share a brief report on his recent class visit to a mango farm.		
d.	Reema wants to present a discussion on constellations that she learned through a book. She wants the presentation to be creative and engaging.		

4. **Shyama drew a beautiful drawing of a flower, which she wanted to paint in purple colour. However, her paint box only had white, black, blue, green, red and yellow colours. She learned somewhere that purple colour can be made by mixing blue and red colours. Therefore, she mixed the two colours to make a shade of purple.**

Shyama decided to tabulate some more colour combinations using MS Word so that she can save them for later use and even share this with her friends. Can you help her prepare a table with the following colours?

a. Consult with your art teacher and friends, research on Google and find out the colour combinations for the following colours.

b. Use the Merge Cell option and format the cells with the respective colour.

c. Use a font style and colours of your choice.

d. Add more rows of colours as per your wish!

Sr. No.	Colour	Colour combinations		
1.	Purple	Red	Blue	-
2.	Lavender	Red	Blue	White
3.	Orange			
4.	Pink			
5.	Brown			
6.	Teal			
7.	Sea Green			
8.	Yellow Ochre			

Congratulations! You have successfully created your own repository of colours!

Worksheet 2 (Chapters 4, 5, 6 and 7)

Competency-based question

Technology Literacy

1. **The Principal of your school has given you the responsibility of inviting students, parents and alumni to the Independence Day celebrations in your school. The invitation will be sent via email. Create an invitation using the Mail Merge features and include required information. Add elements to make it appealing.**

2. **Did you know forests are home to 80% of Earth's terrestrial animals and cover 31% of the landmass? Create a presentation on any of the world's forests and explain what makes it unique. Include pictures, transitions and audio to make the presentation interesting and engaging.**

3. **Pick a topic/sub-topic from a chapter from your favourite subject, then think about some interesting activities to teach the topic. Create a five-slide presentation to teach the topic to your class. The presentation should be engaging and fun.**

4. **Which Scratch blocks will you use to apply the following effects on the sprite? What are the respective effects called?**

	Effect	Blocks used
a.		
b.		
c.		

5. **Create a story with a sprite that talks about different shapes, such as triangle, square and pentagon. The sprite should explain how many sides each of these polygons have.**

   a. Which sprite will you use?

   ___

   b. Which tool will you use to draw these polygons?

   ___

   c. How will you make the story interesting?

   ___

6. **Create a story where a dragon, a fairy, a wizard and a witch talk to each other about creating a magical spell to solve a huge problem faced by nature. Imagine the witty conversation and record the voices with the help of your friends using the record feature of Scratch.**

An example is given here:

Problem	Magic that will help solve it
Humans dumping plastic in the sea.	A spell that makes humans consume less plastic and recycle more.

7. **Vikram has recently started using Scratch and is creating a new project. Could you help him out with the blocks required for the following actions?**

	Action	Blocks required
a.	When the spacebar is pressed, the main character moves forward by 20 steps.	
b.	Ten seconds after the story starts, the sun hides and the background becomes dark blue.	
c.	Three seconds after, the main character says "It is a full moon day today", and then the moon appears in the sky.	
d.	If the main character decides to go to sleep, the story ends.	

8. **Look at the following blocks of code and answer the questions.**

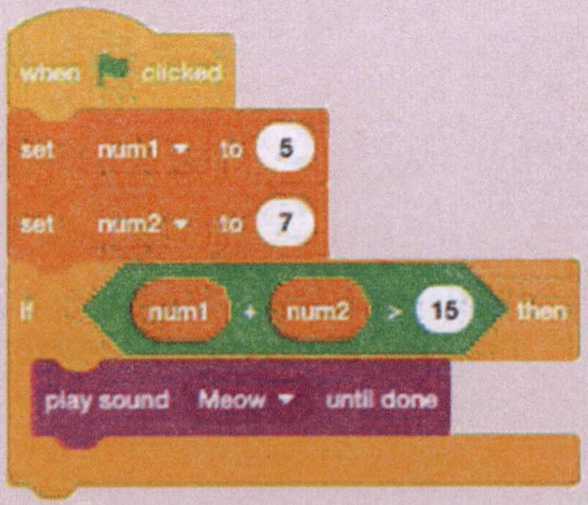

a. Will the Meow sound play when the program runs?

____

b. If yes, for how long does it run?

____

c. What can be changed in the program for the sound to not be played?

____

Worksheet 3 (Chapters 8, 9 and 10)

1. Underline the errors in the following codes based on the given output.

Output	Code
Jupiter is the largest planet.	<h6>Jupiter is the largest planet.</h6>
The second largest planet is Saturn.	<h5>The second largest planet is Saturn. </h5>
The third largest planet is Uranus.	<h4>The third largest planet is Uranus. </h4>
The fourth largest planet is Neptune.	<h3>The fourth largest planet is Neptune.</h3>

2. Classify the following into container elements and empty elements.

<p>, <head>..</head>, <h1>..</h1>, <body>..</body>, <title>..</title>,

Container elements	Empty elements

3. Tick (✔) the proper email etiquettes. Else, mark (✘).

Effect	Blocks used
 a. Bombarding the inbox of friends and family with lots of emails	 b. Using the proper salutations
 c. Mentioning that the email contains an attachment	 d. Using too many acronyms

4. **Suggest suitable subject lines to compose an email for the following situations.**

	Situation	Subject line
a.	Your chess team has won the district-level tournament. The team is very happy. You have to write an email to the Principal, thanking him/her for their support in your participation.	
b.	You recently went to a zoo and clicked many pictures. You have to write an email to your cousin, telling him/her all about your experience along with the pictures.	

5. **Social enterprises refer to organizations that work towards a social cause while creating a profitable enterprise. For example, an e-commerce company that enables artisans in the rural areas to sell their products online. Could you think of a social problem that can be addressed with the help of a social enterprise? Write down three such ideas.**

a.	b.	c.

6. **Research on the internet and write down top three educational blogs and podcasts.**

Top three educational blogs	Top three educational podcasts

7. **If you had to start your own blog or podcast, what would it be? Think on the following lines and write/draw your ideas.**

- Theme of the blog/podcast
- Various topics covered
- Unique features of the blog
- The target audience
- Number of times a week/month that you will be posting
- Platform you will choose to create the blog/podcast

Additional Worksheet

1. Correct the following statements to make them accurate.

a. Today was a very exciting day as I played in the ground all morning. When I got back home, I found that the lift was not working. I had to climb up five floors to reach my house. I freshened up and had my lunch. After a small nap, I was all set to go down and play again. The lift, however, was still not working. It was easier to climb up four flights of stairs than to going down. I met my friends again and we happily played for the next few hours.

b. I went to the market to buy fruits for my cousins. I bought 1 kg of bananas, 1 kg watermelon and 2 kg mangoes. I love mangoes and summers are incomplete without them. I carried 5 kg of fruits and vegetables home and shared them with relish with everyone.

c. I had a wonderful trip last weekend. We went to a nearby beach and the water was fun to play in. We left the beach at around 9 pm on Saturday. The journey was 12-hour long and the train was on time. We live very close to the railway station. We reached home mid-afternoon the next day.

2. Solve the following puzzles.

a. Circle the correct shadow.

b. Spot any five differences.

3. Detective Sam has found a scroll that contains the hints to unlock the combination for a lost treasure. The scroll has a story of a bird that gives clues along its way to hide the treasure. Can you help the detective decipher the clues?

Hints	
Sequence 1: I started my journey when I was five years old. The powerful king's palace was two dozen kilometres away from the sea. The kingdom knew how to measure only in miles. Approximately how far will I travel (in miles)? **Hint:** There are 0.62 miles in a kilometre. __________________	**Sequence 2:** I love to eat fruits. The kind villagers had orchards with fruits that were twice as many as the number of miles I had travelled. How many fruits were there? __________________
Sequence 3: The scorching sun had little effect on me since my way was filled with ponds, where I could stop to take a sip. The number of ponds was 100 times my age. How many ponds were there? __________________	**Sequence 4:** I flew from one end of the country to another to lock the treasure I carried. I met several other birds on the way. The birds were seven times the number of days in a week, added to the number of days in July. How many birds were there? __________________

Final sequence in the correct order (starting from sequence 1 to 4): ________________

Fun Activity

In groups of four to six, play an event controller game. For this, take a carboard sheet and draw a smiley on it. Ask your friends to place a finger on eyes, nose or mouth of the smiley. Whenever your friend touches these parts, all the group members should make a sound. We suggest:

- Eyes → Say 'ting, ting!'
- Nose → Say 'aachhu! (sneezing sound)'
- Mouth → Say 'ha ha!'

Continue till all the members become an even controller.

CLASS 6

QUESTION PAPER SET A

NCO

SOF NATIONAL CYBER OLYMPIAD 2021-22

DO NOT OPEN THIS BOOKLET UNTIL ASKED TO DO SO

Total Questions: 50 | Time: 1 hr.

Guidelines for the Candidate

1. You will get additional ten minutes to fill up information about yourself on the OMR Sheet, before the start of the exam.
2. Write your **Name, School Code, Class, Roll No.** and **Mobile Number** clearly on the **OMR Sheet** and do not forget to sign it. We will share your marks / result and other information related to SOF exams on your mobile number.
3. The Question Paper comprises three sections:
   Logical Reasoning (10 Questions), **Computers and Information Technology** (35 Questions) and **Achievers Section** (5 Questions).
   Each question in Achievers Section carries 3 marks, whereas all other questions carry one mark each.
4. All questions are compulsory. There is no negative marking. Use of calculator is not permitted.
5. There is only ONE correct answer. Choose only ONE option for an answer.
6. To mark your choice of answers by darkening the circles on the OMR Sheet, use **HB Pencil** or **Blue / Black ball point pen** only. E.g.
   Q.16: Which of the following is a type of printer?
   A. Cathode Ray Tube B. Light Emitting Diode
   C. Thermal Flatbed D. Liquid Crystal Display
   As the correct answer is option C, you must darken the circle corresponding to option C on the OMR Sheet. 16. Ⓐ Ⓑ ● Ⓓ
7. Rough work should be done in the blank space provided in this booklet.
8. Return the OMR Sheet to the invigilator at the end of the exam.
9. Please fill in your personal details in the space provided on this page before attempting the paper.

SOF
SCIENCE OLYMPIAD FOUNDATION
Inspiring Young Minds Through Knowledge Olympiads

Name:..

SOF Olympiad Roll No.:.. Contact No.:..

1. Five members D, E, F, G and H are living in a family. D is the father-in-law of F. H is the son of E. G is the sister of H. F is married to E. Then, how is H related to D?

   A. Son
   B. Daughter
   C. Grandson
   D. Granddaughter

2. Count the number of rectangles in the given figure.

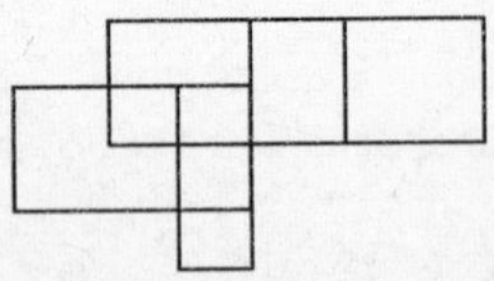

   A. 15
   B. 16
   C. 14
   D. More than 16

3. If '+' denotes '×', '÷' denotes '–', '×' denotes '÷' and '–' denotes '+', then 120 × 8 – 14 + 4 ÷ 16 = ?

   A. 35
   B. 45
   C. 55
   D. 65

4. Select a figure from the options which will complete the given figure matrix.

A	C	D
F	?	O
H	Q	Y

   A. U
   B. T
   C. I
   D. J

5. Which of the following Venn diagrams best represents the relationship amongst, "Papers, Pens and Books"?

   A. 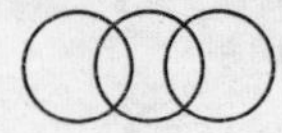
   B. 
   C. 
   D. 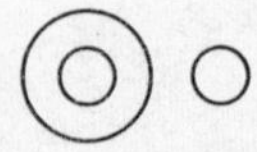

6. How many cubes are there in the given figure?

   A. 14
   B. 15
   C. 16
   D. 18

7. In a certain code language, if CREATE is written as ACEERT, then how will BRIGHT be written in that language?

   A. BHGRIT
   B. GHBITR
   C. BGHIRT
   D. CSJHIU

8. A square transparent Sheet (X) with a pattern and a dotted line on it is given. Select a figure from the options as to how the pattern would appear when the transparent sheet is folded along the dotted line.

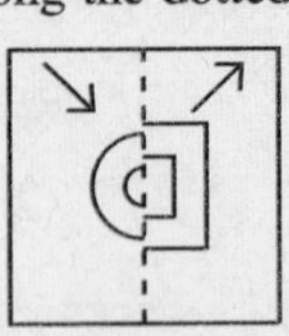

Sheet (X)

   A. 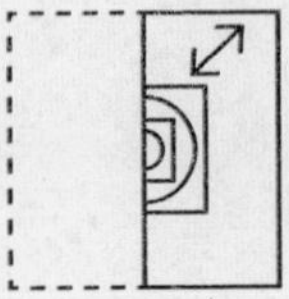
   B. 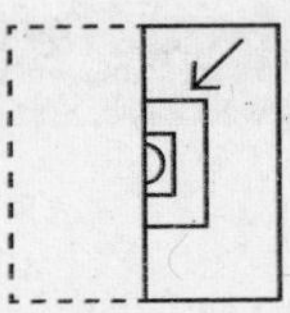

C. 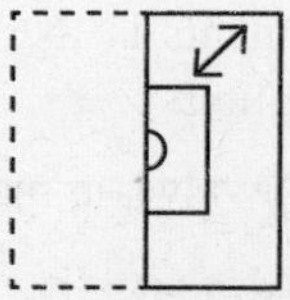

D. 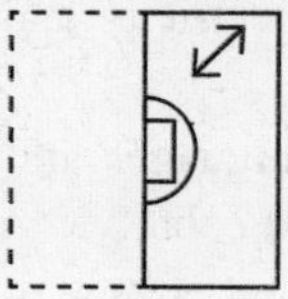

9. Select the odd one out.

A. 415

B. 165

C. 325

D. 247

10. Find the correct water image of the given figure.

A. 

B. 

C. 

D. 

COMPUTERS AND INFORMATION TECHNOLOGY

11. Which of the following options states the CORRECT difference between RAM and ROM memory?

	RAM	ROM
A.	It is read only memory.	It is read and write memory.
B.	It is non-volatile memory.	It is volatile memory.
C.	Types of RAM are PRAM, EPRAM.	Types of ROM are SROM and PROM.
D.	Data in RAM can be modified.	Data in ROM cannot be modified.

12. Select the INCORRECT match of icons present in the Layout tab of Table Tools with respect to MS-Word 2010.

A.  – Repeat Header Rows

B.  – Convert to Text

C.  – Properties

D.  – Merge cells

13. Identify the given device.

- It is a kind of solid semiconductor device.
- It has many functions such as detecting, rectifying, amplifying, switching, voltage stabilizing, signal modulating and so on.

A. Integrated chip

B. Transistor

C. Vacuum tube

D. Cathode ray tube

14. 1000^6 bytes = ________.

A. 1 Exabyte

B. 1 Zettabyte

C. 1 Yottabyte

D. 1 Petabyte

15. Which of the following options of Page Layout tab shows a faded background image that displays behind the text in a document of MS-Word 2010?

A. Page Color

B. Watermark

C. Page Borders

D. No Color

16. Identify the type of computer from the given description.

- They are the large computers with bigger storage capacity.
- They can store a huge database and can also process the data with more speed.
- They are being used by the big companies, banks, etc. as a centralised computer system.

A. Mini computers

B. Mainframe computers

C. Super computers

D. Palmtop computers

17. Select the odd one out.

A. 

B. 

C. 

D. 

18. Which of the following devices can sense hand-drawn marks such as small circles or rectangles made on pre-printed forms?

A. 

B. 

C. 

D. 

19. Which of the following statements is CORRECT about the compiler?

A. It translates high-level program code into machine level one line at a time.

B. It translates whole high-level program code into machine code in one go.

C. It is a general purpose language providing very efficient execution.

D. It translates object code into source code.

20. A CD-R is also known as ________.

A. WORM

B. WORO

C. WMRO

D. ROWM

21. In Qbasic, text that you wish to appear on the screen while your program runs should be written inside ________.

A. Slashes

B. Quotes

C. Brackets

D. Braces

22. Which of the following statements is INCORRECT about first generation of computers?

A. They used vacuum tubes or valves as main electric component.

B. They consumed lot of electricity and produced excessive heat.

C. They used high level languages and assembly languages like fortran and cobol.

D. They were huge in size and creates maintenance problem.

23. What would be the output of the given Qbasic code?

```
CLS
LET X = 25
IF (X more than equals 25) THEN
    PRINT "X is equal to 25"
    ELSE
PRINT "X is less than equal to 25"
END IF
```

A. X is equal to 25 X is less than equal to 25

B. X is equal to 25

C. X is less than equal to 25

D. Compilation failed

24. Identify the following.

- It is not discrete computer.
- It is used to store data in a continuous form of physical quantities.

A. Hybrid computer

B. Analog computer

C. Digital computer

D. Super computer

25. Which of the following statements is INCORRECT regarding the Recycle Bin?

A. When you delete a file from a hard-disk, the deleted file is stored in the recycle bin.

B. The deleted file can be recovered from recycle bin until you empty the recycle bin.

C. It is a directory where deleted files are temporarily stored.

D. The deleted files moved to recycle bin do not occupy space.

26. Select the odd one out (regarding Windows 10).

A. 

B. 

C. 

D. 

27. Which of the following statements hold(s) true about the given snapshot of MS-Word 2010?

Statement 1 : It can be used to represent the outer edge of a document.

Statement 2 : It allows to place edge on any or all four sides of selected text, paragraph and pages.

A. Only Statement 1
B. Only Statement 2
C. Both Statement 1 and Statement 2
D. Neither Statement 1 nor Statement 2

28. Which of the following protocols is used to receive e-mail messages on internet?

A. File Transfer Protocol
B. Hyper Text Transfer Protocol
C. Simple Mail Transfer Protocol
D. Terminal Emulation Protocol

29. Identify the term 'X' and 'Y' (which represents types of optical storage devices) with the help of given description.

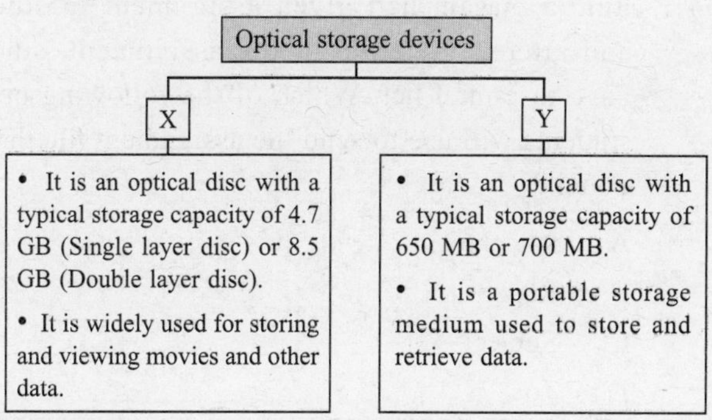

	X	Y
A.	DVD	CD
B.	CD	Pen Drive
C.	Pen Drive	DVD ROM
D.	DVD ROM	Pen Drive

30. Reena has created a table in MS-Word 2010 and now she wants to add 3 more rows to it. Which of the following options would she use to add the new rows to the table?

A. Right click inside table → Insert → Insert Rows Left
B. Right click inside table → Insert → Insert Rows Above
C. Click on any row → Layout tab → Insert Left/ Insert Right
D. Right Click → Insert → Add → Rows

31. Match the generation of computers given in Column-I with their relevant interactions given in Column-II.

Column-I	Column-II
(a) First generation	(i) Keyboards and monitors
(b) Second generation	(ii) Microprocessor and GUI
(c) Third generation	(iii) UNIVAC and ENIAC
(d) Fourth generation	(iv) COBOL and FORTRAN

A. (a) – (iii), (b) – (iv), (c) – (i), (d) – (ii)
B. (a) – (i), (b) – (iii), (c) – (ii), (d) – (iv)
C. (a) – (ii), (b) – (iii), (c) – (i), (d) – (iv)
D. (a) – (i), (b) – (ii), (c) – (iv), (d) – (iii)

32. Which of the following is NOT a Dynamic Content transitions effect of MS-PowerPoint 2010?

A. Blinds
B. Ferris Wheel
C. Conveyor
D. Fly Through

33. When talking about networking and internet, what is a port?

A. An external output device.
B. It is a type of internet software.
C. It is the protocol that e-mail messages have to follow to travel over the internet.
D. It's a data connection that allows information transfer to and from a specific server process.

34. Which of the following statements hold(s) true about the Section Breaks option in MS-Word 2010?

Statement 1 :  Inserts a section break and starts the new section on the same page.

Statement 2 :  Inserts a section break and starts the new section on the next even-numbered page.

A. Only Statement 1
B. Only Statement 2
C. Both Statement 1 and Statement 2
D. Neither Statement 1 nor Statement 2

35. Match the options given in Column-I with their descriptions given in Column-II with respect to Qbasic.

	Column-I		Column-II
(a)	LET	(i)	Output statement
(b)	FOR-NEXT	(ii)	Conditional statement
(c)	IF-THEN-ELSE	(iii)	Assignment statement
(d)	PRINT	(iv)	Loop statement

A. (a) – (iii), (b) – (ii), (c) – (i), (d) – (iv)
B. (a) – (iii), (b) – (iv), (c) – (ii), (d) – (i)
C. (a) – (iv), (b) – (iii), (c) – (ii), (d) – (i)
D. (a) – (ii), (b) – (iv), (c) – (iii), (d) – (i)

36. In the given diagram, features of different generation of computers are given in boxes, marked as X, Y and Z. Identify the generations of computer.

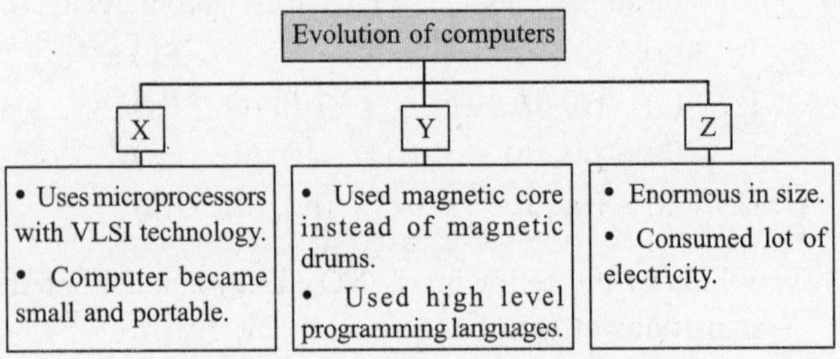

	X	Y	Z
A.	2ND	3RD	1ST
B.	4TH	2ND	1ST
C.	3RD	1ST	2ND
D.	2ND	3RD	4TH

37. What would be the result when you select the data shown in table and click on A Z↓ icon of MS-Word 2010?

4
59
1
23
12
8

A. It will only sort the numbers in descending order.
B. It will arrange items systematically either in ascending or descending order.
C. It displays all spelling and grammatical mistakes.
D. It will arrange the selected data in alphabetical order only.

38. Which of the following options allows users to find information based on keywords on internet?

A. IP address
B. World Wide Web
C. Search Engine
D. Electronic mail

39. Which of the following options in Windows 7 allows user to modify system settings and controls, settings for the mouse, display, sound, network and keyboard?

A. Windows Update
B. Control Panel
C. Search Engine
D. Electronic Mail

40. Identify the given device.

– It is designed by English mathematician and computer pioneer Charles Babbage.
– It was programmable using punched cards and has many essential features found in modern computers.

A. Difference Engine
B. Analytical Engine
C. Pascaline
D. Blaise Pascal

41. Sunita ma'am had given assignment to students and after completion of the assignment, students have to e-mail her. Which of the following options students will use to send the assignment file through e-mail?

A. Attachment
B. Reply
C. Subject
D. To

42. Select the CORRECT match.

A. ENIAC - Electronic Numerical Integrator and Computation
B. EDVAC - Electrical Discrete Variable Automatic Computer
C. UNIVAC I - Universal Automatic Computer-I
D. IBM - Integrated Business Machines

43. ________ is the process of detecting and removing computer program bugs or errors.

A. Downloading
B. Uploading
C. Debugging
D. Defragmentation

44. Identify the following with respect to CPU speed.

- It is used to represents how many cycles a CPU executes per second.
- It is also referred to as clock-rate.

A. Processing
B. CPU cycle
C. Clock Speed
D. Memory Speed

45. ________ is a concept or idea that spreads "virtually" from one person to another via the internet. It could be anything from an image to an e-mail or a video file.

A. Internet Shopping
B. Internet Banking
C. Internet Access
D. Internet Meme

ACHIEVERS SECTION

46. Match the Qbasic math functions and operators given in Column-I with their correct options given in Column-II.

	Column-I		Column-II
(a)	\	(i)	Calculates the square root of a number.
(b)	^	(ii)	Performs remainder division.
(c)	SQR	(iii)	Performs integer division.
(d)	MOD	(iv)	Raises a number to a power of another number.

A. (a) – (iii), (b) – (iv), (c) – (i), (d) – (ii)
B. (a) – (i), (b) – (iv), (c) – (ii), (d) – (iii)
C. (a) – (iii), (b) – (i), (c) – (ii), (d) – (iv)
D. (a) – (ii), (b) – (i), (c) – (iii), (d) – (iv)

47. A teacher asked students to insert data in a table as shown in Table-1 in MS-Word 2010. But after some time, teacher asked students to change the table as shown in Table-2. Which of the following features will help students to achieve this?

ABC School		
Name	Roll no	Class
Priya	0489	6th
Aman	0321	6th
Shri	0986	6th

Table-1

ABC School		
Name	Roll no	Class
Priya	0489	6th
Aman	0321	6th
Shri	0986	6th

Table-2

A. Merge Cells
B. Split Cells
C. Split Table
D. Autofit

48. What would happen when you click on the "Save as..." option from the right click pop-up as shown in the given snapshot of Google home page?

A. It will save the page as in the form of web page and also save the link.
B. It will save the web-page as in the form of MS-Word document.
C. It will save the web page as in the form of image.
D. It will reload that web page in hard disk.

49. Select the INCORRECT match.

A. Compiler : It converts all the source code into machine code, creating an intermediary object code.
B. Interpreter : It converts source code to machine code.
C. Translator : Compiler, Interpreter and Assembler are form of translator.
D. Assembler : It converts all machine code into Interpreter form.

50. Using Animation Delay you can ________ in MS-PowerPoint 2010.

A. Play the animation in full screen.
B. Play the animation after certain number of seconds.
C. Specify the length of animation.
D. Preview the animations applied on the current slide.

SPACE FOR ROUGH WORK

ANSWER KEYS

1.	(C)	**2.**	(D)	**3.**	(C)	**4.**	(C)	**5.**	(D)	**6.**	(C)	**7.**	(C)
8.	(A)	**9.**	(D)	**10.**	(A)	**11.**	(D)	**12.**	(D)	**13.**	(B)	**14.**	(A)
15.	(B)	**16.**	(B)	**17.**	(B)	**18.**	(B)	**19.**	(B)	**20.**	(A)	**21.**	(B)
22.	(C)	**23.**	(D)	**24.**	(B)	**25.**	(D)	**26.**	(D)	**27.**	(C)	**28.**	(C)
29.	(A)	**30.**	(B)	**31.**	(A)	**32.**	(A)	**33.**	(A)	**34.**	(C)	**35.**	(B)
36.	(B)	**37.**	(B)	**38.**	(C)	**39.**	(B)	**40.**	(B)	**41.**	(A)	**42.**	(C)
43.	(C)	**44.**	(C)	**45.**	(D)	**46.**	(A)	**47.**	(A)	**48.**	(A)	**49.**	(D)
50.	(B)												